VICARIOUS TRAUMA AND DISASTER MENTAL HEALTH

Vicarious Trauma and Disaster Mental Health focuses on the clinician and the impact of working with disaster survivors. Floods, hurricanes, tornadoes, mass shootings, terrorism and other large-scale catastrophic events have increased in the last decade and disaster resilience has become a national imperative. This book explores vicarious traumatization in mental health providers who respond to massive disasters by choice or by circumstance. What happens when clinicians share the trauma and vulnerability from the toll taken by a disaster with the victims they care for? How can clinicians increase resilience from disaster exposure and provide mental health services effectively? *Vicarious Trauma and Disaster Mental Health* offers insight and analysis of the research and theory behind vicarious trauma and compares and contrasts with other work-impact concepts such as burnout, compassion fatigue and secondary traumatic stress. It proposes practical evidence-informed personal strategies and organizational approaches that address five cognitive schemas (safety, esteem, trust, control and intimacy) disrupted in vicarious trauma. With an emphasis on the psychological health and safety of mental health providers in the post-disaster workplace, this book represents a shift in perspective and provides a framework for the promotion of worker resilience in the standard of practice in disaster management.

Gertie Quitangon, M.D., is a clinical assistant professor of psychiatry at the New York University School of Medicine and is on faculty at the NYU Public Psychiatry Fellowship. She is currently the medical director at Chapel Street Center, a community-based outpatient clinic of the Department of Veterans Affairs New York Harbor Healthcare System.

Mark R. Everce ... director of psychiatry at the New York University S... :or of mental health at the WTC Health Prog... cal Center of Excellence.

Routledge Psychosocial Stress Series

Charles R. Figley, Ph.D., Series Editor

1. Stress Disorders Among Vietnam Veterans, *Edited by Charles R. Figley, Ph.D.*
2. Stress and the Family Vol. 1: Coping with Normative Transitions, *Edited by Hamilton I. McCubbin, Ph.D., and Charles R. Figley, Ph.D.*
3. Stress and the Family Vol. 2: Coping with Catastrophe, *Edited by Charles R. Figley, Ph.D., and Hamilton I. McCubbin, Ph.D.*
4. Trauma and Its Wake: The Study and Treatment of Post-Traumatic Stress Disorder, *Edited by Charles R. Figley, Ph.D.*
5. Post-Traumatic Stress Disorder and the War Veteran Patient, *Edited by William E. Kelly, M.D.*
6. The Crime Victim's Book, Second Edition, *By Morton Bard, Ph.D., and Dawn Sangrey.*
7. Stress and Coping in Time of War: Generalizations from the Israeli Experience, *Edited by Norman A. Milgram, Ph.D.*
8. Trauma and Its Wake Vol. 2: Traumatic Stress Theory, Research, and Intervention, *Edited by Charles R. Figley, Ph.D.*
9. Stress and Addiction, *Edited by Edward Gottheil, M.D., Ph.D., Keith A. Druley, Ph.D., Steven Pashko, Ph.D., and Stephen P. Weinsteinn, Ph.D.*
10. Vietnam: A Casebook, *By Jacob D. Lindy, M.D., in collaboration with Bonnie L. Green, Ph.D., Mary C. Grace, M.Ed., M.S., John A. MacLeod, M.D., and Louis Spitz, M.D.*
11. Post-Traumatic Therapy and Victims of Violence, *Edited by Frank M. Ochberg, M.D.*
12. Mental Health Response to Mass Emergencies: Theory and Practice, *Edited by Mary Lystad, Ph.D.*
13. Treating Stress in Families, *Edited by Charles R. Figley, Ph.D.*
14. Trauma, Transformation, and Healing: An Integrative Approach to Theory, Research, and Post-Traumatic Therapy, *By John P. Wilson, Ph.D.*
15. Systemic Treatment of Incest: A Therapeutic Handbook, *By Terry Trepper, Ph.D., and Mary Jo Barrett, M.S.W.*
16. The Crisis of Competence: Transitional Stress and the Displaced Worker *Edited by Carl A. Maida, Ph.D., Norma S. Gordon, M.A., and Norman L. Farberow, Ph.D.*
17. Stress Management: An Integrated Approach to Therapy, *By Dorothy H. G. Cotton, Ph.D.*
18. Trauma and the Vietnam War Generation: Report of the Findings from the National Vietnam Veterans Readjustment Study, *By Richard A. Kulka, Ph.D., William E. Schlenger, Ph.D., John A. Fairbank, Ph.D., Richard L. Hough, Ph.D., Kathleen Jordan, Ph.D., Charles R. Marmar, M.D., Daniel S. Weiss, Ph.D., and David A. Grady, Psy.D.*
19. Strangers at Home: Vietnam Veterans Since the War, *Edited by Charles R. Figley, Ph.D., and Seymour Leventman, Ph.D.*
20. The National Vietnam Veterans Readjustment Study: Tables of Findings and Technical Appendices, *By Richard A. Kulka, Ph.D., Kathleen Jordan, Ph.D., Charles R. Marmar, M.D., and Daniel S. Weiss, Ph.D.*
21. Psychological Trauma and the Adult Survivor: Theory, Therapy, and Transformation, *By I. Lisa McCann, Ph.D., and Laurie Anne Pearlman, Ph.D.*
22. Coping with Infant or Fetal Loss: The Couple's Healing Process, *By Kathleen R. Gilbert, Ph.D., and Laura S. Smart, Ph.D.*
23. Compassion Fatigue: Coping with Secondary Traumatic Stress Disorder in Those Who Treat the Traumatized, *Edited by Charles R. Figley, Ph.D.*
24. Treating Compassion Fatigue, *Edited by Charles R. Figley, Ph.D.*
25. Handbook of Stress, Trauma and the Family, *Edited by Don R. Catherall, Ph.D.*
26. The Pain of Helping: Psychological Injury of Helping Professionals, *By Patrick J. Morrissette, Ph.D., RMFT, NCC, CCC.*
27. Disaster Mental Health Services: A Primer for Practitioners, *By Diane Myers, R.N., M.S.N., and David Wee, M.S.S.W.*
28. Empathy in the Treatment of Trauma and PTSD, *By John P. Wilson, Ph.D. and Rhiannon B. Thomas, Ph.D.*
29. Family Stressors: Interventions for Stress and Trauma, *Edited by Don. R. Catherall, Ph. D.*
30. Handbook of Women, Stress and Trauma, *Edited by Kathleen Kendall-Tackett, Ph.D.*
31. Mapping Trauma and Its Wake, *Edited by Charles R. Figley, Ph.D.*
32. The Posttraumatic Self: Restoring Meaning and Wholeness to Personality, *Edited by John P. Wilson, Ph.D.*
33. Violent Death: Resilience and Intervention Beyond the Crisis, *Edited by Edward K. Rynearson, M.D.*
34. Combat Stress Injury: Theory, Research, and Management, *Edited by Charles R. Figley, Ph.D. and William P. Nash, M.D.*
35. MindBody Medicine: Foundations and Practical Applications, *By Leo W. Rotan, Ph.D. and Veronika Ospina-Kammerer, Ph.D.*
36. Understanding and Assessing Trauma in Children and Adolescents: Measures, Methods, and Youth in Context, *By Kathleen Nader, D.S.W*
37. When the Past Is Always Present: Emotional Traumatization, Causes, and Cures, *By Ronald A. Ruden, M.D., Ph.D.*
38. Families Under Fire: Systemic Therapy with Military Families, *Edited by R. Blaine Everson, Ph.D. and Charles R. Figley, Ph.D.*
39. Dissociation in Traumatized Children and Adolescents: Theory and Clinical Interventions, *Edited by Sandra Wieland, Ph.D.*
40. Transcending Trauma: Survival, Resilience and Clinical Implications in Survivor Families, *By Bea Hollander-Goldfein, Ph.D., Nancy Isserman, Ph.D., and Jennifer Goldenberg, Ph.D., L.C.S.W*
41. School Rampage Shootings and Other Youth Disturbances: Early Preventative Interventions, *By Kathleen Nader, D.S.W.*

Editorial Board

VICARIOUS TRAUMA AND DISASTER MENTAL HEALTH

Understanding Risks and Promoting Resilience

Edited by
Gertie Quitangon
Mark R. Evces

Routledge
Taylor & Francis Group

NEW YORK AND LONDON

First published 2015
by Routledge
711 Third Avenue, New York, NY 10017

and by Routledge
27 Church Road, Hove, East Sussex BN3 2FA

Routledge is an imprint of the Taylor & Francis Group, an informa business

© 2015 Gertie Quitangon and Mark R. Evces

Library of Congress Cataloging-in-Publication Data

Vicarious trauma and disaster mental health: understanding risks and promoting resilience / [edited] by Gertie Quitangon and Mark R. Evces.
    pages cm. — (Psychosocial stress series)
    Includes bibliographical references and index.
  1. Mental health personnel and patient.   2. Mental health personnel—Psychology.   3. Disasters—Psychological aspects.
4. Disaster victims—Psychology.   5. Psychic trauma.   6. Resilience (Personality trait)   I. Quitangon, Gertie.   II. Evces, Mark R.
    RC480.8.V53 2015
    616.85'21—dc23
    2014031066

ISBN: 978-1-138-79329-3 (hbk)
ISBN: 978-1-138-79330-9 (pbk)
ISBN: 978-1-315-76134-3 (ebk)

Typeset in Bembo
by Apex CoVantage, LLC

Printed and bound in Great Britain by
TJ International Ltd, Padstow, Cornwall

Dedicated to
St. Vincent's Hospital Manhattan
"Respect, Integrity, Compassion, Excellence"
1849–2010

CONTENTS

SECTION V
Navigating Resources on Vicarious Trauma and Disasters

CONTRIBUTORS

Yeshwant Chitalkar, M.D.
Psychiatrist, Project Renewal
New York, NY

Spencer Eth, M.D.
Associate Chief of Staff for Mental Health
Miami VA Healthcare System
Professor of Clinical Psychiatry
University of Miami Miller School of Medicine
Miami, FL

Mark R. Evces, Ph.D.
Assistant Director of Mental Health
NYU School of Medicine WTC Health Program
Clinical Center of Excellence
Clinical Instructor
Department of Psychiatry
NYU School of Medicine
New York, NY

Jeffrey B. Freedman, M.D.
Director, Division of Psychosomatic Medicine
Mt. Sinai Roosevelt and St. Luke's Hospitals
New York, NY

Jane Hammerslough, LMFT
Clinical Coordinator, Marriage and Family Therapist
Brooklyn Vet Center
Department of Veterans Affairs

New York Harbor Healthcare System
Brooklyn, NY

Mudassar Iqbal, M.D.
PGY IV Resident
Department of Psychiatry
SUNY Downstate Medical Center
Brooklyn, NY

Danielle Kaplan, Ph.D.
Director, NYU-Bellevue Predoctoral Psychology Internship
Clinical Assistant Professor
Department of Psychiatry
NYU School of Medicine
New York, NY

Craig L. Katz, M.D.
Director, Professional Development Program in Mental Health
Associate Clinical Professor of Psychiatry and Medical Education
Mount Sinai School of Medicine
New York, NY

Tamar Lavy, M.D.
PGY IV Resident
Department of Psychiatry
SUNY Downstate Medical Center
Brooklyn, NY

April Naturale, Ph.D.
Senior Technical Specialist, ICF International
Senior Advisor, Disaster Technical Assistance Center (DTAC)
Substance Abuse and Mental Health Services Administration (SAMHSA)

Charles Nelson Ph.D., C.Psych
Psychologist, Operational Stress Injury Clinic
Parkwood Hospital, London, Ontario
Adjunct Clinical Professor of Psychology University of Western Ontario
London, Ontario

Kevin O'Brien, Ph.D.
Team Leader, Brooklyn Vet Center
Department of Veterans Affairs
New York Harbor Healthcare System
Brooklyn, NY

Gertie Quitangon, MD
Medical Director
Chapel Street Center

Department of Veterans Affairs New York Harbor Healthcare System
Clinical Assistant Professor of Psychiatry
NYU School of Medicine
New York, NY

Helen Ryu, M.D.
PGY IV Resident
Department of Psychiatry
SUNY Downstate Medical Center
Brooklyn, NY

Kate St. Cyr, M.Sc.P.P.H.
Research Associate
Operational Stress Injury Clinic
Parkwood Hospital
London, Ontario, Canada

Patricia J. Watson, Ph.D.
Senior Educational Specialist
National Center for PTSD

SERIES EDITOR FOREWORD

This book is about wisdom and hope. Wisdom reflected in lessons learned and shared as professionals faced extraordinary adversities and risks well beyond their training and capacities. Hope for all of us, as no matter the adversity, we are able to rise up from where we were thrown and help the community, neighbors, and loved ones carry on and even benefit from the wake of disaster in the rebuilding.

Resilience is endurance over adversity and adaptability always towards thriving. Those who are resilient are confident in their own survival and have a strong belief and desire for their own definition of thriving. There is no settling for anything less. We are born with a set of skills that are nurtured in different degrees—with or without intention—in resource rich or not so rich learning environments, forcing us to learn how to cope. It is easier for some than others. We only now understand the complex dynamics of trauma resilience.

It is then, with considerable enthusiasm that the Editorial Board and I welcome Gertie Quitangon and Mark R. Evces's *Vicarious Trauma and Disaster Mental Health: Understanding Risks and Promoting Resilience* to the Psychosocial Stress Series. The Series was established in 1978 with the publication of *Stress Disorders among Vietnam Veterans*. Both books share common cores of focus: stress, trauma, resilience, research analysis, and theoretical innovation.

Dr. Gertie Quitangon is the Medical Director at Chapel Street Center, a community-based outpatient clinic of the Department of Veterans Affairs New York Harbor Healthcare System. She is a Clinical Assistant Professor of Psychiatry at the New York University School of Medicine and on faculty at the NYU Public Psychiatry Fellowship. She also holds a private practice in Manhattan.

Right before the September 11 attacks in 2001, Dr. Quitangon received a house staff grant for a pilot study on vicarious traumatization in child psychiatrists and psychologists in training. She subsequently conducted a study exploring vicarious traumatization in mental health professionals who provided services to

9/11 victims and has presented at local and international conferences including the annual meeting of the American Psychiatric Association (APA). She is an elected Fellow of the APA.

Dr. Mark R. Evces is Assistant Director of Mental Health at the NYU School of Medicine World Trade Center Health Program Clinical Center of Excellence, established to provide care for 9/11 first responders. He is also a Clinical Instructor of Psychiatry at the NYU School of Medicine, where he provides and supervises psychotherapy.

Dr. Evces completed a doctoral degree in Counseling Psychology at the University of Georgia and a clinical internship at NYU-Bellevue Hospital Center. He was a postdoctoral fellow and chief intern at NYU-Bellevue Hospital Center before assuming a full-time position as a psychologist in the NYU Department of Pediatrics, Division of Pediatric Infectious Diseases. Dr. Evces maintains a private practice in Manhattan and consults with organizations seeking to prevent and address employee burnout and vicarious traumatization.

This book represents the cutting-edge of trauma scholarship and practice because it focuses on worker resilience of those exposed to high-stress jobs involving suffering people. In the context of disaster resilience, understanding the risks enables us to be prepared when we face them; to be prepared mentally and physically. Disaster preparedness is a common theme in disaster management standards of practice. I urge the reader, therefore, to consider the importance of the title of this new and innovative book: Vicarious trauma—the trauma by association with the traumatized; trauma generated by human empathy toward the traumatized; it is challenging to measure because of its subtle nature and the importance of culture and context of both those in harm's way and the vicarious trauma from working with them.

We are now in our second decade of study in resilience. We are now benefiting from the summary and applications of these studies toward enabling practitioners to transform the lives of the traumatized from being burdened by the past to being inspired by the past.

This book is also part of the emergence of modern disaster management with standards of practice that focus on the caregiver as well as the trauma survivors. Disaster management and mitigation operational plans now include effective training, education, preparation, coaching, supervision, guidance, and support for those who do the work of recovery and who are vulnerable to behavioral health challenges.

I wish to congratulate the editors and those who contributed to this potential game changer in effectively expanding our disaster mental health attention to include vicarious trauma and other challenges of those working with survivors. We are all the better for this shift in the field that is promoted by this important book.

Charles R. Figley, Ph.D.
Series Editor
Tulane University Kurzweg Chair in Disaster Mental Health
New Orleans

ACKNOWLEDGMENTS

We deeply appreciate the support, encouragement, and involvement of the following individuals throughout the development of this endeavor:

Manuel Baldemor, Manuel Trujillo, M.D., Elva Naco, M.D., Joy Pentecostes-Lansang, Ph.D., MPH, Adam D. Grossman, J.D., M.B.A.

Jennifer Bertoni, Cathy Gaytan, L.C.S.W., William Boggess, Denise Harrison, M.D., Peter Haugen, Ph.D., Trace Rosel, L.C.S.W., and colleagues at the World Trade Center Health Program-NYU School of Medicine Clinical Center of Excellence

We are most grateful to the contributors who made this book possible:

Charles Nelson, Ph.D., C.Psych., Kate St. Cyr, M.Sc.P.P.H., Danielle Kaplan, Ph.D., April Naturale, Ph.D., Patricia J. Watson, Ph.D., Jane Hammerslough, L.M.F.T., Mudassar Iqbal, M.D., Helen Ryu, M.D., Tamar Lavy, M.D.

Spencer Eth, M.D., Jeffrey B. Freedman, M.D., Yeshwant Chitalkar, M.D., Craig Katz, M.D., Kevin O'Brien, Ph.D.

Finally, we thank our editors, Anna Moore and Elizabeth Graber, for their guidance and expert advice, and Charles Figley, Ph.D., for his inspiration and unwavering zeal for this project.

INTRODUCTION

Gertie Quitangon and Mark R. Evces

> In becoming intimate with tragedy, terrible losses, and immense heartbreak, disaster mental health workers absorb psychological pain and despair. This can lead to their own difficulties with self-regulation and perspective.
>
> (Halpern & Tramontin, 2007, p. 11).

Vicarious Trauma and Disaster Mental Health: Understanding Risks and Promoting Resilience shifts attention to the mental health clinician and the impact of disaster mental health work. With the increase in both natural events and incidents of mass violence over the past decade that propelled the evolution of disaster mental health, the ethical principle "First do no harm" from the Hippocratic Oath applies to mental health providers as it does to patients. As mental health providers take on many different roles and responsibilities and learn new models of providing trauma-informed care throughout the disaster timeline, there is a growing need to address the unintended negative impact of the work on providers, first, for their overall wellness and safety and, second, for them to perform their roles effectively.

The original concept of this project was a casebook on vicarious trauma and 9/11 as both editors have had unique perspectives on the psychological impact of the unprecedented catastrophic event on friends, colleagues, teachers and mentors in the mental health field acutely and long term. On the tenth-year anniversary of 9/11, New York City paid tribute to the occasion by holding forums graced by leading experts on every facet of life changed by the tragedy, and at a 9/11 mental health conference held at the New York Academy of Medicine, the first question from the audience was "What about vicarious trauma?". It was in the mind of a clinician representative of others whose line of work involves bearing witness to intimate details of adversities disclosed in the confidence of a therapeutic relationship. What were the lessons learned on vicarious trauma a decade after 9/11? In the following year, Hurricane Sandy battered the East Coast, there was a school shooting in Newtown, Connecticut, and a bombing at the Boston Marathon finish line. In New York, both editors witnessed up close the laudable disaster response to Sandy at Bellevue Hospital Center, NYU-Langone Medical Center and the VA-New York Harbor, honed by 10 years of intense and repeated disaster preparations in the city from 2001 after 9/11 to 2011 when Hurricane Irene hit. But the question remains, what about vicarious trauma? In response to the recent spate of disasters, the editors decided to expand the book to vicarious trauma (VT) in mental health providers and disasters of all kinds. The challenge was to write a book on VT that is both academically rigorous and has practical application given the limitations in existing research. The editors present a wide view of the field while remaining close to the individual experiences of clinicians "on the ground" who have experienced the effects of disaster response work first hand. This book is for individual clinicians who would like to further understand the theoretical rationale for VT and the practical applications of concrete steps to manage identified challenges. It is for managers, supervisors, and administrators who play an active role in the management of employee health, work performance, and productivity and who are interested to advance mental health in the workplace by taking meaningful action in promoting resilience and addressing VT. It is also for researchers who are tasked to design innovative research studies on workplace mental health that can provide conceptual and empirical validation of VT in the post-disaster context. The editors hope that this book will contribute to a larger effort in promoting resilience in mental health providers compelled to work with survivors of overwhelming traumatic challenges.

This book is organized in five sections: Section I, "Understanding Vicarious Trauma," Section II, "Understanding Disasters," Section III, "Understanding Vicarious Resilience," Section IV, "Managing Vicarious Trauma in Disasters," and Section V, "Navigating Resources in Vicarious Trauma and Disasters." The "Personal Reflections" section woven in between chapters are personal essays written by mental health providers who were exposed to a massive traumatic event. Each essay tells a story from the perspective of the person behind the clinician who lived through a disaster.

In the first section, Chapter 1 provides readers with the theory, etiology, and presentation of VT as a normal response to indirect exposure to trauma via empathic engagement with patients based on over 20 years of research literature. It reviews the construct and compares and contrasts vicarious trauma with other work-impact concepts such as burnout, compassion fatigue, secondary traumatic stress, and countertransference. Vignettes are used to illustrate the concepts and the chapter closes with challenges for further research and intervention. Chapter 2 discusses the findings of a study conducted on a group of mental health professionals at St. Vincent's Hospital in Manhattan on the first-year anniversary of 9/11, and it reviews the literature on the impact of providing services to 9/11 victims

10 years later. Risk and protective factors are identified but further studies are warranted before any conclusion can be drawn due to the lack of conceptual clarity and methodological limitations across all existing studies. The concept of VT has been studied for over two decades and while no one disputes the importance of the topic, barriers to addressing the issue persist. Chapter 3 explores significant challenges that individuals and organizations face in tackling vicarious trauma.

The increase in frequency and magnitude of disasters globally has raised awareness of the impact of catastrophic events and highlighted the challenges of disaster response and recovery. Section II begins with Chapter 4, an overview of the disaster context—definitions and types of disasters, the phases of disasters, types of disaster exposure and the US disaster response system. It also discusses the role of mental health providers at various stages of the disaster timeline. Chapter 5 describes the history and evolution of Psychological First Aid (PFA). It discusses the theory behind PFA, as well as its goals and principles, its strengths and limitations. The context of early post-disaster intervention does not lend itself to applying a full array of treatment strategies and this factor may contribute to vicarious traumatization, when mental health providers cannot meet their own expectations about what their efforts can achieve in the context of immediate post-disaster intervention. Future directions in the field of immediate post-disaster intervention are also discussed. Chapter 6 compares the federal disaster behavior health response to several large-scale events such as the terrorist attacks of 9/11, the Newtown school shooting, the Boston Marathon bombing, Hurricane Katrina, the Joplin tornado, and a huge spate of other tornados that tore through the southern section of the US in 2011. Mental health providers, substance abuse counselors, faith-based workers and other community volunteers are being called for multiple and longer term disaster mental health deployments than ever before even though they are disaster survivors themselves. The disaster preparedness and training activities conducted in communities can have a significant impact on the development or mitigation of vicarious traumatic effects on disaster mental health responders. Chapter 6 also discusses the federal disaster behavioral health response, the risks to responders, as well as making meaning, attending to self-care and enhancing resilience.

Section III features the positive aspects of trauma work that can enhance professional development and satisfaction. Chapter 7 covers the formulation of the concept of vicarious resilience, or posttraumatic growth, as a process by which clinicians experience positive transformation and empowerment through their empathic engagement with victims of trauma (Hernandez, Gangsei, & Engstrom, 2007). Chapter 8 evaluates the positive perception of self and abilities, positive acceptance of changes to self as a result of working with victims of trauma, the role of organizational support, involvement with family, peers, and leisure activities, and religion and spirituality. Chapter 9 illustrates the work of mental health clinicians by discussing case examples of victims of military, civilian, and mass trauma. Both risk factors for developing symptoms of vicarious trauma and protective factors promoting vicarious resilience are highlighted. Particular attention is paid to the factors associated with vicarious resilience outlined in previous chapters.

Section IV offers concrete steps in the evaluation and management of VT. A number of self-administered tools which assess symptoms of vicarious trauma are available for mental health professionals. Chapter 10 provides an overview of these tools including their development, scoring instructions, and psychometric properties. The use of one of these tools at regular intervals may help with the early identification of a potential problem and, while not to be used as diagnostic tools, they may be used to determine the need for further investigation and intervention. Chapter 11 reviews the core schemas that are most vulnerable to disruption through vicarious traumatization as delineated by Pearlman and Saakvitne (1995) and discusses self-care and organizational strategies that have conceptual and empirical support for addressing these disruptions. Therapists and other helping professionals who dedicate a large part of their work life to the care of trauma survivors are vulnerable to the disruption in their core schemas about self, world, and others. Self-care strategies that are targeted at building resilience in these areas are identified. Chapter 12 proposes a practical framework for organizations to systematically address vicarious trauma and build resilience in mental health providers who respond to large scale disasters by choice or by circumstance. Studies have suggested that interventions such as providing opportunities for peer consultation (Figley, 1995; Pearlman & Saakvitne, 1995), increasing professional support and frequency of individual supervision (Brady, Guy, Poelstra, & Browkaw 1999; Follette & Batten, 2000), and maintaining a balanced caseload (e.g. Chrestman, 1999) may reduce symptoms of VT among disaster mental health disaster workers. These approaches, together with strategies for worksite health promotion and occupational health and safety that are backed by research evidence are tailored to prevent and mitigate disruption of the trauma-focused schemas of safety, esteem, trust, control, and intimacy throughout the disaster mental health response timeline. It is hoped that these organizational approaches will lay the groundwork for the development of research and best practices that decrease the risks of vicarious trauma and promote resilience in disaster mental health response.

The last section is devoted to citing useful resources for mental health providers. Chapter 13 provides an objective account of the nature of services offered on VT by a wide range of organizations as well as a summary of works available through print and electronic resources. Relevant literature can be useful in building a broader base of understanding of the phenomena of vicarious trauma, secondary traumatic stress, and compassion fatigue and can be used as an adjunct to this book. Chapter 14 outlines the roles of major organizations—multiple tiers of government, private and non-profit organizations, both locally and internationally—as providers of mental health services to victims of disaster. Functions include enhancing disaster preparedness, providing direct psychological first aid, and at times providing longer term follow up. In addition, organizations are involved in research, service coordination, and training of responders to further develop a robust resource pool.

Helping others can motivate and inspire but it also has the potential to do harm. Repeated exposure to human suffering can take a toll on mental health providers, particularly in the post-disaster context when clinician resources can be depleted from increased caseloads of traumatized patients and disruptions of the normal course of life. There is a gap in the understanding and management of vicarious trauma that cannot be filled by the reification of a new "disorder" or the blaming of trauma survivors or clinicians who do not become models of self-care and a balanced life. Rather, the mental health field, particularly in the area of crisis and disaster response, must continue to find ways to understand the risks and address the impact of intense and repeated exposure to the most difficult of human experiences. The editors believe that vicarious trauma can and should be addressed proactively to manage risks, deviate from the potential adverse impact and steer towards the intangible rewards of delivering services to disaster victims. This book advocates for the psychological health and safety of mental health providers and offers a framework for the promotion of worker resilience in the standard of practice in disaster management.

References

Brady, J.L., Guy, J.D., Poelstra, P.L., & Browkaw, B. (1999). Vicarious traumatization, spirituality, and the treatment of sexual abuse survivors: A national survey of women psychotherapists. *Professional Psychology Research and Practice*, 30(4), 386–393.

Chrestman, K.R. (1999). Secondary exposure to trauma and self-reported distress among therapists. In B.H. Stamm (ed.), *Secondary traumatic stress: Self care issues for clinicians, researchers, and educators* (2nd ed., pp. 29–36). Baltimore, MD: Sidran Press.

Figley, C.R. (1995). Compassion fatigue as secondary traumatic stress disorder: An overview. In C. Figley (ed.), *Compassion fatigue: Coping with secondary traumatic stress disorder in those who treat the traumatized* (pp. 1–20). New York, NY: Brunner/Mazel.

Follette, V.M., & Batten, S.V. (2000). The role of emotion in psychotherapy supervision: A contextual behavioral analysis. *Cognitive and Behavioral Practice*, 7, 306–312.

Halpern, J., & Tramontin, M. (2007). *Disaster mental health: Theory and practice*. Belmont, CA: Thomson Brooks/Cole.

Hernandez, P., Gangsei, D., & Engstrom, D. (2007). Vicarious resilience: A new concept in work with those who survive trauma. *Family Process, 46*(2), 229–241.

Pearlman, L.A., & Saakvitne, K.W. (1995). *Trauma and the therapist: Countertransference and vicarious traumatization in psychotherapy with incest survivors*. New York, NY: W.W. Norton & Co.

SECTION I

Understanding Vicarious Trauma

1

WHAT IS VICARIOUS TRAUMA?

Mark R. Evces

Susan worked in a mental health clinic serving World Trade Center survivors. She previously worked in an outpatient mental health clinic in an urban hospital center, and she considered herself to be developing as a specialist in treating trauma. In an effort to keep up with the latest treatment research, she actively engaged in continuing education and supervised training in several evidence-based interventions. Though at times her work was draining and the administrative demands frustrating, Susan enjoyed working with her patients and cared deeply for them. She was working in lower Manhattan when the 9/11 attacks occurred and found helping others recover to be a part of her own healing process. Over time, as she heard story after story of death and destruction related to the WTC attacks, Susan began to find herself dwelling on her patients' experiences. She became increasingly concerned about another terrorist attack and tried to convince her partner that they should live outside of the city. When asked why she wanted to move, Susan responded, "Now that I know what people are capable of, I realize it's just a matter of time before this happens again. It's not safe to be here."

Introduction: Direct versus Vicarious Trauma

Psychological trauma is, by nature, overwhelming. Extreme threat and loss flood the normal processes of human experience. Basic functioning such as perception, memory, and emotional experience become unreliable, compounding the traumatic event's initial threat to stability, predictability, and safety. Fundamental beliefs and assumptions about the world, our relationships and ourselves can be transformed, sometimes permanently so. For many, trauma eventually leads to a greater appreciation of life and a deeper sense of meaning. However, shifts in meaning following a trauma can also cause significant distress, and the consequences can be severe.

Traumatic events, those involving actual or witnessed threat to life and safety, are both statistically common in human experience (Norris, 1992) and uniquely out of place in a survivor's life. While the vast majority of people who experience or witness a traumatic event recover, many do not do so without treatment (Kessler, Sonnega, & Bromet, 1995). Survivors who are unable to successfully integrate traumatic events become stuck in a cycle of intrusive, distressing memories and attempts to avoid those memories (Horowitz, 2011). The accompanying intense emotions such as fear, anxiety, anger, shame, and guilt become too much to bear. The words that would describe and integrate the meaning of the trauma become unspeakable.

The nature of helping others heal from trauma includes speaking of the unspeakable. Most mental health treatments for traumatized patients involve some form of exposure to trauma-related material including memories, thoughts, and emotions (e.g. Foa, Steketee, & Rothbaum, 1989; Resick & Schnicke, 1993). While the intent of patient exposure is to relieve posttraumatic stress, in facilitating exposure the treatment provider is secondarily, or indirectly, exposed to the survivor's traumatic material. In contrast to primary or direct exposure, in which an individual experiences or observes a threat of or actual harm or loss, secondary exposure involves exposure to the traumatic memories, thoughts, feelings, and behaviors of others. Helping professionals become indirectly exposed to the traumatic experiences of their patients via graphic descriptions of death and disaster, senseless and brutal acts, and random acts of destruction. There is little doubt among clinicians that helping people recover from trauma impacts everyone involved: survivors, their family and friends, and treatment providers from a variety of occupations (Figley, 1989). Secondary, or indirect, traumatic exposure is not limited to mental health providers. Anyone who repeatedly and empathically engages with traumatized individuals can be at risk for distress and impairment due to indirect exposure to others' traumatic material. The results of indirect, occupational trauma exposure are increasingly considered in diagnostic classification. Recent changes in the definition of Posttraumatic Stress Disorder include specific mention of experiencing "first-hand or repeated exposure to aversive details of the traumatic event (not through media, pictures, television or movies unless work-related)" (American Psychiatric Association, 2013). The addition of symptom Criterion D, negative alterations in cognitions and mood, includes "persistent (and often distorted) negative beliefs and expectations about oneself or the world."

Many occupations involve repeated exposure to aversive details of others' traumatic experience. Most obvious are first responders, and medical and mental health professionals, whose job duties include exposure to the details of survivors' traumatic memories and distress. Volunteer helpers, social service workers, lawyers, and the clergy may also be indirectly exposed. Professional helpers rely on training and professional experience to manage any unintended or overwhelming negative effects they may experience as a consequence of indirect trauma exposure.

However, in the event of the collective trauma associated with large-scale disasters, it is more likely that many workers will experience sudden, repeated, and intense indirect trauma exposure. Even the most experienced and well-trained clinicians may feel overwhelmed if the level of indirect exposure exceeds their ability to cope. Many will lack the training and support for prevention and remediation of any lasting effects. Whether it's a gradual accumulation, as in clinical outpatient work, or the sudden and enveloping collective trauma of large-scale disaster response, clinicians often find themselves engaging with some of the most painful aspects of human experience (Palm, Polusny, & Follette, 2012).

There is little doubt that exposure to the suffering of others can have an impact on people. This is not to be confused with blaming a trauma survivor: it is the traumatic material, not the traumatized person that is the source of distress related to a helping professional's indirect exposure. Anecdotal and empirical data indicate that clinicians can be professionally and personally affected, even impaired, by working with traumatized clients (Elwood, Mott, Lohr, & Galovski, 2011; Sabin-Farrell & Turpin, 2003). Several constructs have appeared in the literature to describe these effects of indirect trauma exposure on professional helpers. However, recent reviews describe a lack of conceptual clarity and consistent empirical evidence to describe the effects of indirect trauma exposure on professional helpers (Baird & Kracen, 2006; Elwood et al., 2011; Jenkins & Baird, 2002).

To address this apparent contradiction between anecdotal experience and academic research, this chapter will review and present examples from peer-reviewed journals of constructs of the effects of indirect trauma exposure on professional helpers: vicarious trauma (VT), burnout, secondary traumatic stress, compassion fatigue, countertransference, and shared trauma. An emphasis will be placed on VT as its effects can disrupt deeply held beliefs, assumptions, and expectations. Other indirect trauma-related constructs are not specific to professional helpers (e.g., burnout), not specific to work with trauma survivors (e.g., compassion fatigue), short-lived (e.g., countertransference), or not due to repeated exposure (e.g., secondary traumatic stress). VT is the only construct that specifically describes the cumulative, long-lasting effects on professional helpers working specifically with trauma survivors.

Vicarious Trauma: A General Pattern

McCann and Pearlman (1990) first described VT, or vicarious traumatization, as changes in a therapist's inner world resulting from repeated empathic engagement with clients' trauma-related thoughts, memories, and emotions. VT often specifically refers to negative changes in a professional helper's fundamental beliefs about the world, self, and others (McCann & Pearlman, 1990). The cumulative effects of empathically engaging with survivors while they relate their most difficult experiences can deeply affect and even impair clinicians. In some cases, helpers experience PTSD-like intrusive images of their patients' traumatic material, and other sensory and behavioral disruptions. Helpers may also begin to feel the fear, mistrust, and isolation of their patients in a way that is personal, deeply affecting, and difficult to recover from without help. Particular emphasis continues to be placed on beliefs related to basic human needs for safety, self-esteem, trust, control, and intimacy. VT has been described as a common, long-term response to working with traumatized populations, and as part of a continuum of helper reactions ranging from vicarious growth and resilience to vicarious traumatization and impairment. Its originators hypothesized that VT is widespread in the helping professions and when not addressed could be detrimental to the well-being and effectiveness of clinicians and organizations.

Prevalence

In reviewing 10 years of secondary traumatization research across 41 studies, Elwood et al. (2011) identified 10 different assessment instruments used to measure variously defined constructs of secondary trauma symptoms, including VT. The Traumatic Stress Institute Belief Scale (TSIBS; Traumatic Stress Institute, 1994) and subsequent revisions (Revision L; Pearlman (1996)); and the Trauma Attachment Belief Scale (TABS; Pearlman (2003)) measure frequency and severity of VT among helping professionals (see Chapter 11). Reviewed studies reported TSIBS scores among various populations as well as correlations with other measures of secondary traumatization. Frequency and intensity of secondary trauma effects varied widely. However, the studies reviewed did not report means for TSIBS or revised versions, preventing specific conclusions about the prevalence of VT.

Elwood et al. (2011) concluded that there is insufficient evidence of a significant correlation between secondary traumatization and therapist exposure to traumatic material, therapist trauma history, or professional role as a trauma therapist. However, trauma therapists do experience specific areas of distress. There is a lack of consistent evidence to support the notion that trauma therapists are more generally distressed than others in the helping professions, such as therapists with little or no cases of traumatized patients, or social service workers who are not providing psychotherapy. The prevalence of distress and impairment associated with indirect exposure, including changes in the trauma-related schemas of those helping trauma survivors is basically unknown and more research studies are needed.

Etiology and Presentation

Pearlman and Saakvitne (1995) conceptualize both direct and indirect (vicarious) traumatization using a constructivist self-development theory (CSDT) of personality, integrating psychodynamic and constructivist theory, and cognitive theories of social learning and cognitive development. From the constructivist perspective, individuals actively create meaning out of their experiences, constructing narratives in order to adapt to an ever-changing world and to maintain personal and interpersonal stability. CSDT defines direct traumatization as a disruption of human development and adaptation. A survivor's most basic assumptions about the world can be transformed when those assumptions are violated by traumatic experience; however, most survivors are able to successfully cognitively assimilate and accommodate a trauma's meaning. For some, however, adaptive attempts to construct meaning lead to distress and impairment. As listed previously, CSDT conceptualizes five categories of beliefs fundamental to human development and adaptation: safety, self-esteem, trust, control, and intimacy. Disruptions in these schemas can result in distress and impairment. The basic predictability and safety of the world become suspect or lost. People seem more capable of cruelty. Trust in others becomes difficult or impossible. An individual's specific posttraumatic adaptations are shaped by the interaction between the specific circumstances of a traumatic experience, the survivor's personality and personal history, and social and cultural context. Specific aspects of the developing and adapting self that are affected by trauma exposure are presented in Table 1.1.

TABLE 1.1 Constructivist Self-Development Theory: Aspects of the Self Impacted by Psychological Trauma, and Corresponding Examples of Vicarious Traumatization (Adapted from Pearlman & Saakvitne, 1995)

Aspect of Self Affected	Examples of Symptoms of VT
Frame of Reference	
• Worldview	"My view of the world has changed: most people don't care about other people."
• Identity	"Being a therapist was part of my identity. Now I'm not sure who I am."
• Spirituality	"I had a sense of purpose and a connection to a greater meaning in life. Now, I feel lost and disconnected."
Self Capacities	
• Tolerate Strong Affect	"I just can't be around strong feelings anymore, including my family's."
• Maintain Positive Sense of Self	"I don't think I'm very effective at helping others."
• Maintain inner sense of connection with others	"I feel distanced from my clients and the people in my personal life. I feel lonely."
Ego Resources	
• Self-Awareness skills	"People are telling me I'm becoming cynical, but I'm sure I'll know when I'm affected by my work."
• Interpersonal and self-protective skills	"My colleague and I don't get along anymore. I can't tell her about my work anymore without feeling criticized."

(Continued)

TABLE 1.1 (*Continued*)

Aspect of Self Affected	Examples of Symptoms of VT
Psychological Needs and Related Cognitive Schema	
• Safety	"I have trouble walking home now. It's too dangerous."
• Esteem	"I've failed my clients. They need someone better than me."
• Trust	"I don't date anymore. You can't trust anyone to tell you the truth about themselves."
• Control	"I don't know if either of us could control our anger if I expressed myself to my coworker."
• Intimacy	"My wife and I don't really talk anymore. We're just too busy, I guess."
Memory System	
• Verbal	"I can't remember our session from last week."
• Affect	"I can tell you about my patients, but I'm having trouble identifying my feelings about them."
• Imagery	"I can't get the image of my client running from the building collapse out of my mind."
• Somatic	"I've been away from work for a week with lower back pain."
• Interpersonal	"I feel like I'm bullying my clients, like I'm interrogating them."

From the CSDT perspective, VT is a disruption of clinicians' efforts to adapt to repeated exposure to their patients' traumatic memories and emotional responses, in the context of empathic engagement. Story after story of human suffering begins to affect the way the clinician sees themselves, others, and the world. Like the survivor of direct trauma, the clinician adapts to and makes meaning of exposure to intense emotional pain. *If so many people have been assaulted, the world must be a very dangerous place. Most people are cruel. I can never feel safe.* As in direct traumatization, efforts at adaptation can also lead to posttraumatic growth and vicarious resilience. *I can make a difference in other people's lives. People are resilient. The world is full of stories of positive transformation.* These shifts in beliefs may be a normal consequence of indirect exposure, often resolving on their own and without lasting effects. Proactive measures such as self-care, maintaining manageable caseloads and competent supervision measures protect vulnerable clinicians from lasting, negative impact. However, some negative effects on inner experience may persist, leading to distress and impairment associated with VT and indicating intervention (Quitangon, Lascher, DeFrancisci, Rovine, & Eth, 2003).

The majority of VT literature has focused on changes in trauma-focused schemas (e.g. safety, esteem, trust, control and intimacy) as a primary outcome, rather than the full range of aspects of self as described by Pearlman and Saakvitne (1995). The Traumatic Stress Institute Belief Scale (TSIBS; Traumatic Stress Institute, 1994), for example, assesses changes in schemas of safety, self, and others, and does not query for intrusive, avoidant, or hyperarousal symptoms also associated with VT. A focus on changes in fundamental beliefs about the world, self, and other, sets VT apart from other similar constructs such as compassion fatigue and burnout. Intrusions, avoidance, and hyperarousal are more often associated with secondary traumatic stress and compassion fatigue (e.g. Figley, 1995), described later in this chapter.

In their comprehensive review of VT and related constructs, Sabin-Farrell and Turpin (2003) describe other possible mechanisms for VT including countertransference, empathy, emotional contagion, cognitive theory, and organizational/work and therapist factors, including therapist history of trauma. Others have speculated that VT is the result of emotional and physical exhaustion (Devilly, Wright, & Varker, 2009), as in burnout, or is better explained by failures of the clinician to effectively manage the therapeutic relationship (Hafkenscheid, 2005). Neurobiological aspects of empathy have also been considered to play a role (Rothschild & Rand, 2006). As there is no clear consensus on the active mechanism leading to VT, there is also no consensus regarding risk factors, though researchers have identified therapist history of personal trauma (Baird & Kracen, 2006) and caseload size (Creamer & Liddle, 2005) as potential factors.

Other Effects of Helping Trauma Survivors

There are a variety of perspectives and constructs describing the effects of one person being exposed to another's distress. The section below includes the more commonly described concepts and is not intended to be an exhaustive list. Others, including counter-trauma (Gartner, 2014), projective identification (Klein, 1946), and the role of empathy response (Rothschild & Rand, 2006) are relevant and important but are not included in this chapter.

Countertransference

Mike felt strong protective feelings for his new patient, a female Army officer who presented for treatment of combat trauma. The patient had difficulty expressing anger at her commanding officers who she felt made terrible decisions during a fire fight. Mike developed intense anger towards the patient's commanding officers and found himself referring to the officers using expletives during the therapy. Surprised at the intensity of his anger, Mike sought peer supervision and discussed the similarities between the patient and Mike's younger sister who had been assaulted as a teenager. Having explored the origins of his identification with the patient, Mike felt more in control of himself during sessions, and more able to focus on his patient's sense of being betrayed by her superiors.

Trauma survivors often have powerful emotional responses to trauma and its consequences. These responses can be directed at the therapist. Thoughts, feelings, and behaviors that distort a patient's experience of the therapist are commonly referred to as *transference* (Wilson & Lindy, 1994). Thoughtful attunement to patients' transference can yield important information about the patient's traumatic experience and its consequences. Prolonged empathic engagement with a patient's intense emotions, including transference, can result in the therapist straining to maintain empathy for the patient.

Countertransference describes the immediate, often unconscious, emotional reactions of mental health providers to their patients. While there is a diverse literature describing countertransference, many clinicians agree that therapist emotional reactions to patients are expected, useful, and not necessarily problematic unless unrecognized and disruptive. Countertransference reactions can be particularly intense with trauma survivors, whose powerful affects are often related to being harmed by another person (Herman, 1992). Therapists may over-identify with patients, leading to excessive self-disclosure, loss of boundaries, and preoccupation with the patient (Wilson & Lindy, 1994). Alternatively, the therapist may withdraw or avoid the patient, leading to emotional distancing, intellectualizing, or denial of the survivor's traumatic experience. When a therapist has an unrecognized emotional reaction to a patient, he or she may lose empathy for the patient, weakening the therapeutic relationship and threatening the clinician's thoughtful control over clinical decision-making. In the absence of a safe and empathic environment, patients may become stuck in or terminate treatment.

A specific type of countertransference, *event countertransference*, describes a therapist's reaction to the nature of their patient's trauma, as in therapist reactions to the Holocaust while treating Holocaust survivors. Rather than reacting to the patient, the therapist has an emotional response to the nature of the trauma which has the potential to disrupt treatment (Danieli, 1994).

Freud (1910/1959) initially considered feelings towards the patient and about the treatment to be a barrier to therapeutic progress. Countertransference was conceptualized as a manifestation of a therapist's unresolved neurotic conflicts. However, subsequent theorists have considered countertransference as normal, inevitable and potentially useful for conceptualization and intervention, including thoughtful disclosure to the client (Wilson & Lindy, 1994). When adequately recognized and addressed, transference and countertransference provide useful information for patient and clinician, leading to a safer, more collaborative therapeutic relationship.

Secondary Traumatic Stress

One patient, in particular, affected Susan deeply. The patient had seen several coworkers die during a building collapse, and the horrific images the patient described evoked strong feelings of sadness and fear in Susan. Susan noticed these feelings remained long after therapy sessions, and though she tried not to think about the patient's stories, horrific images appeared in her mind. She found herself becoming tearful after sessions. After two months of meeting with the patient, Susan developed insomnia and avoided anything that might make her sad or afraid. She felt she might be overwhelmed by these feelings. During sessions, she found herself avoiding discussion of the patient's memories, once ending a session early because she read the wall clock incorrectly. She felt irritation with anyone who brought up potentially sad or frightening material, including her family and friends. Her husband noticed that Susan seemed distant and emotionally numb.

Figley (1989) described the secondary traumatization of trauma survivors' family members as well as caregivers exposed to survivors' traumatic material (Figley & Kleber, 1995). Stamm (1995) published a volume on secondary traumatic stress and self-care during the same year. Originally called *secondary traumatic stress syndrome*, the symptoms paralleled those of PTSD: intrusive traumatic images, thoughts and memories; subsequent efforts to avoid such affectively charged material; and hyperarousal resulting from overstimulation and hypervigilance.

Compassion Fatigue

Susan's intense clinical work proved exhausting. Her caseload was well over the normal number of patients for her clinic. Her patients trusted her with their most difficult memories and intense emotions during therapy sessions, including strong feelings towards Susan. Increasing exhaustion led to difficulties concentrating and she began to feel less effective as a clinician. A patient informed her, "You're not getting it. I can see that you're somewhere else." Normally, Susan would see such a rupture as an opportunity for exploration. Instead, she felt incompetent and resentful of the patient for pointing out her limitations. Unable to track her patients' narratives and emotional states, her ability to empathize slowly faded until she found herself experiencing relief when patients cancelled, and resentment when they came to appointments with strong feelings or complaining of distress.

Following his work on secondary traumatic stress in families of trauma survivors, Figley (1995) described compassion fatigue as the empathic strain and general exhaustion resulting from caring for people in distress. Thought to be a less stigmatizing term than secondary traumatic stress disorder, compassion fatigue is most often associated with those in the helping professions, including first responders, physicians, and disaster recovery workers (Figley, 1995).

Recent literature has focused on emotional and physical exhaustion rather than PTSD-like symptoms as the primary effects of compassion fatigue (Elwood et al., 2011). PTSD-like symptoms are considered to be more characteristic of secondary traumatic stress disorder. Unlike burnout, compassion fatigue is specifically related to exposure to others' suffering and loss of empathy. Unlike VT, compassion fatigue does not focus on changes in trauma-related schemas due to exposure to traumatic memories of survivors. Rather, it is a gradual erosion of physical and emotional resources leading to indifference and antipathy towards those in need.

Burnout

When Susan started work at the trauma clinic, she made efforts to leave work at 5 p.m., but soon she found herself staying an hour later to finish paper work. After the first six months, she began to come to the office early to work on treatment plans and catch up on reading. Her caseload was large but manageable. After her first year, her supervisor asked Susan to increase her caseload size and to supervise trainees. Susan began to find herself rushing through the day, worrying that she might not get her notes finished on time. Her days stretched past 8 hours to 10 or more. In order to compensate for the increased work demands, she stopped her regular exercise in the mornings so she could arrive earlier. She drank more coffee to push through the fatigue in the morning and, eventually, in the afternoon. She cancelled any optional meeting or work activity in order to keep up with her work, including lunch and increasingly avoided all contact with coworkers.

Burnout is a persistent feeling of exhaustion, cynicism and inefficacy resulting from chronic exposure to work-related stress (Maslach, Schaufeli, & Leiter, 2001). Originally a term used to describe the depleting effects of long-term drug abuse, burnout was first used by psychiatrists and social psychologists in the 1970s to describe the negative, chronic effects of human services and education work. Subsequent research has expanded the concept to other professions (e.g., law enforcement, military, management), including those that do not include a primary interpersonal focus (e.g., computer services).

Three core aspects of burnout have been identified (Garden, 1987). The central characteristic of job burnout is *emotional exhaustion* resulting from feeling overworked and exhausted of physical and emotional resources. *Depersonalization, or cynicism*, is a negative and detached interpersonal experience towards coworkers and clients, including distrust of organizations. Cynical emotional responses include hostility, lack of empathy, or detachment and may represent an attempt to cope with feelings of exhaustion and overwhelm. *Lack of self-efficacy* includes a reduced sense of personal achievement, productivity, and competence, and may also emerge from feeling exhausted and without sufficient emotional and physical resources. While these elements are also common to depression, burnout is considered to be specific to work and have less or no effect on the individual's life outside of work. The primary cause of job burnout is thought to be overload: too many hours, too many tasks, and too many clients in the context of too little social support and poorly defined or conflicting work roles.

Burnout can be differentiated from vicarious traumatization in that burnout is not primarily interpersonal in nature, does not include active engagement with clients' traumatic material, and does not result in behavioral, cognitive, or emotional shifts outside of the workplace. Burnout is similar to VT in that it results from work-related stress and includes physical and emotional exhaustion, interpersonal cynicism and detachment, and a lack of self-efficacy. The much wider scope of VT's effects, and its relationship to indirect exposure to trauma, suggest that it may be more useful to consider the two constructs related but conceptually distinct, with some overlap of effects.

Shared Trauma

Susan came to work two days after the attacks of September 11, 2001. Her apartment building was closed due to dust contamination, and she stayed with her parents for months. The first two nights she spent crying in her bedroom, calling friends and family and hoping they were safe. When she returned to her clinic, she was waiting to hear if a close friend had survived the attacks and worried that another attack might occur. Her first patient sat down in her office and said, "You look awful. I came here to see if you were still alive. I was terrified that you might have been killed. Do you know if your family is ok?" Susan felt vulnerable and unable to contain her fear and sadness. The usual feeling of focused curiosity and concern for her patients was replaced by an intense desire to leave the room and find a place to cry. Susan responded, "I'm ok. I'm here. I appreciate you checking on me. It sounds like you were worried I might not be here today." The patient responded, "I was. I guess we are both dealing with a lot."

Shared trauma, "shared reality" or "shared traumatic reality" occurs when professional helpers and their clients are exposed to the same potentially traumatic event or its consequences (Dekel & Baum, 2010). Large-scale disasters are likely to affect entire communities, including professional helpers and the people they assist. As members of the same disaster-stricken community, both patient and clinician may experience similar disruptions of shelter, transportation, access to social and material supports, and communication with loved ones. Mental health workers are also increasingly included as part of post-disaster response (Watson, Brymer, & Bonanno, 2011), raising the likelihood of direct exposure to the immediate after-effects of disasters such as threat to life, bodily injury, and exposure to injured or killed victims. Whereas clinicians may be directly exposed to the very same life-threatening events as their patients, they may have quite different reactions (Baum, 2010). Reports have described the effects on clinicians of terrorist attacks in Oklahoma City (Wee & Myers, 2002) and New York (Baum, 2010; Tosone et al., 2003), and the aftermath of Hurricane Katrina in New Orleans (Boulanger, 2013).

Boulanger (2013) describes shared trauma experiences of therapists in the aftermath of Hurricane Katrina as "working in an echo chamber" (p. 37) in which patients' descriptions of shared traumatic events or consequences trigger intense emotion in mental health providers. Therapeutic relationships develop a "fearful symmetry" in which therapists face similar emotional and cognitive disruptions as their patients and are forced to disclose personal aspects of a shared trauma's effects. Normal markers of safety such as a consistent office space and uninterrupted sessions might also be disrupted, making the boundaries and therapeutic frame necessary for effective clinical work difficult or impossible to maintain. How can therapists adapt? Boulanger (2013) describes therapists using self-disclosure in new ways to reassure their patients and explain unavoidable realities (e.g., an office destroyed by flooding). These shifts in frame and boundaries require clinician flexibility and thoughtful adaptation. Clinicians are particularly vulnerable to vicarious traumatization when they themselves have experienced direct trauma exposure, as in the case of a shared trauma (Saakvitne, 2002). Considering the increased risk of therapist VT and threats to the most fundamental aspects of the therapeutic relationship, shared trauma presents a particularly challenging time in the course of any mental health treatment.

Challenges

Helping people heal from tragedy and human cruelty can both inspire and deplete us. Through helping others, we are changed. Yet, reviews have effectively documented the lack of knowledge about this phenomena that professional helpers largely agree to be an important aspect of clinical work. While exposure to suffering can have an effect on mental health professionals, the field has yet to consistently define and differentiate constructs and collect data indicating as much. Reviews indicate that conceptual ambiguity and overlap, inconsistent/lacking assessment tools and inadequate methods and statistical analyses have limited the conclusions of empirical studies. It is not easy to measure the effects of indirect exposure on clinicians. Future studies will need to address these issues to identify the occupational hazards of working with trauma survivors. Significant challenges remain towards understanding, preventing, and remediating the effects of repeated and intense indirect exposure on clinicians.

Inspiration can sustain and positively transform professional helpers, while physical and mental exhaustion can accumulate, distress, and impair. If helpers do not replenish what exposure to others' trauma can deplete, a process of chronic, vicarious traumatization can occur: lasting negative changes in a provider's fundamental beliefs resulting from repeated exposure to human suffering. Burnout describes a more general sense of physical and emotional exhaustion from overwork, and compassion fatigue describes a specific form of burnout resulting from caring for others. Countertransference describes the providers' moment-to-moment emotional reactions to their patients, which, if unmonitored and addressed, can lead to compassion fatigue. VT is a phenomenon specific to working with traumatized individuals, likely exacerbated by shared or prior traumatization of the therapist. VT is particularly salient to disaster mental health workers, who may have been directly exposed to and/or affected by a community-wide disaster and who may be suddenly faced with long hours and an increased caseloads of recently traumatized patients.

Why a Book on Vicarious Traumatization?

Compassion moves us to help those who are struggling, and empathy allows us to understand and facilitate healing. For most clinicians, assisting others is a predominantly rewarding and challenging endeavor: the "prognosis" for such clinicians is good. Clinicians may be inspired when they see others healing from terrible and frightening experiences. Over time, clinicians may develop vicarious resilience (described in Chapter 7; Hernández, Gangsei, & Engstrom, 2007), further strengthening their ability to survive and even thrive in the face of difficult experiences in their personal and professional lives. However, our reactions to others' traumatic memories and responses may also include emotional pain, which can persist if our fundamental beliefs in the safety and predictability of ourselves and our world are shaken, as in the case of vicarious traumatization. Recovering from shaken beliefs may occur naturally as part of a common reaction to indirect exposure, but for some the reverberations of others' suffering may result in lasting distress and impairment. Every clinician faces the risk of feeling worn down and overwhelmed by listening to others' most difficult experiences. Assertive self-care and informed interventions allow clinicians to stay healthy and effective. For this reason, VT is the focus of this chapter. Among the constructs describing the effects of exposure to others' suffering, VT is conceptually the most specific to those who help trauma survivors and perhaps the most impactful when left unaddressed. Government, educational, and health institutions are beginning to address the acute and long-term effects of trauma- and disaster-related work on professional helpers. It is hoped that this book will be a useful tool for organizations and individuals to understand, prevent, and treat the long-term effects of helping others.

Vicarious Trauma and Disaster Mental Health

It is important to advance methods of effectively coping with and recovering from the mental health effects of disaster. Informed and proactive disaster response plans can better serve survivors if mental health responders are trained to cope with the stories and distress of those they are helping.

Further understanding the effects of trauma work will lead to more effective identification and support for distressed clinicians, particularly in disaster response when professional helpers are most at risk for sudden, intense, and repeated exposure to others' suffering. During and following disasters, clinicians are at increased risk for direct and indirect trauma exposure, while their material, social, and institutional resources may be rendered unavailable or destroyed. Further study of VT will lead to improved clarification of the construct, measurement, and identification of risk and protective factors. Preventative and remedial interventions at the individual and organizational level will promote provider resilience, improving our ability to respond to large-scale disasters and their consequences. For over 20 years, clinicians and researchers have found evidence for lasting changes in the fundamental beliefs of professional helpers. We must continue to acknowledge and explore the impact of vicarious traumatization.

References

American Psychiatric Association. (2013). *Diagnostic and statistical manual of mental disorders 5.* Arlington, VA: American Psychiatric Publishing.

Baird, K., & Kracen, A.C. (2006). Vicarious traumatization and secondary traumatic stress: A research synthesis. *Counselling Psychology Quarterly, 19*(2), 181–188.

Baum, N. (2010). Shared traumatic reality in communal disasters: Toward a conceptualization. *Psychotherapy: Theory, Research, Practice, Training, 47*(2), 249.

Boulanger, G. (2013). Fearful symmetry: Shared trauma in New Orleans after Hurricane Katrina. *Psychoanalytic Dialogues, 23*(1), 31–44.

Creamer, T.L., & Liddle, B.J. (2005). Secondary traumatic stress among disaster mental health workers responding to the September 11 attacks. *Journal of Traumatic Stress, 18*(1), 89–96.

Danieli, Y. (1994). *Countertransference, trauma, and training.* New York, NY: Guilford Press.

Dekel, R., & Baum, N. (2010). Intervention in a shared traumatic reality: A new challenge for social workers. *British Journal of Social Work, 40*(6), 1927–1944.

Devilly, G.J., Wright, R., & Varker, T. (2009). Vicarious trauma, secondary traumatic stress or simply burnout? Effect of trauma therapy on mental health professionals. *Australian and New Zealand Journal of Psychiatry, 43*(4), 373–385.

Elwood, L.S., Mott, J., Lohr, J.M., & Galovski, T.E. (2011). Secondary trauma symptoms in clinicians: A critical review of the construct, specificity, and implications for trauma-focused treatment. *Clinical Psychology Review, 31*(1), 25–36.

Figley, C. (1989). *Treating stress in families.* Philadelphia: Brunner/Mazel.

Figley, C. (1995). *Compassion fatigue: Coping with secondary traumatic stress disorder in those who treat the traumatized.* New York, NY: Routledge.

Figley, C.R., & Kleber, R.J. (1995). *Beyond the "victim": Secondary traumatic stress.* New York, NY: Plenum Press.

Foa, E.B., Steketee, G., & Rothbaum, B.O. (1989). Behavioral/cognitive conceptualizations of post-traumatic stress disorder. *Behavior Therapy, 20*(2), 155–176.

Freud, S. (1910/1959). Future prospects of psychoanalytic psychotherapy. In J. Strachey (Ed. and Trans.), *The standard edition of the complete psychological works of Sigmund Freud* (Vol. 11, pp. 139–151). London: Hogarth.

Garden, A.M. (1987). Depersonalization: A valid dimension of burnout? *Human Relations, 40*(9), 545–559.

Gartner, R. (2014). Trauma and countertrauma: On being simply human. Paper presented at Division of Psychoanalysis (39) 34th Annual Spring Meeting. New York, NY.

Hafkenscheid, A. (2005). Event countertransference and vicarious traumatization: Theoretically valid and clinically useful concepts? *European Journal of Psychotherapy & Counselling, 7*(3), 159–168.

Herman, J.L. (1992). Complex PTSD: A syndrome in survivors of prolonged and repeated trauma. *Journal of Traumatic Stress, 5*(3), 377–391.

Hernández, P., Gangsei, D., & Engstrom, D. (2007). Vicarious resilience: A new concept in work with those who survive trauma. *Family Process, 46*(2), 229–241.

Horowitz, M. J. (2011). *Stress response syndromes: PTSD, grief, adjustment, and dissociative disorders.* Lanham, MD: Jason Aronson.

Jenkins, S.R., & Baird, S. (2002). Secondary traumatic stress and vicarious trauma: A validational study. *Journal of Traumatic Stress, 15*(5), 423–432.

Kessler, R.C., Sonnega, A., & Bromet, E. (1995). Posttraumatic stress disorder in the National Comorbidity Survey. *Archives of General Psychiatry, 52*, 1048–1060.

Klein, M. (1946). Notes on some schizoid mechanisms. In *The Writings of Melanie Klein*, Vol. 3, 1–24. London: Hogarth Press.

Maslach, C., Schaufeli, W.B., & Leiter, M.P. (2001). Job burnout. *Annual Review of Psychology, 52*(1), 397–422.

McCann, I.L., & Pearlman, L.A. (1990). Vicarious traumatization: A framework for understanding the psychological effects of working with victims. *Journal of Traumatic Stress, 3*(1), 131–149.

Norris, F.H. (1992). Epidemiology of trauma: Frequency and impact of different potentially traumatic events on different demographic groups. *Journal of Consulting and Clinical Psychology, 60*(3), 409.

Palm, K.M., Polusny, M.A., & Follette, V.M. (2012). Vicarious traumatization: Potential hazards and interventions for disaster and trauma workers. *Prehospital and Disaster Medicine, 19*(01), 73–78.

Pearlman L. A. (1996). Psychometric review of TSI Belief Scale Revision L. In B.H. Stamm (Ed.) *Measurement of stress, trauma and adaptation*. Lutherville, MD: Sidran Press.

Pearlman, L.A. (2003). *The Trauma Attachment Belief Scale manual*. Los Angeles, CA: Western Psychological Services.

Pearlman, L.A., & Saakvitne, K.W. (1995). *Trauma and the therapist: Countertransference and vicarious traumatization in psychotherapy with incest survivors*. New York, NY: W.W. Norton.

Quitangon, G., Lascher, S., DeFrancisci, L., Rovine, D. & Eth, S. (2003). Vicarious traumatization at a Manhattan hospital on year after the 9/11 tragedy. Poster presented at the American Psychiatric Association, New York, NY.

Resick, P.A., & Schnicke, M. (1993). *Cognitive Processing Therapy for rape victims*. New York, NY: Sage.

Rothschild, B., & Rand, M. (2006). *Help for the helper*. New York, NY: W.W. Norton.

Saakvitne, K.W. (2002). Shared trauma: The therapist's increased vulnerability. *Psychoanalytic Dialogues, 12*(3), 443–449.

Sabin-Farrell, R., & Turpin, G. (2003). Vicarious traumatization: Implications for the mental health of health workers? *Clinical Psychology Review, 23*(3), 449–480.

Stamm, B.H. (1995). *Secondary traumatic stress*. Brooklandville, MD: Sidran Press.

Tosone, C., Lee, M., Bialkin, L., & Martinez, A., Campbell, M., Martinez, M., . . . Stefan, A. (2003). Shared trauma: Group reflections on the September 11th disaster. *Psychoanalytic Social Work, 10*(1), 57–77.

Traumatic Stress Institute. (1994). *The TSI Belief Scale*. South Windsor, CT: Author.

Watson, P.J., Brymer, M.J., & Bonanno, G.A. (2011). Postdisaster psychological intervention since 9/11. *American Psychologist, 66*(6), 482.

Wee, D.F., & Myers, D. (2002). Stress responses of mental health workers following disaster: The Oklahoma City bombing. In C.R. Figley (Ed.), *Treating compassion fatigue* (pp. 57–83). New York, NY: Brunner-Routledge.

Wilson, J.P., & Lindy, J.D. (1994). *Countertransference in the treatment of PTSD*. New York, NY: Guilford Press.

2

WHAT FACTORS CAN PREDICT SUSCEPTIBILITY TO VICARIOUS TRAUMA?

Gertie Quitangon, Kate St. Cyr, and Charles Nelson

Introduction

The terrorist attacks on September 11, 2001 caused massive death and destruction, widespread trauma, and financial repercussions, and the malicious intent behind the unprecedented tragedy triggered lasting psychological effects. It resulted in the loss of many lives, and a profound disturbance in self-perceived safety nationwide (Galea et al., 2003). In the wake of the catastrophic event, Posttraumatic Stress Disorder (PTSD) received considerable media and academic attention. Schlenger et al. (2002) found that one to two months after 9/11, the prevalence of probable PTSD in NY metropolitan area was approximately 11.2%. The prevalence of PTSD for New Yorkers who lived south of Canal Street (i.e. near World Trade Center) was approximately 20% (Galea et al., 2002).

The impact of treating PTSD and other comorbidities in victims of large-scale disasters has been less widely studied. "Vicarious Traumatization at a Manhattan Hospital a Year After 9/11" (2003) (see Figure 2.1) was a pilot study that took a closer look at a group of mental health professionals who delivered services to 9/11 victims and explored variables that may predict susceptibility to the development of symptoms of vicarious trauma (VT). This represented the first effort to investigate vicarious traumatization of mental health clinicians in a tertiary care hospital setting after a national tragedy. On the tenth year anniversary of 9/11, a systematic review of published studies on VT and 9/11 was conducted to explore the knowledge base in the field, update the literature review of the pilot study in 2003 and compare and contrast findings.

Literature Review

Pearlman and Mac Ian (1995) studied 188 trauma therapists to identify variables associated with vicarious traumatization. Participants answered a questionnaire that included questions on work experience and personal trauma history and they completed the following instruments: Traumatic Stress Institute Belief Scale, Impact of Events Scale, Symptom Checklist 90–revised. The authors found that therapists with a *history of trauma* experienced significantly more disruption of schema from their work than those without a personal trauma history. Among those with trauma history, those with *less than two years of experience* reported more distress and disrupted schema.

Schauben and Frasier (1995) studied vicarious traumatization in 118 female psychologists and 30 female counselors in a Midwestern state. Participants completed the following: Traumatic Stress Institute Belief Scale, PTSD symptom checklist, Brief Symptom Inventory, Maslach Burnout Inventory, the Coping Inventory (COPE), and a questionnaire inquiring on work history and the extent to which they identified themselves as experiencing VT. They found that a *caseload* of survivors of sexual violence correlated with more disruptions in schema, more PTSD symptoms and increased self-report of vicarious traumatization. They did not find significant correlation with personal trauma history.

Brady, Guy, Poelstra, and Browkaw (1999) conducted a national survey of 1,000 randomly selected female psychotherapists who work with sexual abuse survivors. Respondents were surveyed on work-related characteristics, history of personal psychotherapy and personal trauma. They completed the following instruments: Impact of Events Scale, Traumatic Stress Institute Belief Scale, and the Spiritual Well-Being Scale. The survey revealed that if they have a higher *caseload* of sexual abuse clients or if they see a greater number of survivors over the course of their careers, they are more likely to experience symptoms of trauma themselves, but no more likely to experience significant disruption in cognitive schema. However, trauma symptoms were found to be relatively mild, and *spiritual well-being* was higher for those clinicians who saw more sexual abuse survivors.

VT has also been documented in those who provide mental health services to victims of mass disasters, such as hurricanes, earthquakes, and civil war (Culver, McKinney, & Paradise, 2011; Wee & Myers, 2002). Ten years post 9/11, "Vicarious Trauma in Mental Health Profressionals following 9/11: The Impact of Working with Trauma Victims" (2011), a systematic literature review of published studies on VT and 9/11 generated over 300 studies on VT, secondary traumatic stress and other related concepts but only 5 studies focused on 9/11 and examined variables of interest similar to the pilot study in 2003 (Adams, Figley, & Boscarino, 2006; Colarossi, Heyman, & Phillips, 2005; Creamer & Liddle, 2005; Daly et al., 2008; Eidelson, D'Alessio, & Eidelson, 2003). As summarized below, most of the studies examined the relationship between both personal (i.e., age, marital status, history of trauma) and professional factors (i.e., years of experience, caseload, hours of supervision) and the unintended negative outcomes of disaster mental health work.

Eidelson et al. (2003) specifically examined the impact of *distance from Ground Zero* on 592 psychologists in New York, New Jersey, Connecticut and Pennsylvania. Respondents completed a 15-item survey on how they were affected by 9/11. They found that those who worked closer to Ground Zero and those who had the highest percentage of 9/11 victims in their caseload reported higher work-related stress and stronger feelings of being unprepared. *Female* respondents reported higher levels of fearfulness. Those who had *more years of professional experience* reported less work stress. Volunteering in 9/11 activities was an important positive predictor of increased positive feelings about work.

Colarossi et al. (2005) analyzed the effects of certain stressors, such as *proximity to Ground Zero*, on developing symptoms using subscales of depression, anxiety, somatization, and posttraumatic stress. The survey consisted of a personal questionnaire, a patient health questionnaire and an NIH instrument designed to measure effects of 9/11. The study revealed that among the 777 social work students and MSW practitioners in the NY metropolitan area surveyed, those living within 10 miles of the World Trade Center site reported increased symptoms of depression, anxiety, somatization and traumatic stress. *Providing services directly to 9/11 survivors* positively related to depression, anxiety and traumatic stress symptoms. *Directly witnessing the disaster* and knowing someone who died or was injured increased anxiety, somatic, and traumatic stress symptoms. *Displacement from work* after the attack increased likelihood of somatic symptoms. *Caucasians and Asians* reported higher levels of depression and anxiety. Females reported higher levels of symptoms but they also reported more clients affected by 9/11.

Creamer and Liddle (2005) studied symptoms of secondary traumatic stress (STS) using the Impact of Events Scale and the Life Events Checklist. They surveyed 80 disaster mental health workers who responded to 9/11 from 28 states, as well as Washington, DC, and Alberta, Canada. Higher STS was found in those who had a *heavier caseload prior to 9/11*, those who were *younger and had less professional experience*, those with a *longer length of assignment*, and those with a *caseload* of children, firefighters, and clients with morbid material. Gender and personal trauma history was not significantly related to STS.

Adams et al. (2006) surveyed 274 New York City–based social workers who provided services to individuals experiencing distress following the 9/11 terrorist attacks and the study focused on compassion fatigue and its two components—work burnout and secondary trauma. The respondents completed the following validated scales: Compassion Fatigue Scale–Revised, General Health Questionnaire (GHQ-12), Negative Life Events Scale, Lifetime Traumatic Events Scale, September 11 Counseling Experience Scale, Social Support Scale and Sense of Mastery Scale. The authors found that *providing counseling services to those impacted by 9/11* was not significantly associated with compassion fatigue, work burnout or secondary trauma. *Age* was inversely associated with secondary trauma but there was no association with work burnout or compassion fatigue. *Gender* was not a significant predictor of any of the variables while *being married* was protective against compassion fatigue. A *history of negative life events* was significantly associated with compassion fatigue, work burnout and secondary trauma.

Daly and colleagues (2008) hypothesized that symptoms of PTSD, depression, anger, alcohol abuse, and functional impairment would increase on the first year *anniversary of 9/11*. Using a sample of 108 disaster mental health workers, they found a significant increase in depressive symptoms and functional impairment on the first year anniversary of 9/11. This study administered seven instruments: Clinician Administered PTSD Scale (CAPS), PTSD Checklist, Beck Depression Inventory (BDI), Profile of Mood States-Brief Profile (POMS-BP), Multidimensional Anger Inventory (MAI), Alcohol Dependence Scale, and Subjective Symptoms Scale.

9/11 Disaster Mental Health Response

Prior to September 2001, there were only six disasters in the US with fatality rates greater than a thousand and approximately 15 disasters resulted in greater than 40 injuries a year (Zibulewsky, 2001). With the exponential increase in frequency of large-scale disasters since 9/11, mental health professionals have played many important roles in helping communities prepare and respond to massive disasters. Universal interventions such as information, education, and a comforting therapeutic presence take on a different meaning in the confusion and chaos of a disaster and this is further complicated by the fact that both clinicians and victims share the experience of a massive traumatic event. In this study, all of the mental health clinicians surveyed worked at a teaching hospital most proximal to the World Trade Center, controlling for the variable of proximity to Ground Zero, and the array of services provided to address the mental health implications from the magnitude and devastation of 9/11 is briefly described below.

After the planes struck the twin towers, St. Vincent's Hospital Manhattan (SVH), a trauma center approximately one mile north of the World Trade Center, was put on high alert. The disaster plan was activated, all operating rooms were cleared for emergency cases and an emergency triage center was established outside the doors of the Emergency Department. In the first two hours after the attacks, nearly 400 patients were received and a second wave of patients was expected to arrive based on the hospital's experience from the 1993 World Trade Center bombing. However, only a few made it to the hospital.

Hours later, the SVH Department of Psychiatry organized the Family Support Center, a crisis center for families seeking missing loved ones. The center was quickly overwhelmed by the high volume of individuals looking for friends or family and long lines stretched several blocks, prompting relocation to a bigger space offered by the New School nearby. The Family Support Center was open 24/7 for 10 days after the attacks staffed by psychiatrists, social workers and psychotherapists from SVH as well as priests, rabbis and ministers from the community. There were a total of 6,900 visits, 16,000 calls to crisis lines, 1,200 individuals sent to the emergency room out of whom 148 were admitted, and 1,200 visits for anthrax concerns for which 248 tests were conducted.

New York City was declared a federal disaster area and became eligible for a range of Federal Emergency Management Agency (FEMA) programs. The New York State Office of Mental Health (OMH) applied for federal assistance and within six weeks received a total of \$155.2M from the Crisis Counseling Assistance and Training Program (CCP), jointly operated by FEMA and the Center for Mental Health Services (CMHS), to fund short-term programs designed to meet the immediate disaster-related mental health needs in New York for the next nine months (Felton, 2002). By the middle of October, Project Liberty was up and running, and SVH was one of over a hundred participating providers who provided free outreach and crisis counseling services to individuals and groups and referral to longer term formal mental health treatment when appropriate over the course of the year. SVH designed programs for specific populations including surviving firefighters and their families, the Port Authority Police, and the New York City Corrections Department Emergency Unit Officers who remained at Ground Zero during the cleanup. SVH also extended services to three schools located a block from Ground Zero—the High School of Economics and Finance, the High School of Leadership and Public Service and Elementary School PS89. Children and adolescents at risk for PTSD, depression, and high-risk behaviors such as drug use were identified and counseled while a Parent and Teachers Assistance Program was established to help the adults cope with emotional issues related to the tragedy. Free acupuncture and massage was also offered on a walk-in basis in the community through the Integrative Stress Management Program.

Method

A survey was conducted at SVH Department of Psychiatry on the first year anniversary of the 9/11 terrorist attack. The study was approved by the hospital Institutional Review Board. Informed consent was obtained and participation was voluntary and anonymous. The following standardized tools were administered: Impact of Events Scale revised (IES-r), Compassion Fatigue Self-Test (CFST), and Trauma Symptom Inventory (TSI). Respondents were also asked to complete a questionnaire about themselves and their level of 9/11 exposure (see Table 2.2), including involvement with victims of 9/11 immediately following the event and one year later, caseload, frequency of individual supervision received, demographic information such as age, religious participation, and marital status; and psychiatric history, including past personal trauma (see Table 2.3), and symptoms of depression and anxiety before and after 9/11. A total of 35 respondents participated in the study. Correlation analyses were conducted to estimate the association between TSI subscale scores, psychiatric variables, and demographic variables, while chi-square analyses were used to identify differences between groups of participants.

Vicarious Traumatization at a Manhattan Hospital One Year After the 9/11 Tragedy

Gertie Quitangon, M.D., Steven Lascher D.V.M., Lea DeFrancisci M.D., Deborah Rovine M.D., Spencer Eth, M.D.

Behavioral Health Services, Saint Vincent's Catholic Medical Centers of New York and Department of Psychiatry, New York Medical College

In the aftermath of the terrorist attacks on September 11, 2001,large numbers of New York City residents developed psychiatric symptoms and sought intervention by mental health professionals. This study examines a group of mental health professionals and the impact of working with 9/11 trauma victims.

Method

A survey was conducted in the Department of Psychiatry of a Manhattan teaching hospital located near the World Trade Center one year after the 9/11 terrorist attack. The study was approved by the hospital IRB, and participation by therapists was voluntary and anonymous. The following measures were administered: Personal Questionnaire, Impact of Events Scale revised (IES-r), Compassion Fatigue Self Test, and Trauma Symptom Inventory (TSI). A total of 35 respondents participated in the study. Statistical analysis of the responses was conducted.

Immediately post 9/11, 90.3% of respondents provided professional services to 9/11 trauma victims including individual and group psychotherapy, and medication management. One year later, only 9.6% reported 9/11 trauma victims as part of their caseload. If the respondent had a caseload of 9/11 rescue workers, they were at greater risk for significantly elevated intrusion score on IES-r.

Individual supervision that occurred more than once a week was protective from significantly elevated intrusion scores compared with less frequent supervision (chi2=3.85, p=0.05).

Respondents who endorsed symptoms of depression on the personal questionnaire prior to the 9/11 tragedy were at higher risk for significantly elevated intrusion scores compared with those who did not report depressive symptoms (chi2 6.039, p=0.014). <graph 1>.

Post 9/11 symptoms of depression and anxiety on personal questionnaire were positively correlated with the following scales on the Trauma Symptom Inventory (TSI):intrusive experiences (.38), defensive avoidance (.34), dissociation (.29), sexual concerns (.43) and tension reduction behaviors (.42).

Past trauma was significantly related to post 9/11 symptoms. Of those who had no previous trauma, 35% acknowledged having some post 9/11 symptoms, whereas of those who had previous trauma, 67% acknowledged having some post 9/11 symptoms.

TSI scales that were positively correlated with past trauma include anxious arousal (.31), depression (.39), anger/irritability (.45), intrusive experiences(.32), defensive avoidance (.35), sexual concerns (.29), and tension reduction behaviors (.45) <graph 2>.

Married status was inversely related to symptoms of depression (–.30) and dysfunctional sexual behaviors(–.30) on the TSI scale. Age(–.38) and religious participation(–.31) was inversely related to symptoms of defensive avoidance on the TSI scale.

Conclusion

Further studies are necessary to delineate more fully the impact of the evaluation and treatment of victims of mass traumatic events on the emotional well-being of mental health professionals. It does appear that vicarious traumatization occurs in certain therapists engaging in disaster work

REFERENCES

Brady, J.L., Guy, J.D., Poelstra, P.L., & Brokaw, B.F. (1999). Vicarious traumatization, spirituality, and the treatment of sexual abuse survivors: A national survey of women psychotherapists. Professional Psychology: Research and Practice, 30(4), 386–393. / Briere, J. (1995) Trauma symptom inventory professional manual. Odessa, FL: Psychological Assessment Resources. / Figley, C(2002). Treating Compassion Fatigue. New York: Brunner-Routledge Psychosocial Stress Series / Jenkins, S.R. & Baird, S. (2002). Secondary Traumatic Stress and Vicarious Trauma: A Validational Study. Journal of Traumatic Stress. 15(5), 423–432 / McCann, I.L. & Pearlman, L.A. (1990). Vicarious traumatization: a framework for understanding the psychological effects of working with victims. Journal of Traumatic Stress, 3(1), 131–149./ Weiss, D. & Marmar, C.(1997). The impact of event scale â€" revised. In J. Wilson & T. Keane (Eds.), Assessing psychological trauma and PTSD. New York: Guilford.

Graph 1: Mental Health Professionals with Depression/Anxiety Symptoms Prior to 9/11 Were at Higher Risk for Elevated Intrusion Score

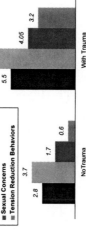

Legend: ■ Intrusion Score

- Endorsed Depression/Anxiety Symptoms Before 9/11: 14.7
- Did Not Endorse Depression/Anxiety Symptoms Before 9/11: 6.05

Graph 2: Mental Health Professionals with History of Personal Trauma were at Greater Risk for PTSD Symptoms (TSI Score)

Legend:
- ■ Intrusive Experiences
- ■ Defensive Avoidance
- ■ Sexual Concerns
- ■ Tension Reduction Behaviors

No Trauma: 2.8, 3.7, 0.6, 1.7
With Trauma: 5.5, 6.7, 4.05, 3.2

History of Personal Trauma Before 9/11

FIGURE 2.1 Vicarious traumatization at a Manhattan hospital one year after the 9/11 tragedy.

Quitangon, G., Lascher, S., DeFransisci, L., Rovine, D., & Eth, Sp. (2003). Vicarious traumatization at a Manhattan hospital one year after the 9/11 tragedy. Poster presentation at the American Psychiatric Association Annual Meeting in New York, NY, on May 3, 2004.

Results

Over 90% of respondents provided services to 9/11 trauma victims immediately after the event including individual and group psychotherapy and medication management. One year later, only 9.6% reported 9/11 victims as part of their caseload. The demographic characteristics of the respondents are summarized in Table 2.1.

Married Status

Married mental health clinicians reported fewer symptoms of depression and fewer dysfunctional sexual behaviors in those TSI subscales ($r = -0.30$ for both subscales; $p < 0.05$).

Race

Respondents of Asian descent obtained clinically significant avoidant scores in the IES (χ^2 8.45; $p=0.004$).

Religious Participation

Religious participation was inversely related to TSI defensive avoidance scale (-0.31; $p < 0.05$). The study indicated that frequency of religious participation may have a protective effect against VT.

TABLE 2.1 Demographic Information ($n = 35$)

AGE	Mean	SD			
	36.03	8.65			
GENDER	Male	Female			
	12	23			
MARITAL STATUS	Single	Married	Partnered	Divorced/ Separated	Other
	15	12	4	3	1
ETHNICITY	Caucasian	Hispanic	African American	Asian	Other
	20	2	2	9	1
PROFESSIONAL DISCIPLINE	Psychiatry	Psychology	Social Work	Other	
	22	1	4	8	
	Attending				
	5				
	Fellow				
	6				
	Resident				
	11				
RELIGION	Jewish	Catholic	Protestant	Hindu	Other
	8	10	3	3	11
LEVEL OF RELIGIOUS OBSERVANCE	None	Minimal	Moderate	Significant	
	7	15	8	5	

Post-9/11 Symptoms

23.3% of the respondents reported PTSD symptoms immediately after 9/11. One year later, only one self-reported persistent PTSD symptoms. Symptoms of depression after 9/11 were positively correlated with the following TSI subscales: past trauma (.39), current stress (.34), sexual concerns (.43), tension reduction behaviors (.42), dissociation (.29), intrusive experiences (.38).

Depression Prior to 9/11

Respondents who reported experiencing depressive symptomatology prior to the 9/11 terrorist attacks had significantly higher IES-r intrusion scores than those who did not report depression symptoms before 9/11 (χ^2 = 6.04, p = 0.014). Those respondents receiving individual psychotherapy had more clinically significant intrusion scores than those not in psychotherapy (χ^2 = 8.119 p = 0.004). Those taking psychotropic medications obtained clinically elevated avoidant scores (χ^2 = 4.14; p = 0.042).

Personal Trauma History

A history of trauma was significantly associated with post-9/11 symptoms (.39). Of those who had no previous exposure to traumatic events, 35% reported experiencing some post-9/11 symptoms of psychological distress; while 67% of participants who acknowledged a history of trauma described experiencing post-9/11 symptoms. Symptoms include increased anxious arousal (.31), depression (.39), anger/irritability (.45), intrusive experiences (.32), defensive avoidance (.35), sexual concerns (.29), and tension reduction behaviors (.45). TSI significant correlations p < .10 had the strongest correlations with the scale scores.

TABLE 2.2 Level of 9/11 Exposure

(n=35*)			
WHERE WERE YOU ON 9/11?	SVH	Other	
	20	13	
HOW WERE YOU AFFECTED BY 9/11?	Minimal	Moderate	Severe
	6	24	3
DO YOU KNOW ANYONE PERSONALLY WHO DIED ON 9/11?	Yes	No	
	26	7	
DO YOU KNOW ANYONE WHO WAS IN THE WTC AREA ON 9/11?	Yes	No	
	29	4	

*some missing answers

TABLE 2.3 History of Trauma

(n=35)		
HISTORY OF PHYSICAL ABUSE	Yes	No
	32	3
HISTORY OF SEXUAL ABUSE	Yes	No
	3	32
WITNESS TO VIOLENCE	Yes	No
	11	24

Caseload

Respondents who had a caseload of 9/11 rescue workers had significantly elevated intrusion scores compared with those without rescue workers in their caseload. However, caseload was unrelated to any of the TSI subscales.

Supervision

Mental health professionals who reported receiving individual supervision at least once a week had lower IES-r intrusion scores than those who received individual supervision less frequently ($X^2 = 3.85, p = 0.05$).

Limitations of the Study

There were a number of factors limiting the interpretation of results from this study. The small sample size precludes identification of clear predictors of VT among mental health workers who provided services to victims of 9/11. It may also be limited by selection bias as the mental health workers who agreed to participate in the study may differ from those who did not. Finally, the study may be limited by its cross-sectional design. A longitudinal design would allow for additional inferences about predictors of VT to be made.

The literature on VT and mental health disaster response has yet to come together in longitudinal and comprehensive theoretically driven studies. The lack of consensus in concept and the methodological differences across published studies including variability in instruments used to measure these differing concepts hinders anyone's ability to compare results and may explain much of the inconsistencies in certain findings.

Conclusion

Clinicians must increase recognition of VT and their own vulnerabilities and, together with administration and leadership of organizations, share the responsibility of preventing and mitigating VT in disaster mental health work. Over a decade after 9/11, we learn that there is a lack of empirical evidence to determine variables that predict susceptibility to VT in mental health professionals who lived through 9/11 and simultaneously delivered services in the aftermath of an unprecedented national tragedy. This study identified several factors that may promote resilience in disaster mental health response and decrease the risk of VT but further research is warranted to validate these findings. Conceptual and empirical validation of VT and the risk and resilience factors that have been identified is integral in addressing VT in disaster mental health work.

Case Study

Emma immigrated to New York in the mid-1990s to join her father, who was an esteemed and celebrated psychiatrist from Egypt. She completed psychiatry residency training at St. Vincent's Hospital in downtown Manhattan and was hired to stay on as an attending psychiatrist after graduation at the St. Vincent's Behavioral Health Outpatient Clinic. Emma is dedicated to her work and feels a particular closeness and loyalty to her private Egyptian patients, many of them indigent and undocumented. She even sees some of them pro bono. Emma had just returned from a trip to her home country when 9/11 occurred.

"They told us it was an emergency. I ran from my office on the sixth floor of the O'Toole Building down to the streets where people had converged to watch the burning towers," she said. "We were called to a meeting in the resident's lounge and told to buy gallons of water at Duane Reade. Don't ask why, but we did. It was organized chaos. We waited for hours to help in the ER but no one came. I was anxious to hear from my husband, John, who worked downtown," Emma remembers. "It was such a relief that none of my family, friends, or patients were hurt. Everyone called to make sure we were fine—friends from New York and Egypt. That evening, John and I took our daughter Olivia and we joined others on the streets, mourning together, looking at pictures, and lighting candles."

Emma and John were childhood sweethearts who had married in their teens. John was a handsome, fun, and outgoing man. He was thriving in New York's high energy, but he also had become heavily involved in gambling. "It was a very confusing period in New York and for me personally. I had fallen in love with someone else and breaking the news to John weighed heavily on my mind." After years of bailing him out from enormous debts, Emma decided she wanted a divorce. She longed to return to Egypt and felt detached from New York. At work, she was not her usual sensitive and empathic self.

"I found myself detached when it came to 9/11—not only due to the enormity and suddenness of the event, but also because of the helplessness and vulnerability that came with it. It could happen to anyone, anytime. My reaction vacillated in a range of emotions, from feeling sad to trying to be more understanding, then feeling accused for their sufferings to avoiding hearing their stories altogether. I tried hard not to cry with my patients. There was this one woman I will not forget." Emma regularly saw a homeless woman in her forties who lost her brother on 9/11. He had been working as a janitor in one of the towers and the woman had desperately searched for him. She usually called in a state of crisis but never followed through with any assistance or treatment offered. "She made me feel terribly sad. I wanted to help her but what could I possibly do? She said her problems only started after 9/11, but I suspected

her psychiatric condition had deeper roots. I am not sure why I was more invested in this patient while others I evaded. Like that patient at my new job. . ."

Nine years after 9/11, St. Vincent's Hospital went bankrupt and closed. Emma trans-ferred to a community-based clinic affiliated with SUNY Downstate Medical Center in Brooklyn. By this point, she had remarried and her relationship with her ex-husband John had become more amicable in the months since her father passed from an aggressive form of bone cancer.

"On my first day at work, I heard a hesitant knock on the door. A young man walked in the room with trepidation, his gaze averted. He was pale, thin, and his blue eyes were sunken. He sat down at the edge of the chair, as if ready to walk out of my office any sec-ond," she recalls. *"He was extremely irritable, did not want to talk, told me to read his chart and yelled, 'Just give me my Ativan!'"*

After a long anxiety-filled silence, Emma engaged him in a brief conversation. He said he had never been the same since 9/11, when he witnessed a man jump from the tower, fall at his feet, and blood splatter all over him. He reported that he had been very depressed and suffered from panic attacks on a regular basis. He had no appetite, did not want to do anything, and was always angry.

"I heard myself say, 'That must have been so traumatic,' but I really didn't want to hear anymore. My first thought was how glad I was that it didn't happen to me. Then I felt anguish . . . like I was drawn into a fog," she says. *"I could not halt my imagination. It was as if I saw a blood-soaked white sheet thrown over his body covering him and his face. I kept looking at the clock, wishing the session would end. He stopped talking and I did not pursue any more information,"* she said. *"I felt guilty those thoughts crossed my mind. I felt even guiltier that I did not dig deeper."* Emma says that at that moment, a wave of helplessness ran through her.

Discussion

Emma's story illustrates the complex interplay of several variables that can contribute to vicarious traumatization. Her response to treating patients who experienced 9/11-related trauma occurred within a social and personal context that left her more vulnerable to being negatively impacted by empathic engagement with her patients. The shared exposure to 9/11 further complicated her capacity to effectively treat her patients. Emma experienced fear, anxiety, and sadness in response to the scale and unexpected nature of 9/11. She struggled to come to terms with her feelings of vulnerability, even while she focused on helping patients cope with distress and find meaning in the disaster. Working at SVH in close proximity to Ground Zero and difficult life events such as divorce, death of a parent, and a recent change of employment further increased Emma's risk for developing symptoms of vicarious traumatization. The specific symptomatology in this vignette includes intrusive traumatic imagery, avoidance, guilt, detachment, loss of empathy, helplessness, and anguish related to empathic engagement with her patients.

When a depressed and anxious man reluctantly described his traumatic experience on 9/11, Emma felt relieved that she was spared the horror and the resultant posttraumatic distress of her patient. Her alternating engagement and avoidance of this patient's traumatic experience paralleled his attempts to avoid his own intrusive traumatic thoughts, memories and emotions. When she engaged and listened to the graphic details of his traumatic material, Emma became overwhelmed by intrusive images of her patient covered with blood. Intrusive imagery is a hallmark of post-trauma adaptation (Brett & Ostroff, 1985; Horowitz, 2011), and in this case, an important sign of vicarious traumatization. Emma's patient may have sensed her avoidance, and in turn, expressed less than he would have otherwise. Emma felt intense guilt for colluding in his avoidance and straying from her mission of emotional engagement. Her guilt was compounded by the knowledge that by engaging rather than avoiding, she may have been more successful in relieving the man's anxiety, depression, and anger.

As this patient sought relief from his suffering, he generated feelings of helplessness, sadness, and guilt in Emma, feelings that can be spawned from intensely traumatic experiences. Helplessness is an understandable response to profound feelings of failure, guilt, and loss of capacity to help a patient. According to the Constructivist Self Development Theory (CDST), the foundation for the concept of vicarious traumatization, there are five major psychological needs that are sensitive to traumatic events: safety, trust, esteem, intimacy, and control (Saakvitne & Pearlman, 1996). In Emma's case, helplessness could have resulted from a disruption in her feelings of safety and control evoked by the combination of her personal experience of a horrific terrorist attack and her patient's tragic account.

Acknowledgments

This chapter reviews findings based on two studies presented at the American Psychiatric Association (APA) Annual Meeting: "Vicarious Traumatization at a Manhattan Hospital A Year After 9/11" (2003) and "Vicarious Trauma in Mental Health Professionals Following 9/11: The Impact of Working with Trauma Victims" (2011).

The authors wish to acknowledge the following contributors to "Vicarious Traumatization at a Manhattan Hospital A Year After 9/11": Steven Lascher, D.V.M., Ph.D., M.P.H., Lea DeFrancisci, M.D., Deborah Rovine, M.D., Spencer Eth, M.D.

References

Adams, R.E., Figley, C.R., & Boscarino, J.A. (2006). The Compassion Fatigue Scale: Its use with social workers following urban disaster. *Research on Social Work Practice, 18*(3), 238–250.

Brady, J.L., Guy, J.D., Poelstra, P.L., & Browkaw, B. (1999). Vicarious traumatization, spirituality, and the treatment of sexual abuse survivors: A national survey of women psychotherapists. *Professional Psychology Research and Practice, 30*(4), 386–393.

Brett, E., & Ostroff, R. (1985). Imagery and posttraumatic stress disorder: An overview. *American Journal of Psychiatry, 142*, 417–424.

Colarossi, L., Heyman, J., & Phillips, M. (2005). Social workers' experiences of the World Trade Center disaster: Stressors and their relationship to symptom types. *Community Mental Health Journal, 41*(2), 185–198.

Creamer, T.L., & Liddle, B.J. (2005). Secondary traumatic stress among disaster mental health workers responding to the September 11 attacks. *Journal of Traumatic Stress, 18*(1), 89–96.

Culver, L.M., McKinney, B.L., & Paradise, L.V. (2011). Mental health professionals' experiences of vicarious traumatization in post–Hurricane Katrina New Orleans. *Journal of Loss and Trauma, 16*(1), 33–42.

Daly, E.S., Gulliver, S.B., Zimering, R.T., Knight, J., Kamholz, B.W., & Morissette, S.B. (2008). Disaster mental health workers responding to Ground Zero: One year later. *Journal of Traumatic Stress, 21*(2), 227–230.

Eidelson, R.J., D'Alessio, G.R., & Eidelson, J.I. (2003). The impact of September 11 on psychologists. *Professional Psychology Research and Practice, 34*(2), 144–150.

Felton, C.J. (2002). Project Liberty: A public health response to New Yorkers' mental health needs arising from the World Trade Center terrorist attacks. *Journal of Urban Health: Bulletin of the New York Academy of Medicine, 79*(3), 429–433.

Galea, S., Ahern, J., Resnick, H,. Kilpatrick, D., Bucuvalas, M., Gold, J., & Vlahav, D. (2002). Psychological sequelae of the September 11 terrorist attacks in New York City. *New England Journal of Medicine, 346*(13), 962–967.

Galea, S., Vlahov, D., Resnick, H., Ahern, J., Susser, E., Gold, J., . . . Kilpatrick, D. (2003). Trends of probable post-traumatic stress disorder in New York City after the September 11 terrorist attacks. *American Journal of Epidemiology, 158*(6), 514–524.

Horowitz, M. J. (2011). *Stress response syndromes: PTSD, grief, adjustment, and dissociative disorders*. Lanham, MD: Jason Aronson.

Pearlman, L.A., & Mac Ian, P.S. (1995). Vicarious trauma: An empirical study of the effects of trauma work on trauma therapists. *Professional Psychology Research and Practice, 26*(6), 558–565.

Saakvitne, K.W., & Pearlman, A. (1996). *Transforming the pain: A workbook on vicarious traumatization*. New York, NY: W.W. Norton.

Schauben, L.J., & Frasier, P.A. (1995). Vicarious trauma: The effects on female counselors of working with sexual violence victims. *Psychology of Women Quarterly*, 19, 49–64.

Schlenger, W.E., Caddell, J.M., Ebert, L., Jordan, B.K., Rourke, K.M., Wilson, D., . . . Kulka, R.A. (2002). Psychological reactions to terrorist attacks: Findings from the National Study of Americans' Reactions to September 11. *Journal of the American Medical Association, 288*(5), 581–588.

Wee, D.F., & Myers, D. (2002). Stress responses of mental health workers following disaster: The Oklahoma City bombing. In C.R. Figley (Ed.), *Treating compassion fatigue* (pp. 57–84). New York, NY: Brunner-Routledge.

Zibulewsky, J. (2001). Defining disaster: The emergency department perspective. *BUMC Proceedings*, 14, 144–149.

3

WHAT ARE THE BARRIERS TO ADDRESSING VICARIOUS TRAUMA?

Jane Hammerslough

At a small social service agency that works with victims of crime, a young therapist is arriving later and later to work each day. When the issue is raised by her supervisor, she reports that she has trouble sleeping because she is thinking so much about work, and "can't get my clients' stories out of my head."

The employee turnover rate at a counseling center that works with families displaced by a natural disaster is higher than ever, and the process of continually training new clinicians only to have them leave after a few months is getting more and more difficult for the staff that remains. Their caseloads are growing, and because the center is so short-staffed, time off is now restricted. Morale is at an all-time low.

Because of recent budget cuts, the city's crisis intervention program has had to cut way back on trauma-specific training and no longer offers continuing education or other professional development for clinicians. The program's director is disturbed by the increasing number of sick days staff have taken in recent months, but is not sure what to do about the issue.

In a town where a tragic, large-scale shooting has occurred, mental health workers are working to make sure that victims' families get the support and care they need in the hours, days, and weeks that follow the event. In time, some of the caregivers are feeling overwhelmed and helpless themselves.

What Can be Done to Help the Helpers?

While it may lead to personal and professional growth, treating trauma—as a result of a disaster or another traumatic experience—can also take a toll on mental health clinicians: more than two decades of studies show that those who work with helping people who have experienced trauma may be susceptible to compassion fatigue, burnout, and/or some other symptoms of distress or symptoms of PTSD themselves (Baird & Kracen, 2006). Clinicians who provide individual and group psychotherapy and other mental health services to traumatized populations may be especially subject to developing Secondary Traumatic Stress (STS) or Vicarious Traumatization (VT) (Sabin-Farrell & Turpin, 2003).

Although there is no generally accepted theory of Secondary Traumatization or its implications, STS has been defined as the development of some PTSD symptoms—hypervigilance, nightmares, and others—via exposure to and knowledge of a traumatizing event experienced by another person (Figley, 1995).Vicarious Trauma (VT) also refers to exposure to others' trauma experiences, but it is distinct in that it refers not only to various symptoms, but to changes to clinicians' schemas, view of the world, and their relationships with others, similar to the changes that happen in a person who has experienced trauma (Pearlman & Mac Ian, 1995).

The difference between STS and VT is subtle but distinct, and the different definitions of what, exactly, constitutes adverse clinician responses is an obstacle in addressing the issue. Is vicarious traumatization a disorder, an occupational hazard or condition, or both? Is it a temporary state that is resolved, or one that is more permanent? Or is it resolved, but returns via triggers in the future? A significant barrier to addressing the issue is in understanding and defining it, as there is no one universal theory or definition of secondary traumatization.

Because vicarious traumatization occurs in the context of work and workplaces, and is a result of exposure to work-related stressors, it is as much an occupational hazard as any other injury that occurs on the job.Yet the area of clinician vulnerability to and symptom development of VT is a gray one. Some people who work with people who have experienced trauma develop severe symptoms of VT, while others do not.While there is no doubt that trauma clinicians may be personally, adversely affected by their work—which, in turn, can have an adverse effect on their ability to effectively work with patients, function as members of clinical teams, or competently contribute to an agency or institution in other ways—the issue is complex. The collateral damage of working with the traumatized may impact a great many other people, even affecting the functionality of institutions as a whole—yet the barriers to addressing it are numerous.

What happens when the people who help the hurt are themselves hurt by the experience? And what can be done about this issue? The acknowledgment that working with the traumatized can lead to trauma is relatively new, and a current, key barrier to treating people who experience VT is the fact that it was not named or studied until recently. Although STS and VT have been explored more in the past 20 years than ever before, research and literature on the subject is still in its infancy (Voss Horrell, Holohan, Didion, & Vance, 2011) and much remains uncertain about the short or long-term effects of working with traumatized populations.

Another important barrier to addressing VT is found in the limitations of existing research. A review of literature about vicarious traumatization by Sabin-Farrell and Turpin (2003) found limitations in measuring areas of distress—and their impact—on practitioners. Additionally, various studies have found that certain practitioners may be more vulnerable than others, but results are inconsistent; demographics do not correlate directly to incidence of VT or STS (Meichenbaum, 2007).

While we know that people are affected by working with trauma, the existing research does not consistently show clear cause and effect of vicarious traumatization symptoms. To complicate matters further, there is little consensus in research on the circumstances that might lead to VT or STS symptoms developing—or how they might be prevented (Elwood, Mott, Lohr, & Galvoski, 2011). And there are even fewer studies on effective ways to address the issue of VT or STS—and help those clinicians who help others work through trauma on an individual, group, agency, and other levels. Clearly, inconsistencies in research present a barrier to addressing the issue.

Additionally, the research gap in the issue of addressing STS and VT in mental health clinicians is both glaring and wide. While possible psychological, physical, occupational, and other effects of working with traumatized populations is now acknowledged, possible ways of addressing those effects is much less explored. More research into both the effects of working with people who have experienced disasters and other traumatic events and ways that problems might be prevented is necessary to fully explore the issue (Elwood et al., 2011).

What are the other barriers to addressing the issue of clinician VT or STS? One possible answer lies in the fact that for the most part, VT and STS affect individuals who often work within a much larger organization or institution—a clinic, hospital, or government agency—yet it has most often been viewed as a problem of individuals. As Bober and Regehr note, the research that does exist tends to focus on the response and responsibility of individual practitioners for coping with their own STS or VT, "implying that those who feel traumatized may not be balancing life and work adequately and may not be making effective use of leisure, self-care, or supervision" (Bober & Regehr, 2006) .

This implication, quite naturally, might lead an individual practitioner to dismiss his or her own distressing symptoms. This dismissal—symptoms of trauma as a result of working with the traumatized are a sign of incompetency or weakness, for example—potentially puts the individual clinician at risk, along with possibly impairing his or her capacity to serve the needs of patients and interact with colleagues, among others. Both burnout and "compassion fatigue"—referring to individuals in the helping professions who experience a reduced capacity or interest in being empathic toward clients as a result of exposure to patients' issues combined with a continual expenditure of empathy toward those patients—highlight a proposed consequence of the symptoms (Elwood et al., 2011).

Simply put, it may become much harder to function empathically when one is constantly exposed to stories that may be potentially traumatic to hear, possibly resulting in disengagement (or worse) when working with patients. Because those who work with traumatized populations often do so by choice, this emotional exhaustion may be perceived as a failure, or even more destructive, a way of being, both by clinicians themselves and throughout their work environments.

Clearly, the implication that STS and VT are somehow a clinician's "fault"—a result of not practicing effective self-care or benefitting from supervision in a way that will help inoculate him or her from the effects of secondary traumatization—serves as a barrier to acknowledging secondary trauma symptoms (Bober & Regehr, 2006). And certainly, such causality and implied blame of the individual practitioner—along with the idea that clinicians develop VT as a result of easily-rectified, deficient individual coping strategies—is quite likely to serve as a barrier to addressing it. It is not surprising, then, that clinicians might be reluctant to report symptoms of VT.

The current focus on individual clinicians may detract from considering the issue of VT and STS from a systemic perspective, and in fact, addressing it on an organizational level, from workplace policies to structural issues. What factors in groups, agencies, or institutions might influence or impede addressing the issue?

Clinician time, and its management, is important to addressing the issue of VT and STS. Several studies indicate that the primary predictor of higher traumatization scores in clinicians is the amount of time a clinician spends treating traumatized people. Moreover, counseling traumatized individuals for more time correlated to an increase in clinicians' stress levels. Additionally, more time spent treating traumatized people also produced higher levels of intrusive symptoms in clinicians (Bober & Regehr, 2006).

Lack of time and other resources may also result in deficits in ongoing training, research, and supervision opportunities for clinicians; not having trauma-specific training has been linked to VT symptoms (Adams & Riggs, 2008). Therefore, the costs associated with enhancing trauma-informed care—from deeper training for clinicians working with trauma-specific patients to educating supervisors for improving trauma-informed supervision—may intrude on addressing VT in the most effective way possible.

Time is also a factor when it comes to clinician caseloads serving as a barrier to addressing VT: while treating patients who are angry, aggressive, and/or at risk for suicide most of the time may place undue strain on clinicians (Voss Horrell et al., 2011), it also may be difficult to avoid when working with people who have experienced trauma. And although balancing clinicians' workloads with a diverse set of clients is recommended (Meichenbaum, 2007), it is not always possible.

In line with the issue of time is diversification of caseloads. Clinicians who work primarily with patients who have experienced one particular type of trauma—for example, recovering from the effects of a disastrous storm or sexual trauma—to the exclusion of seeing a number of different types of patients, adds to clinician stress and burnout rates (Voss Horrell et al., 2011). The lack of diversity of patients in working with victims of disaster may be a barrier to preventing or addressing secondary or vicarious traumatic responses.

Finally, organizational and agency structures and issues may serve as a barrier to addressing VT. Different care settings—hospital-based, social service and other community-based organizations, and private practices—offer different challenges for addressing VT. Regardless of the setting, however, creating a more supportive environment for staff who work with traumatized populations can be effective in "inoculating" them against possible trauma themselves. Ensuring that staff have balanced caseloads and are supported in taking care of themselves—with generous break and vacation time, supporting self-care, assisting in managing boundaries, offering ongoing opportunities for professional growth, and fostering spiritual or other renewal, for example (Meichenbaum, 2007), may help address VT—but may also be impossible within existing budgets or organizational structures.

Eliminating barriers to identifying and responding to VT and STS requires further research. This research might be twofold: to explore the issue of how and why individuals might develop trauma responses to working with traumatized patients, as well as how those individual clinicians might be supported in a larger context. Further research and consideration for the role and impact of groups, agencies, or institutions—and the ways they may better function to serve the needs of clinicians who are vulnerable to experiencing occupational trauma, recognizing that the issue is not simply personal, but institutional and possibly even political—might help eliminate barriers to preventing, identifying, and treating VT and STS.

References

Adams, S.A., & Riggs, S.A. (2008). An exploratory study of vicarious trauma among clinician trainees. *Training and Education in Professional Psychology, 2*, 26–34. doi:10.1037/1931-3918.2.1.26

Baird, K., & Kracen, A.C. (2006). Vicarious traumatization and secondary traumatic stress: A research synthesis. *Counselling Psychology Quarterly, 19*(2), 181–188.

Bober, T., & Regehr, C.D. (2006). Strategies for reducing secondary or vicarious trauma: Do they work? *Brief Treatment and Crisis Intervention, 6*(1), 1–9.

Elwood, L.S., Mott, J., Lohr, J.M., & Galvoski, T.E. (2011). Secondary trauma symptoms in clinicians: A critical review of the construct, specificity, and implications for trauma-focused treatment. *Clinical Psychology Review, 31*(1), 25–36.

Figley, C. (1995). Compassion fatigue: Towards a new understanding of the costs of caring. In B. Stamm (Ed.), *Secondary traumatic stress: Self-care issues for clinicians, researchers, and educators* (pp. 3–28). Lutherville, MD: Sidran Press.

Meichenbaum, Donald. (2007). Self-care for trauma psychotherapists and caregivers: individual, social and organizational interventions. Retrieved from: http://www.melissainstitute.org/documents/Meichenbaum_SelfCare_11thconf.pdf Accessed on October 10, 2013.

Pearlman, L.A., & MacIan, P.S. (1995). Vicarious traumatization: An empirical study of the effects of trauma work on trauma therapists. *Professional Psychology: Research and Practice, 26*(6), 558.

Sabin-Farrell, T., & Turpin, G. (2003). Vicarious traumatization: Implications for the mental health of health workers. *Clinical Psychology Review*, 23, 449–480.

Voss Horrell, S.C., Holohan, D.R., Didion, L.M., & Vance, G.T. (2011). Treating traumatized OEF/OIF veterans: How does trauma treatment affect the clinician. *Professional Psychology: Research and Practice, 42*(1), 79–86.

PERSONAL REFLECTIONS

My Story

On September 11, 2001, my staff at the Brooklyn Vet Center was throwing a birthday party for a co-worker and me (my birthday is September 12th and his later in the month) when we heard a rumble and the building seemed to shake. Several of us went to the window where we saw smoke begin to come across from Manhattan past our windows. Much of the memories are vague, because unfortunately I didn't keep a journal or think about the events at the time. I just seemed to operate on autopilot. As Team Leader it was my responsibility to assure that staff and clients were safe as we learned about the events that transpired through the morning and into the afternoon.

It was shortly after this that a second plane crashed into the second tower where there was a clear burst of noise and a rumble, and we witnessed it on the television. I went up to the roof of our building at his point to see the wreckage, I was taken aback and began to cry. Quickly recovering, and stuffing my feelings, I saw that both towers were engulfed in smoke and flame, and that mixed debris was being thrown out windows and off the rooftops. It was only after watching the two towers collapse that it registered that the debris was falling men and women jumping to earth rather than burning alive. I froze and did my best to remain composed and spoke to my staff about this as we processed some of what went down and prepared to close the Center a few hours later and make my way home on foot. We had no working phone lines, and I thought it best for each employee to go home to his or her respective family.

On September 13, I volunteered to do counseling with the police canine and POPPA units and began offering debriefings for the fire departments. One in particular stands out as having been exceptionally difficult. It was in late September and I arrived about twenty minutes early and everyone else was late. However, the whole unit was there and eager to talk during my time there, as I sat in the back kitchen area so we casually chatted about their lives and about 9/11 and their losses and how each was impacted by the losses. It was all very casual and easy going, over coffee and food. They told me about their friends and the significance of the losses to their unit and how the formality of the debriefing was a crock and not really necessary to go through. I let down my guard and joined the group, in their grief. They had lost more than half their house unit of brothers. I was devastated for and with them.

It was then I found out my partner was not coming and that I was going to do this debriefing alone. Not having done a debriefing on my own before, and not wanting to let these guys down, I accepted anyway. I began the debriefing, which started off with explaining typical issues of loss, and feelings, and how we would break into small groups after. Then it struck, panic. I felt fraudulent and I had no place telling these guys how to process their grief when I hadn't yet looked at my own. As I over-identified with the losses of each member just casually told to me minutes before it exacerbated my sense of overwhelm, panic, and fear, until finally, the room got darker, and I passed out.

I was in the kitchen with the cook and several men taking care of me. Overwhelmed with shame I didn't have the wherewithal to use this as a learning tool for understanding over-exhaustion or to see the need for self-care. I simply apologized and did my best to save face. This would have been a good opportunity to speak to the use of self as an example of how the body can only take so much stress, and how it needs to be cared for. It needs stress release, be it through therapy or physical exercise. I simply minimized my reaction, thanking them and getting out of there as quickly as possible. I was absolutely physically and emotionally exhausted and worn out. I realized I had nothing else to give, and needed to regroup and conserve my strength.

It needs to be said that I did not deal with this well. This was my last debriefing, and my last 9/11 work until my dissertation proposal three years later. The bulk of my focus had to change, and I had to begin caring for myself. The healer needed healing, and I sought out help, dove into my research on resilience and trauma and slowed down on my drinking. Because prior to that time my drinking had increased as did my own PTSD symptoms, I refused to speak about them in therapy or to my committee and stoically trudged onward, studying trauma and resilience. Finally in 2003 when I finally had enough, I had to seek outside help for my depression, PTSD, and drinking and took a brief break from my studies and completed my PhD in 2006 on resilience and the etiology of post-traumatic stress disorder, where I sampled more than 125 New Yorkers including first responders measuring their reactions to 9/11.

Since then I continue to thrive running my clinic, at the VA, and a private practice in New York City where I specialize in trauma and substance abuse as well as a host of other conditions. But my belief is that we can all live the best possible lives if we get the help we need, when we are ready for that help. Humans are exceptionally resilient and can thrive following the worst circumstances given the opportunity and a little guidance from experienced clinicians.

Kevin O'Brien, Ph.D.
Team Leader
Brooklyn Vet Center
Private Practitioner NYC

SECTION II
Understanding Disasters

4

WHAT DO WE NEED TO KNOW ABOUT DISASTERS?

Gertie Quitangon

Introduction

In order to mount an effective disaster mental health response, mental health providers must have basic information on disasters, in addition to training on public health approaches and evidence-informed mental health interventions following large-scale catastrophic events. This chapter will present an overview of the definitions and classification of disasters and the disaster response system in the United States. It will describe the degrees of disaster exposure, the expected population-based responses at various phases of a disaster, and the corresponding interventions addressing stage-specific challenges.

Definition of "Disaster"

A disaster has been defined as "a sudden accident or a natural catastrophe that causes great damage or loss of life" (*Oxford English Dictionary*, 2013) or "a sudden calamitous event bringing great damage, loss, or destruction" (*Merriam-Webster Dictionary*, 2004). Both definitions reflect the adverse impact of an unpredictable phenomenon to a community qualified by degrees of loss and damage. In *local* disasters, infrastructures are left intact and the local government conducts business as usual but local medical resources could be overwhelmed. *Regional* disasters affect a larger geographic area, there is greater damage to infrastructure and resources of the community but government and public services remain fully functional. A *federal* disaster is declared when there is severe community disruption and governmental infrastructure is significantly damaged. The Federal Emergency Management Assistance (FEMA) defines a disaster as "an occurrence that has resulted in property damage, deaths, and/or injuries to a community" (FEMA, 1990). FEMA was established in 1979 by the Carter administration as an independent unit of the executive branch whose mission is "to support our citizens and first responders to ensure that as a nation we work together to build, sustain, and improve our capability to prepare for, protect against, respond to, recover from, and mitigate all hazards." FEMA remains the lead federal agency for disaster planning, mitigation, coordination, and recovery. In 2003, it became part of the Department of Homeland Security which was instituted in response to the September 11 attacks (Felton, 2002).

Disaster Response Continuum

Knowledge of the disaster response system better prepares mental health clinicians to respond to disasters of all kinds (Garakani, Hirschowitz, & Katz, 2004; Kantor & Beckert 2011) and to understand the complex interplay of local, state, and federal government. When a disaster strikes, local and state governments are principally responsible for alleviating suffering and damage in the community resulting from the catastrophe, repairing essential public facilities and developing plans to cope with major disasters. An Emergency Operations Center (EOC) is established in order to coordinate search and rescue operations (e.g., extinguish fires, manage hazardous materials, locate injured, provide on-site medical treatment), ensure public safety (e.g., restore communications, public utilities, and transportation), and provide immediate relief (e.g., food, water, clothing, shelter). There are locally based volunteer programs that augment the disaster response capabilities of communities, such as the Community Emergency Response Team (CERT) and the Medical Reserve Corps (MRC). Both CERT and MRC are volunteer programs in partnership with the Citizens Corps, which is under the auspices of the Department of Homeland Security. CERTs provide education and training on basic disaster response and preparedness while the MRC assists in credentialing volunteer healthcare providers in order to provide access to their expertise year round in the event of an emergency (Kantor & Beckert, 2011; FEMA, n.d.b.). The American Red Cross is probably the most well-known non-governmental organization at the forefront of assisting communities immediately post-disaster and has extensive experience in providing basic necessities, social supports, health screening, and mental health care (Kantor & Beckert, 2011).

State and federal officials conduct preliminary damage assessment post-disaster in order to establish the need for federal assistance. They determine whether disaster relief is beyond the capabilities of state and local governments depending on the severity of damage, estimated cost, and impact on private and public sectors. FEMA assesses a number of factors in order to determine the severity, magnitude, and impact of a disaster event (FEMA, n.d.a.). When the president declares a state of emergency or a federal disaster, resources are allocated to emergency relief and reconstruction assistance and the federal government bears the major costs of disaster response and recovery efforts through its grant, loan, and insurance programs. Prior to 1950, disaster relief was viewed as a moral responsibility of neighbors, churches, charities, and communities, and the government only provided token financial assistance, usually limited to building flood programs. The Disaster Relief Acts of 1950, 1970, and 1974 expanded the role of the federal government in disaster relief, progressively introducing more comprehensive disaster plans to include emergency response and rescue, infrastructure repair, grants and tax subsidies to the victims, long-range economic recovery programs for major disaster areas, and insurance programs to supplement and replace governmental assistance.

The establishment of FEMA in 1979 was part of a major reorganization of disaster response services and the reorientation of federal disaster policy to emphasize disaster preparedness and prevention in addition to the task of rescue and recovery. The Stafford Disaster Relief and Emergency Assistance Act (Stafford Act) was signed into law in 1988, amending laws dating back to 1950 and constituting statutory authority for most federal disaster response activities. It authorizes FEMA to fund programs that address unmet needs in federally declared disaster areas, including mental health assistance and training and case management.

In 1992, FEMA developed the Federal Response Plan (FRP) in an effort to coordinate multiple disaster services provided by federal agencies and non-governmental organizations, including the American Red Cross. The Stafford Act has been amended in response to lessons learned from various emergencies and by 1996, FEMA launched the "Guide for All Hazards Emergency Operations Planning" for individual states. On the heels of 9/11, the Department of Homeland Security mandated integration of domestic all-hazards prevention, preparedness, response and recovery plans through the National Response Framework (NRF). The NRF provides a model for federal collaboration with state, tribal, and local governments as well the private sector, non-profits, faith-based, and non-governmental organizations. It updated the National Response Plan (NRP) based on lessons learned from the responses to hurricanes Katrina, Wilma, and Rita and built on guiding principles of the National Incident Management System (NIMS) and Incident Command System (ICS) with the ultimate goal of implementing a unified national response to disasters and emergencies.

Funding Sources

How disaster programs are funded influences disaster response strategies and the mental health services provided. Grant programs for three distinct disaster mental health programs are briefly described in this section to familiarize clinicians with the financing mechanisms supporting emergency and disaster mental health services. The Crisis Counseling Program (CCP) is jointly operated by FEMA and the Center for Mental Health Services (CMHS) and addresses the short-term mental health needs of communities affected by federally designated disasters (Felton,

2002). CCP provides community outreach, psychoeducation on traumatic stress reactions and appropriate coping strategies, and short-term supportive counseling. It encourages linkages with social supports and community resources and identifies those who may need referral to formal mental health treatment. There are two grant mechanisms through which state mental health authorities can avail of CCP funding. First is the *Immediate Services Program (ISP)*, which provides funds for the first 60 days following disaster declaration. The ISP is monitored by FEMA but technical assistance is provided by the Substance Abuse and Mental Health Services Administration (SAMHSA). The *Regular Services Program (RSP)* extends funding for the same services for an additional nine months. FEMA designated the sole responsibility for monitoring and technical assistance of all RSP programs to SAMHSA. Another FEMA funded program in accordance with the Stafford Act is the *Disaster Case Management Program (DCMP)*, a supplemental program awarding grants to state and local government agencies in collaboration with private organizations, faith-based, or non-profits (e.g., disability organizations, religious networks, and other community-based organizations) to provide time-limited case management services as well as financial assistance to victims of major disasters. The idea is to provide disaster survivors with a single point of contact to facilitate access to a broad range of services post-disaster, coordinate with multiple disaster response agencies, and minimize duplication of services. The *SAMHSA Emergency Response Grants (SERG)* is considered the funding of last resort when no other funding sources are available and communities struggle to meet the mental health and addiction needs post-disaster (SAMHSA, 2013). Applications for *immediate SERG awards* are accepted within 10 days of the emergency occurring and up to $50,000 is available for use within three months. *Intermediate SERG grants* are awarded based on mental health and/or substance abuse needs assessment during the recovery period and no funding cap is set. Applications are filed within 90 days of the emergency and funds can be used to support mental health services for up to one year.

Types of Disasters

The disaster literature classifies disasters in a number of ways, and every typology is neither precise nor straightforward, in keeping with the chaos, confusion, and uncertainty characteristic of disasters (Myers & Wee, 2005; Eynde & Veno, 1999). This chapter classifies disasters in terms of etiology into two primary categories: *natural* and *man-made*. Man-made disasters are further subdivided into *intentional* (or *acts of commission*) and *unintentional* (or *acts of omission*). Some studies suggest that these dichotomies have a bearing on the mental health impact of disasters (Norris, Friedman, & Watson, 2002; Myers & Wee, 2005; Halpern & Tramontin, 2007; Eynde & Veno, 1999), hence, it is useful to have a general understanding of these distinctions. The scope, intensity, and duration of disasters will be discussed in the next chapter.

Natural disasters are adverse events caused by forces of the physical world and generally refer to severe weather (tornado, hurricane/cyclone, flood, cold environment, heat wave, drought) or geophysical events (earthquake, landslide, tsunami, volcano) that increase in frequency during certain periods of the year in vulnerable "disaster-prone" areas. For example, the coastal areas in the United States are prone to hurricanes, the West Coast is predisposed to seismic activity and earthquakes, and the Midwest is referred to as "tornado alley" because it is highly vulnerable to twisters. The predictability of natural disasters varies as some hazardous weather may have advance warning (e.g., hurricanes and tornadoes) while others are sudden and the timing cannot be predicted with certainty (e.g., earthquakes and wildfires). See Table 4.1.

Man-made disasters are catastrophic events resulting from human error or negligence or the intent to do harm. Acts of omission have been defined as "accidents, failures and mishaps involving the technology and manipulation of the natural environment" (Baum, Fleming, & Davidson, 1983, pp. 333). These events are typically unintentional and vulnerability is increased in populations who live near hazardous material industries or close to transportation lines. Examples of acts of

TABLE 4.1 Types of Disasters

Types of Disasters by Etiology		
Natural Disasters	Drought	
	Earthquake	
	Flood	
	Heat	
	Hurricane, Cyclone, Typhoon, Tropical Storm	
	Landslide	
	Tornado	
	Tsunami	
	Wildfire	
	Winter Storm, Blizzard	
	Volcano	
Man-made Disasters	Acts of Omission	Mass Transportation Accident
		Residential Fire
		Structural Collapse
		Hazardous Material
		Nuclear Accident
	Acts of Commission	Violence
		War
		Terrorism

Source: Centers for Disease Control and Prevention. (n.d.). *Natural disasters and environmental hazards.* Retrieved from: http://emergency.cdc.gov/disasters/. Accesssed on February 10, 2013.

omissions include mass transportation accident, residential fire, structural collapse, industrial and nuclear accidents. A chemical spill is an example of an industrial accident that can harm people's health. The release of hazardous chemical and nuclear materials can be intentional, as in a terrorist attack, when the intent is to demoralize people, induce chaos, and disrupt society (Hall, Norwood, Ursano, & Fullerton, 2003). Terrorism (e.g., bioterrorism, chemical warfare, weapons of mass destruction), war, and violence are examples of acts of commission that are intentional disasters and all populations are at risk independent of location. Weapons of mass destruction are not limited to explosive devices, and they refer to any destructive device, whether chemical, biological, radiological, or nuclear, designed to cause death or serious injury to a significant number of people. Some chemical agents that have been developed by military organizations for use in war that can also be used by terrorist groups are nerve agents (sarin, VX), mustards (sulfur and nitrogen mustards), and choking agents (phosgene). The deliberate release of biological agents, such as the smallpox virus causing a smallpox epidemic or the bacteria *Bacillus anthracis* resulting to anthrax, are examples of bioterrorism.

Disaster Exposure

From a mental health perspective, Norris and colleagues (2002) define a disaster as "a sudden event that has the potential to terrify, horrify, or engender substantial losses for many people simultaneously" (p. 207). There has been a significant increase in literature published on the mental health effects of disasters after the September 11 attacks, and the general consensus is that most people exposed to severe traumatic events are resilient and exhibit normative stress responses for a brief period (Norris, 2006; North, Pfefferbaum, & Hong, 2006). The emergence of psychiatric pathology, such as Posttraumatic Stress Disorder (PTSD) or a Major Depressive Disorder (MDD), is less prevalent and could develop in susceptible individuals several weeks post-disaster (American Psychiatric Association [APA], 2013; Sederer et al., 2011). Findings in the disaster literature on the normality of responses, emphasis on high-risk populations, and the promotion of overall wellness have informed the current disaster mental health response and the integration of public health expertise in disaster and emergency management (North & Pfefferbaum, 2013).

The mental health consequences of a disaster increase as the proportion of victims to non-victims increases (Green, 1982). In a disaster community, the victims who were most directly exposed to the disaster are at greatest risk of negative mental health outcomes, followed by rescue workers, then the general public (Galea, Nandi, & Vlahov, 2005; Sederer et al., 2011). Severity of exposure is one of the most consistent predictors of post-disaster distress (Norris et al., 2002). Disaster trauma exposure has two aspects—the degree of personal loss and the community disruption experienced by a disaster victim. The loss could be direct, experienced as a result of being part of the event, or through the process of identification. Studies have indicated that those who experienced both high personal loss and high community destruction reported greater levels of distress (Norris, Phifer, & Kaniasty, 1994). Bolin (1985) referred to *primary victims* as those who were in direct endangerment and sustained physical injury or personal losses, such as the death of a loved one or loss of property. *Secondary victims* are those who reside in the affected area and whose lives were disrupted by the impact of the disaster on community structures but have no personal injuries or direct losses. *Tertiary victims* are those indirectly exposed, and they do not reside in the affected community but could have witnessed the event on TV or other forms of media, or they experienced the economic, social, and political consequences of the disaster (Flynn & Norwood, 2004). Disasters of extreme magnitude may also have far-reaching effects on populations with less direct exposure (Norris, 2006). For example, all epidemiological studies of the mental health consequences of the 9/11 attacks found significant rates of new onset 9/11-related PTSD in those directly and indirectly exposed in NY and also in persons across the US (Neria et al., 2006, Galea, Ahern, Resnick, & Vlahov, 2006, Cohen-Silver et al., 2006).

In the mobilization of a disaster mental health response, some providers volunteer or are deployed from other locations and may have not been directly exposed to the disaster but could have witnessed the event on TV or social media. Many may have been exposed to the disaster by virtue of living in the vicinity of the disaster-hit area, and they may or may not be involved in a formal disaster response but they work with disaster survivors at their usual place of work. Regardless of personal disaster exposure, mental health clinicians have an additional risk of exposure to intense disaster-related material in their line of work, listening repeatedly to graphic details of injury, loss, and devastation. The revised PTSD criteria in the newly released DSM 5 added criterion A4 citing *"Repeated or extreme indirect exposure to aversive details of the event(s), usually in the course of professional duties"* as a stressor suggesting that mental health professionals could be at risk of developing PTSD from disaster mental health work (APA, 2013).

Psychological Phases of Disaster

Public grief has become part of the shared experience of major disasters, and the interventions are influenced by cultural, political, and socioeconomic factors (Zinner & Williams, 1999). The external public response to an event has been described to follow a sequence of emotional stages characterized by changing levels of activity and arousal, typically decreasing with the progression of time (DeWolfe, 2000). Zunin and Myers's (2000) phases of disaster (see Figure 4.1) has been widely used to understand population-based responses corresponding to points in time during a disaster and it identifies eight phases: warning, threat, impact, heroic, inventory, honeymoon, disillusionment, and reconstruction. Some events allow for a *warning* phase when the public is made aware of a looming disaster, and the most common example is when meteorologists track storm systems during hurricane season in the US. The *threat* phase follows when the disaster becomes imminent and there is a

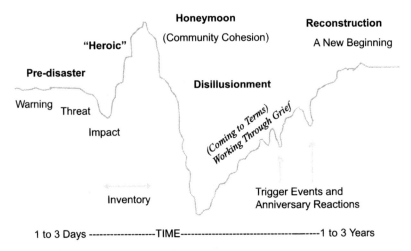

FIGURE 4.1 Psychological Phases of Disaster

Source: Zunin, L.M., & Myers, D. (2000). *Training manual for human service workers in major disasters* (2nd ed.) DHHS Publication No. ADM 90-538. Washington, DC: Department of Health and Human Services.

window of opportunity to empower the community by implementation of safety, evacuation, and contingency plans. *Impact* is often referred to as the "acute trauma phase" and the focus at this moment in time is on survival and enduring the event. This period is characterized by magnified levels of arousal; and although fear and tension is high, historically, panic has been the exception, and demonstration of pro-social behaviors and purposeful and productive acts tends to be the rule. Stories of noble efforts to help victims abound during and just after disaster impact as the *heroic* or rescue phase begins and the influx of resources and mobilization of supports predominates. An immediate goal of any emergency is to stabilize the scene, and during the *inventory* phase, the impact of the disaster is assessed to determine the immediate needs of the community. The *honeymoon* or remedy phase lasts approximately from two weeks to two months but this phase could be longer in large-scale disasters. During this period, energy and morale is high and there is a collective spirit of compassion, hope, and tolerance. Communities pull together and are unified by the validation of suffering and heroism. Pyszczynski (2004) notes that when people are reminded of the possibility of their own death, their worldviews are strengthened and there is a shared increase in patriotism and a sense of national group identification with the victims. However, with the passage of time comes the *disillusionment* phase when the realities of the loss are felt, hardships associated with the extent of the damage prevail, and the camaraderie experienced in the honeymoon phase is replaced with grief and anger (Somasundarum, Norris, Asukai, & Murphy, 2003). This phase is marked by government and insurance bureaucracy and various investigations demanding accountability, whether it be the cause of the disaster or the effectiveness of the disaster response. The *reconstruction* phase lasts from several months to years and the more extreme the destruction, the more monumental the challenges are at rebuilding. Communities readjust to a new normal and move forward with fewer resources relative to the heroic phase. The timing of each of the phases described above are fluid and do not occur in exact sequence; they usually overlap rather than occur discretely and can move forward or back across the timeline, affected by a myriad of variables including the type, scope, and severity of the disaster; the resources available to the affected community; and certain events that could increase the risk of negative mental health outcomes (see Table 4.2). Reminders of community trauma, such as anniversaries and the occurrence of similar catastrophic events, rekindle thoughts and images of the disaster and having local rituals or ceremonies mitigate adverse impacts by providing a venue for collective reflection where survivors can tell their stories and share their insights.

Role of Mental Health Providers

The role of mental health providers in disaster management has grown significantly in the post 9/11 era and it continues to broaden. A recent systematic review of the current disaster response by North and Pfefferbaum (2013) recommends integration of mental health services in existing emergency medicine and trauma care. By the same token, the World Association for Disaster and Emergency Medicine (WADEM) established a Psychosocial Section in 2012 to increase the presence and involvement of disaster mental health specialists in existing disaster response networks. WADEM provides education, research, and training on empirically derived "best practices" and "lessons learned" in disaster preparedness and response for the international disaster-related professional community (WADEM, 2013).

Disaster psychiatrists define disasters as "traumas that affect communities" (Garakani et al., 2004) and the distinction between trauma psychiatry and disaster

TABLE 4.2 Variables that Impact the Disaster Community

High-Risk Events
Evacuation
Ending Search and Rescue
Death Notification
Return to Impacted Area
Funerals and Memorials
Reopening of Public Facilities
Anniversary and Trigger Events

Source: Ligenza, L & Sharp, C. (2013). *Mitigating Disaster Trauma: The Role of the Mental Health Outpatient Clinic*. The National Council for Community Behavioral Health Care. Retrieved from: www.ctacny.com. Accessed November 10, 2013.

psychiatry has been pointed out. Planning interventions for high-risk populations (e.g., children, the elderly, and individuals with serious mental illness) rather than developing individual treatment plans is a shift in practice for disaster psychiatrists (Flynn & Norwood, 2004). Unlike individual traumatic events, the potential psychological consequences of disaster trauma extend even to those indirectly exposed and without direct losses. Norris et al., (2002) posits that research studies could overlook what it means to be a victim of disaster when disaster survivors are studied as if they experienced separate traumatic events, and North and colleagues (2006) assert that what is known from research on post-traumatic response in individual events may not apply to disaster settings. Current disaster mental health studies have shown that the majority of adverse mental health outcomes in the immediate aftermath are not labeled as psychiatric disorders and 40% of those symptomatic individuals evaluated at post-disaster settings such as shelters and family assistance centers had exacerbations of preexisting psychopathology (North & Pfefferbaum, 2013).

In order to focus on the timeline of disaster mental health needs and stage-specific interventions, this section narrows down the psychological phases of disasters into pre-disaster, acute, and post-acute phases. During the *pre-disaster phase*, mental health clinicians can participate in designing policies and programs to prepare for the unexpected and respond to all kinds of disasters. Because disaster mental health care is yet to be incorporated in traditional mental health training, education and training on current evidence-informed disaster mental health interventions integrated in disaster preparedness events and through conferences, workshops, and continuing education forums becomes a priority. Prior to a catastrophic event, familiarity with the basic hierarchy of disaster response, the continuum of emergency services, and the disaster resources available in the community is also important to increase preparedness during the chaos associated with acute disaster situations (Kantor & Beckert, 2011).

The *acute phase* commences from disaster impact and can extend up to two months post-disaster. Disaster mental health needs assessment begins at both the individual and community level (North & Pfefferbaum, 2013), and the goals are to ensure safety, diminish suffering, preserve function, and promote resilience and recovery. Disaster literature has documented that emotional distress may be ubiquitous in exposed populations, but most people are generally resilient even after the most severe traumatic events (North et al., 2006; Norris, 2006). At this stage, most disaster victims require practical assistance; information; access to food, clothing, shelter; and linkage to community resources. Active outreach and resilience-based psychosocial interventions, such as Psychological First Aid (PFA), are provided to symptomatic individuals, and those identified as having extreme reactions are referred for further mental health assessment. A challenge for mental health clinicians in the immediate days and weeks after a catastrophic event is to distinguish normative distress reactions and behaviors from exacerbation of preexisting mental illness and new onset disaster-related pathology. Causes of changes in mental status specific to disaster settings that need to be ruled out include head injury, toxic exposures, medical illness, delirium, dehydration, drug withdrawal or intoxication, and interruption of established medication regimens (Norwood, Ursano, & Fullerton, 2000).

The *post-acute phase* is approximately two months after a disaster and can last for several months to years. Clinicians continue to work in collaboration with disaster community agencies to deal with practical issues and to provide a setting that promotes coping and resilience, particularly for high-risk populations. The psychological tasks of recovery during this phase include regaining a sense of mastery and control, resumption of roles and activities, and development of new normal routine. With the passage of time, individuals who remain symptomatic and reach the threshold of a psychiatric disorder are identified and referred to formal mental health treatment in the more traditional and structured office settings where standard treatments such as psychotherapy and pharmacotherapy are provided. It has been suggested in disaster research that post-disaster symptomatology peaks in the first year then predominantly declines, but the course of recovery has not been uniform (Norris et al., 2002).

Disaster mental health care continues to evolve and mental health clinicians can wear many hats in disaster planning, preparedness, and response. Throughout the course of a disaster, mental health providers can participate in the evaluation of disaster programs and opportunities for empirical research to better understand and meet the mental health needs of the disaster community (see Table 4.3).

TABLE 4.3 Guiding Principles in Disaster Mental Health

- "No one who sees a disaster is untouched by it."
- "There are two aspects of disaster trauma: individual trauma and collective trauma."
- "Most people pull together and function during and after a disaster but their effectiveness is diminished."
- "Many disaster stress reactions are normal responses to an abnormal situation."
- "Psychological reactions to disaster may cause serious psychological impairment."
- "Many emotional reactions of disaster survivors stem from problems of living caused by the disaster."
- "Disaster relief procedures have been called 'the second disaster'."
- "Most people do not see themselves as needing mental health services following disaster and will not seek out services."
- "Disaster survivors may reject disaster assistance of all types."
- "Disaster mental health assistance is often more practical than psychological in nature."
- "Disaster mental health services must be uniquely tailored to the communities they serve."
- "Mental health staff need to set aside traditional methods, avoid mental health labels, and use an active outreach to intervention."
- "Survivors respond to active interest and concern."
- "Interventions must be appropriate to the phase of disaster."
- "Support systems are crucial to recovery."

Source: Myers, D. & Wee, D. (2005). *Disasters and their impact: Disaster mental health services*. New York, NY: Routledge, pp. 24–33.

References

American Psychiatric Association. (2013). *Diagnostic and statistical manual of mental disorders 5.* Arlington, VA: American Psychiatric Publishing.

Baum, A., Fleming, R., & Davidson, L. (1983). Natural disaster and technological catastrophe. *Environment and Behavior, 15*, 333–354.

Bolin, R. (1985). Disaster characteristics and psychosocial impacts. In B. Sowder (Ed.), *Disasters and mental health: Selected contemporary perspectives* (pp. 3–28), Rockville, MD: National Institute of Mental Health.

Centers for Disease Control and Prevention (n.d.). *Natural disasters and environmental hazards.* Retrieved from: http://emergency.cdc.gov/disasters. Accessed February 10, 2013.

Cohen-Silver, R., Holman, Al., McIntosh, D., Poulin, M., Gil-Rivas, V., & Pizarro, J. (2006). Coping with a national trauma: A nationwide longitudinal study of responses to the terrorist attacks of September 11. In Y. Neria, R. Gross, R. Marshall, & E. Susser (Eds.), *9/11: Mental health in the wake of terrorist attacks* (pp. 45–70). Cambridge, UK: Cambridge University Press.

DeWolfe, D. (2000). *Training manual for mental health and human service workers in major disasters* (2nd ed.). DHHS Publication No. ADM 90–538. D. Nordboe (Ed.), Washington, DC: Substance Abuse and Mental Health Services Administration. Retrieved from: http://www.samhsa.gov/dtac/FederalResource/Response/4Training_Manual_MH_Workers.pdf. Accessed February 23, 2013.

Dictionary, O. E. (2013). *Oxford English Dictionary*, 2nd ed.

Eynde, J.V., & Veno, A. (1999). Coping with disastrous events. In R. Gist & B. Lubin (Eds.), *An empowerment model of community healing: Response to disaster* (pp. 167–193). New York, NY: Routledge.

Federal Emergency Management Agency. (1990). Disaster assistance programs, Crisis counseling programs: A handbook for grant applicants (DAP-9). Washington, DC. Retrieved from: http://www.fema.gov/community-emergency-response-teams. Accessed March 13, 2013.

Federal Emergency Management Agency. (n.d.a.) Declaration process fact sheet. Retrieved from: http://www.fema.gov/declaration-process-fact-sheet. Accessed March 13, 2013.

Federal Emergency Management Agency. (n.d.b.). Guide for all hazards emergency operations planning. Retrieved from: http://www.fema.gov/pdf/plan/slg101.pdf. Accessed March 13, 2013.

Felton, C.J. (2002). Project Liberty: A public health response to New Yorkers' mental health needs arising from the World Trade Center terrorist attacks. *Journal of Urban Health: Bulletin of the New York Academy of Medicine, 79*(3), 429–433.

Flynn, B.W., & Norwood, A. (2004). Defining normal psychological reactions to disaster. *Psychiatric Annals, 34*(8), 597–604.

Galea, S., Ahern, J., Resnick, H., & Vlahov, D. (2006). Post-traumatic stress symptoms in the general population after a disaster: implications for public health. In Y. Neria, R. Gross, R. Marshall, & E. Suzzer (Eds.), *9/11: Mental health in the wake of terrorist attacks* (pp. 19–44) Cambridge, UK: Cambridge University Press.

Galea S., Nandi A., & Vlahov D. (2005). The epidemiology of post-traumatic stress disorder after disasters. *Epidemiological Reviews, 27*, 78–91.

Garakani, A., Hirschowitz, J., & Katz, C. (2004). General disaster psychiatry. *Psychiatric Clinics of North America, 27*, 391–406.

Green, B. (1982). Assessing levels of psychological impairment following disaster: Consideration of actual and methodological dimensions. *Journal of Nervous and Mental Disease, 170,* 544–552.

Hall, M., Norwood, A., Ursano, R., & Fullerton, C. (2003). The psychological impacts of bioterrorism. *Biosecurity and Bioterrorism, 1,* 139–144.

Halpern, J., & Tramontin, M. (2007). *Disaster mental health theory and practice.* Belmont, CA: Brooks/Cole.

Kantor, E.M., & Beckert, D.R. (2011). Preparation and systems issues: Integrating into a disaster response. In F.J. Stoddard, A. Pandya, & C. Katz (Eds.), *Disaster psychiatry* (pp. 3–17). Arlington, VA: American Psychiatric Publishing.

Ligenza, L. & Sharp, C. (2013). *Mitigating disaster trauma: The role of the mental health outpatient clinic.* The National Council for Community Behavioral Health Care. Retrieved from: www.ctacny.com. Accessed November 10, 2013.

Merriam-Webster Inc. (2004). *Merriam-Webster's collegiate dictionary,* 11th ed. Merriam-Webster.

Myers, D., & Wee, D. (2005). *Disasters and their impact: Disaster mental health services.* New York, NY: Routledge.

Neria, Y., Gross, R., Olfson, M., Gameroff, M., Das, A., Feder, A., Lantigua, R., Shea, S., & Weissman, M. (2006). PTSD in urban primary care patients following 9/11. In Y. Neria, R. Gross, R. Marshall, & E. Suzzer (Eds.), *9/11: Mental health in the wake of terrorist attacks* (pp. 239–263). Cambridge, UK: Cambridge University Press.

Norris, F. (2006). Community and ecological approaches to understanding and alleviating postdisaster distress. In Y. Neria, R. Gross, R. Marshall, & E. Suzzer (Eds.), *9/11: Mental health in the wake of terrorist attacks* (pp. 141–156). Cambridge, UK: Cambridge University Press.

Norris, F., Friedman, M., & Watson, P. (2002). 60,000 disaster victims speak. *Psychiatry, 65,* 207–260.

Norris, F. Phifer, J., & Kaniasty, K. (1994). Individual and community reactions to the Kentucky Floods: Findings from a longitudinal study of older adults. In R. Ursano, B. McCaughey, & C. Fullerton (Eds.), *The structure of human chaos: Individual and community responses to trauma and disaster* (pp. 378–400), Cambridge, UK: Cambridge University Press.

North, C.S., & Pfefferbaum, B. (2013). Mental health response to community disasters: A systematic review. *Journal of the American Medical Association, 310*(5), 507–518.

North, C.S., Pfefferbaum, B., & Hong, B. (2006). Historical perspective and future directions in research on psychiatric consequences of terrorism and other disasters. In Y. Neria, R. Gross, R. Marshall, & E. Suzzer (Eds.), *9/11: Mental health in the wake of terrorist attacks* (pp. 95–113). Cambridge, UK: Cambridge University Press.

Norwood, A.E., Ursano, R.J., & Fullerton C.S. (2000). Disaster psychiatry: Principles and practice. *Psychiatric Quarterly 71*(3), 207–226.

Pyszczynski, T. (2004). What are we so afraid of? A terror management theory perspective on the politics of fear. *Social Research, 71*(4), 827–849.

Sederer L.I., Lanzara C.B., Essock S.M., Donahue S.A., Stone J.L., & Galea S. (2011). Lessons learned from the New York state mental health response to the September 11, 2001 terrorist attacks. *Psychiatric Services, 62,* 1085–1089.

Somasundarum, D., Norris, F., Asukai, N., & Murphy, R. (2003). *Trauma in war and peace: Prevention, practice, and policy.* New York, NY: Kluwer Academic/Plenum Publishers.

Substance Abuse and Mental Health Services Administration Disaster Technical Assistance Center (2013). Retrieved from: http://www.samhsa.gov/dtac/proguide.asp. Accessed March 13, 2013.

World Association for Disaster and Emergency Medicine (2013, August). Retrieved from www.wadem.org. Accessed March 13, 2013.

Zinner, E.S., & Williams, M.B. (1999). *When a community weeps: Case studies in group survivorship*. Philadelphia, PA: Brunner/Mazel.

Zunin, L.M., & Myers, D. (2000) *Training manual for human service workers in major disasters* (2nd ed.) DHHS Publication No. ADM 90–538. Washington, DC: Department of Health and Human Services.

5

HOW DIFFERENT IS PSYCHOLOGICAL FIRST AID FROM OTHER PSYCHOTHERAPEUTIC MODALITIES?

Patricia J. Watson

Introduction

Many disaster response agencies recommend training in Psychological First Aid (PFA) prior to providing basic mental health interventions in major traumatic events (Hobfoll et al., 2007; National Institute of Mental Health, 2002; Ng & Kantor, 2010). One of the issues with vicarious traumatization following disasters is that mental health providers have high expectations about what they can achieve in their traditional sessions with clients, but the context of early intervention after disasters does not lend itself to applying a full array of treatment strategies. In fact, experts in the field of traumatic stress have indicated that prior to about two weeks following a traumatic stressor there is no algorithm for predicting long-term psychopathology such as PTSD, depression, complicated grief reactions, increased substance use, physical problems, and anxiety disorders. Rather than aiming to treat psychopathology, the recommendation is that the goals of immediate, short-term interventions should be to promote safety, attend to practical needs, enhance coping, stabilize, and connect survivors with additional resources, while intermediate interventions are geared to prevent or treat psychopathological reactions (Bryant & Litz, 2009). Therefore, PFA is designed to fit into a coordinated behavioral health effort by assessing for and either referring on to more intensive behavioral health care or intervening where indicated with a broad range of reactions. It is designed to provide practical and emotional support that bolsters survivors' ability to deal with a variety of needs, without pathologizing their stress reactions. Additionally, because stigma can contribute to individuals not seeking help when needed, PFA aims to convey the message that many people may need a little assistance to feel better or function better, without necessarily needing formal diagnosis or treatment. This chapter will describe the history and evolution of PFA into an evidence-informed disaster mental health intervention. It will familiarize readers with the theory behind PFA and discuss its goals and principles, as well as its strengths and limitations.

Background

PFA was developed on the foundations of crisis intervention as far back as the mid-20th century (Lindemann, 1944; Schneiderman, Farberow, & Litman, 1970). The term "psychological first aid" was first coined in the early disaster work of Raphael (1977) and Farberow (1978).

Disaster behavioral health programs have been available in the United States for decades, but in the last decade, the challenge has been to develop practices based on a synthesis of research, consensus-based best practices guidance, case studies, and program evaluation efforts. In one such effort, starting in 1999, the Center for Mental Health Services (CMHS), located within the Substance Abuse and Mental Health Services Administration (SAMHSA), began collaborating with the Department of Veterans Affairs National Center for Posttraumatic Stress Disorder (NCPTSD), and later with the National Child Traumatic Stress Network (NCTSN) and a select group of highly skilled private consultants, to translate and incorporate current scientific and experiential knowledge into evidence-informed practices for their FEMA–funded Crisis Counseling Assistance and Training Program (CCP).

In the initial phases of their collaboration (2000–2001), NCPTSD and SAMHSA collaborated with a number of federal agencies to co-sponsor a Consensus Workshop on Mental Health and Mass Violence (NIMH, 2002). Subject matter experts identified PFA as one of eight key components for disaster behavioral health intervention, and defined it as a set of basic strategies to reduce psychological distress. The PFA strategies identified are included in Table 5.1.

TABLE 5.1 Expert Consensus Efforts on Components of PFA

1. Orientation to disaster and recovery efforts
2. Reduction of physiological arousal
3. Mobilization of support for those who are most distressed
4. Facilitation of reunion with loved ones and keeping families together
5. Providing education about available resources and coping strategies
6. Using effective risk communication techniques

Source: National Institute of Mental Health. *Mental health and mass violence: Evidence-based early psychological intervention for victims/survivors of mass violence: a workshop to reach consensus on best practices.* NIH Publication No. 02–5138, Washington DC: US Government Printing Office. 2002. Available at: http://www.nimh.nih.gov/health/publications/massviolence.pdf. Accessed 9 June 2013.

TABLE 5.2 Expert Consensus Efforts on Disaster Behavioral Health Intervention

Provide a full spectrum of services, including:

a) Provision of basic needs
b) Assessment at the individual level (triage, screening, monitoring, and formal clinical assessment), and community level (needs assessment and ongoing monitoring, program evaluation)
c) Psychological First Aid / resilience-enhancing support
d) Outreach and information
e) Technical assistance, consultation, and training to local providers
f) Treatment for individuals with continuing distress or decrements in functioning (preferably evidence-based treatments like trauma-focused CBT)

Source: National Institute of Mental Health. *Mental Health and mass violence: Evidence-based early psychological intervention for victims/survivors of mass violence: A workshop to reach consensus on best practices.* NIH Publication No. 02–5138, Washington DC: US Government Printing Office. 2002. Available at: http://www.nimh.nih.gov/health/publications/massviolence.pdf. Accessed 9 June 2013.

Other key components recommended for disaster behavioral health programs are included in Table 5.2. Psychological debriefing, while widely accepted for use with primary survivors of disasters and mass violence prior to 9/11, was not recommended by this consensus effort, in accordance with a mounting evidence base indicating that it does not consistently reduce risks of later adjustment difficulties, and may be harmful for more high-risk individuals. (e.g., Bryant & Litz, 2009).

Other working groups followed, to more fully explore the knowledge base and formulate consensus recommendations for specific disaster mental health-related challenges. For example, regarding the timing of early interventions, experts have posited that timing will vary depending on the type of trauma and post-trauma adversities, the setting, and the service provider. For instance, after mass disasters in which there is significant loss to the individual and the community, the time frame for early interventions that are conducted in the community will be more protracted than those implemented in a hospital setting. Researchers in this arena have recommended that the decision to implement an intervention designed to promote safety, coping, and stability versus one designed to prevent or treat psychopathological reactions should not be based on the length of time after the event, but rather on the extent to which a threat exists for the survivor, and if the survivor has sufficient resources to engage in the intervention.

In an effort to address delivery of services under conditions of ongoing threat, a two-day panel of international experts identified five principles of intervention in mass violence situations which provide a blueprint for disaster intervention. (Hobfoll et al., 2007). The panel published a seminal article (Hobfoll et al., 2007) describing the elements that are consistently related to improved recovery from adversity and traumatic stress, described in Table 5.3.

TABLE 5.3 Five Essential Principles of Intervention for Mass Violence

1. *Promoting a psychological sense of safety* can reduce biological aspects of posttraumatic stress reactions, positively affect cognitive processes that inhibit recovery, and reduce beliefs that "the world is completely dangerous," exaggerations of future risk, and similar thoughts.
2. *Promoting calming* can reduce trauma-related anxiety that survivors may generalize to other situations. Calming can reduce the risks associated with trauma-related anxiety, such as high arousal, numbing, or emotionality. These risks can interfere with sleep, eating, hydration, decision-making, and performance of life tasks, and, if prolonged, result in panic attacks, dissociation, PTSD, depression, anxiety, and somatic problems.
3. *Promoting a sense of self- and community-efficacy* can increase a survivor's belief in his or her ability to manage distressing events, principally through self-regulating thought, emotions, and behavior, and may be the mechanism through which the other four elements improve psychosocial functioning.
4. *Promoting connectedness* increases opportunities to exchange knowledge essential to disaster response and provides opportunities for a range of social support activities, including practical problem-solving, emotional understanding and acceptance, sharing of traumatic experiences, normalization of reactions and experiences, and mutual instruction about coping.
5. *Instilling hope* helps survivors maintain optimism, positive expectancy, a feeling of confidence that life and self are predictable, or other hopeful beliefs (e.g., in God or that there is a high probability that things will work out as well as can reasonably be expected).

Source: Hobfoll, S.E., Watson, P., Bell, C.C., Bryant, R.A., Brymer, M.J., Friedman, M.J., . . . Ursano, R.J. (2007). Five essential elements of immediate and mid-term mass trauma intervention: Empirical evidence. *Psychiatry, 70*, 283–369. PMID:18181708; http://dx.doi.org/10.1521/psyc.2007.70.4.283

The Development of the NCTSN/NCPTSD PFA Model

The consensus conferences and case studies conducted by SAMHSA and NCPTSD consistently identified a gap in a coherent model to guide immediate post-disaster mental health services, prior to the establishment of a formal CCP (which usually occurs 2–4 weeks post-disaster). Those involved indicated that, due to the chaotic post-disaster environment, there was a need for a flexible, multi-modal model, where attention is paid to pragmatic material needs, possible developmental and cultural issues, and multiple recovery needs based on complex variables and risk and resilience factors.

To help fill the identified gap, NCPTSD collaborated with NCTSN to create a PFA Field Guide (Brymer et al., 2006; http://www.ncptsd.va.gov/pfa/PFA.html). The field guide is focused on the needs of distressed survivors in the first hours and days following disaster exposure, and it recommends that disaster mental health responders deliver assistance in a way that is survivor-centered and effective but modest in its goals. It is comprised of eight core helping actions, as described in Table 5.4.

The NCTSN/NCPTSD PFA Field Operations Guide, online training, and mobile app operationalize these core actions with children and adolescents, as well as adults and older adults. In addition to implementing these core actions,

TABLE 5.4 NCTSN / NCPTSD Psychological First Aid Model Core Actions

1. *Contact and engagement,* where the goal is to respond to contacts initiated by affected persons, or initiate contacts in a non-intrusive, compassionate, and helpful manner.

2. *Safety and comfort,* where the goal is to enhance immediate and ongoing safety, and provide physical and emotional comfort.

3. *Stabilization,* where the goal is to calm and orient emotionally overwhelmed/ distraught survivors.

4. *Information gathering,* where the goal is to identify current needs and concerns and gather information to tailor PFA interventions.

5. *Practical assistance,* where the goal is to offer practical help to the survivor in addressing immediate needs and concerns.

6. *Connection with social supports,* where the goal is to reduce distress by helping structure opportunities for brief or ongoing contacts with primary support persons or other sources of support.

7. *Information on coping,* where the goal is to provide the individual with education about stress reactions and coping to help them deal with the event and its aftermath.

8. *Linkage with collaborative services,* where the goal is to link survivors with needed services, and inform them about available services that may be needed in the future.

Source: Brymer, M., Jacobs, A., Layne, C., Pynoos, R., Ruzek, J., Steinberg, A., . . . Watson, P. NCTSN & NCPTSD, 2006; http://www.ncptsd.va.gov/pfa/PFA.html.

PFA requires a certain set of skills in the provider, including the ability to work in chaotic and unpredictable environments, the capacity for rapid assessment of survivors, the skills to provide services tailored to timing of intervention, context, and culture, and the ability to tolerate intense distress and reactions. PFA providers must also be able to accept tasks that are not initially viewed as mental health activities, work with diverse cultures, ethnic groups, developmental levels, and faith backgrounds, and have the capacity for self-care. This self-care can include things such as limiting daily numbers of most severe cases, utilizing the buddy system to share distressing emotional responses, accessing supervision routinely, practicing stress management during the workday, and checking common attitudinal obstacles to self-care, such as feeling like it would be selfish to take time to rest, or that the needs of survivors are more important than the needs of helpers.

How Is PFA Different from Other Psychotherapeutic Modalities?

The NCTSN/NCPTSD PFA model was designed to be consistent with research evidence on risk and resilience following trauma, applicable and practical in field settings, appropriate for developmental levels across the lifespan, culturally informed, and tailored to the needs of disaster survivors in the immediate aftermath of a disaster, when they are most likely to experience distress and difficulty functioning.

PFA does not assume that all individuals will develop severe mental health problems or long-term difficulties. Instead, it is based on an understanding that survivors and others affected by such events will experience a broad range of early reactions (physical, psychological, behavioral, spiritual). Some of these reactions will cause enough distress to interfere with adaptive coping, and recovery may be helped by support from compassionate and caring providers.

Many people will have transient stress reactions in the aftermath of disasters and mass violence, and such reactions may occur, occasionally, even years later. PFA seeks to address a broad range of possible effects of disasters, foster protective mediating factors such as self-efficacy, and reduce vulnerability factors. For instance, the environment after the event (other stressors: physical disability, low income/job loss, etc.) is often related to how long stress reactions last, so PFA aims to reduce and help survivors manage the post-disaster adversities. Rather than traditional diagnosis and clinical treatment, in the early phases post-disaster, most survivors are likely to need support and resources to ease the transition to normalcy. For other survivors with higher risk factors or more severe stress reactions, community and, at times, clinical intervention may be required. That is why one of PFA's core actions is linking survivors with collaborative services such as more intensive clinical care. PFA differs from traditional mental health approaches in a number of ways, as described in Table 5.5.

While the NCTSN/NCPTSD PFA model has not introduced any radical new intervention component to immediate post-disaster response, it has aimed to clearly operationalize and provide an evidence-informed framework of developmentally appropriate actions to help providers provide a range of context-appropriate services for disaster survivors (Vernberg et al., 2008). Because most providers of early interventions will not be mental health professionals, PFA has been adapted for school staff, religious personnel, first responders, homeless youth, and family shelter staff. It has been included in a number of international

TABLE 5.5 Ways that PFA Differs from Traditional Mental Health Services

1. PFA is field-based rather than office-based.
2. PFA assesses needs, strengths, and coping skills rather than being illness-oriented.
3. PFA facilitates resilience rather than targeting existing mental illness.
4. PFA is highly flexible rather than structured.
5. PFA has a non-probing focus on validating expectable reactions and experiences, rather than exploring past experiences' influence on current problems.
6. PFA has a psycho-educational rather than psychotherapeutic focus.

consensus guidelines as an intervention recommended immediately after disasters, along with other community-based outreach efforts to build individual, family, and community resources.

PFA is intended to be flexible to the needs of the survivor, modularized depending on the context and needs, and sensitive to timing, context, age, culture, and preference of the survivor. It also specifically states that not everyone needs PFA; it is intended for only those who are experiencing distress or difficulty functioning. Prior to PFA being routinely implemented, oftentimes providers attempt to "help" everyone. Paradoxically, implying that a disaster survivor "needs" interventions in order to recover from a disaster can indicate that they don't have the resources to recover on their own. They may accept help, which actually removes an opportunity for them to work out their problems on their own, effectively undermining their own abilities and their chances of viewing themselves as a stronger person via having to solve their own problems.

A number of other PFA models have been developed (e.g., Bryant et al., 2010; Center for the Study of Traumatic Stress. Psychological First Aid [CSTS], 2007; IFRC, 2009; Substance Abuse and Mental Health Services Administration [SAMHSA], 2005; van Ommeren, Snider, & Schafer, 2011; Wooding & Raphael, 2010). In general, PFA models aim to reduce distress, foster short- and long-term adaptive functioning, and link distressed or at-risk survivors with additional services. A few models have been developed by comparing existing models and revising them based on either a new context, or based on a consensus process such as the Delphi method. For instance, the World Health Organization (WHO), War Trauma Foundation (WTF), and World Vision International (WVI) produced a PFA model for use in humanitarian crises worldwide, which was based on a review of other psychological first aid models, then pilot tested and revised. The "Curbside Manner" Stress First Aid (SFA) program also created a version of stress first aid for first responders working with citizens, by drawing upon input from focus groups of first responders to create a condensed version of actions described in a number of currently available PFA and SFA peer support models (Gist, Watson, Taylor, & Elvander, 2013). Finally, the creators of Mental Health First Aid (MHFA) organized a recent consensus effort, derived from risk factor research and existing PFA models, to create a version of MHFA that identifies the most helpful principals for assisting others following potentially traumatic experiences (Kelly, Jorm, & Kitchener, 2010). One team is currently conducting a components analysis of PFA models that has, to date, indicated that while there is notable variability in the enumeration and "packaging" of these skills sets, "calming" and "connectedness" are consistent elements in the majority of extant PFA models. In contrast, "safety" is less emphasized; "self-efficacy" and "hope" are more challenging to measure and to relate to the PFA intervention (Shultz & Forbes, 2013); and other components are hard to define as "psychosocial interventions," such as the provision of practical assistance, other than being closely related to problem-solving.

Future Directions

It is important to remain conservative in any assessment of what PFA can accomplish toward prevention of long-term functional and symptomatic impact. For instance, the provision of PFA principles may be more feasible than structured clinical interventions, but it is unknown whether such interventions are associated with significant improvements in functioning in the same way that more formal, intensive mental health treatments have been. As can be seen with the psychological debriefing literature, overstating the proposed effects of an intervention prior to evidence of its impact can result in programs being implemented at the expense of careful consideration of more viable alternatives. Because PFA models are meant to be tailored to the specific needs of each disaster survivor, and to be conducted in the immediate aftermath of disasters, evaluation of their effectiveness is challenging. As stated earlier in this chapter, PFA should be implemented as part of an integrated, stepped care approach to disaster behavioral health, which follows guidelines set by a number of consensus efforts. These guidelines have in common the following elements:

- Plan to provide services for both individuals and the community that are appropriately matched for each phase across the entire developmental recovery period, and are proactive, pragmatic, and flexible.
- Promote sense of safety, connectedness, calming, hope, and efficacy at every level of intervention.
- Make every effort to do no harm by, for instance, implementing coordination groups to learn from others and to minimize duplication and gaps in response, conducting needs assessment that guide interventions based on local resources, staying updated on evidence regarding effective practices, and committing to program evaluation.
- Maximize the participation of local affected populations, and integrate programming into larger systems to reduce standalone services and reach more people.
- Use a stepped-care approach where the initial response requires practical help and pragmatic support to all in need; psychological first aid, education, and resilience-building support to those in distress; and specialized services only for those who require more care.
- Provide both individual- and community-level support by, for example, working with media to prepare the community at large and facilitate appropriate communal, cultural, memorial, spiritual, and religious healing practices.
- Provide a spectrum of services such as provision of basic needs; assessment at the individual and community level; PFA and resilience-enhancing support; outreach and information dissemination; technical assistance, consultation, and training; and treatment for individuals with continuing distress or decreased functioning.

While the PFA model has not received controlled empirical support to date (Bisson & Lewis, 2009; Fox et al., 2012), PFA principles have been promoted by many consensus efforts as the most appropriate, least likely to do harm approaches to early intervention following disasters (e.g., Bisson et al., 2010; Bryant & Litz, 2009; Inter-Agency Standing Committee, 2007; Disaster Mental Health Subcommittee, 2009; National Commission on Children and Disasters, 2010; Brymer et al., 2006). At present, there is little empirical evidence that any immediate intervention offered within hours of trauma can prevent development of mental health problems. Indeed, a recent systematic review of the literature on PFA noted an absence of any solid empirical evidence for PFA effectiveness (Bisson et al., 2010). In the absence of this evidence, the field is currently basing its endorsement of PFA on peer-reviewed consensus statements and guidelines. While the reviewers noted the lack of evidence, they recommended continuing the use of PFA as a first step in ensuring basic care, comfort, and support. Therefore, the current situation juxtaposes a high level of promotion and advocacy for PFA against a low level of evidence of its effectiveness. Importantly, of course, lack of extant evidence does not mean that PFA is not effective; rather, that effectiveness has not yet been demonstrated. It is, however, clear that there is an urgent need to demonstrate the effectiveness—or otherwise—of this widely used early intervention.

There remains a great need for further field research to evaluate the delivery and effectiveness of PFA and MHFA models in a variety of post-disaster contexts (Fox et al., 2012). Researchers wishing to conduct studies on acute interventions following disaster face many methodological challenges. Early interventions typically take place in chaotic and uncontrolled settings, with little preplanning, funding, or coordination between researchers and interventionists; the focus is generally on action and assistance rather than research, and there are often cross-community barriers between local responders and external researchers. However, PFA has been designed to be consistent with current traumatic stress research and theory, and it is hoped that systematization of current thinking about very early intervention within the PFA Field Operations Guide will stimulate research on the effectiveness of the approach. For instance, a controlled trial of the model with crime victims is underway, and an evaluation of training (Allen et al., 2010) suggests that it is well-received by consumers and providers. It has been praised for its flexible, tailored approach to helping solve practical needs, as well as its voluntary nature and allowance of discussing the traumatic incident at the survivor's wish, without insisting on it. A pilot trial of a PFA model in Haiti noted a need to communicate the boundaries of PFA in relation to other support interventions, such as providing material aid and/or clinical mental health care, and the need for a range of programming (Schafer, Snider, & van Ommeren, 2010).

Forbes and colleagues (2011) have suggested that PFA evaluation may be better operationalized and tested in a controlled way in high-risk organizations such as hospital emergency rooms, communities regularly impacted by recurring disasters, and in first responder settings.

Improvement of the field will now depend on its continued movement toward more careful evaluation of PFA services, efforts to integrate PFA principles into high-use settings for disaster survivors (such as primary care medical settings), testing and development of innovative delivery systems (such as mobile app and Internet-based self-management), and improvements in rate and efficacy of referral practices for more intensive mental health services. While the PFA field guide specifically addresses ways to maximize the possibility that survivors will accept mental health referrals, the reportedly low rates of referral and use of traditional mental health services after disasters demands further research into ways of marketing and delivering services that are more acceptable to survivors. None of this work is easily accomplished in an environment where chaos and overwhelming conditions rule. However, it is only by systematically attempting to introduce new phase- and context-specific interventions, while at the same time evaluating and improving services based on feedback gathered, that the field of disaster mental health can move forward to offset the tremendous impact that disasters and mass violence can have on communities and individuals, and improve both natural resilience and recovery for those most affected.

References

Allen B., Brymer M.J., Steinberg A.M., Vernberg E.M., Jacobs A., Speier A.H., & Pynoos, R.S. (2010). Perceptions of psychological first aid among providers responding to Hurricanes Gustav and Ike. *Journal of Traumatic Stress, 23*, 509–13. PMID:20623598; http://dx.doi.org/10.1002/jts.20539

Bisson J.I., & Lewis C. (2009). *Systematic review of psychological first aid*. Commissioned by World Health Organization. Cardiff, Wales: Cardiff University, and Geneva, Switzerland: World Health Organization.

Bisson, J.I., Tavakoly, B., Witteveen, A.B., Ajdukovic, D., Jehel, L., Johansen, V.J., . . . Olff, M. (2010). TENTS guidelines: Development of post-disaster psychosocial care guidelines through a Delphi process. *British Journal of Psychiatry, 196*, 69–74. PMID:20044665; http://dx.doi.org/10.1192/bjp.bp.109.066266

Bryant, R.A., & Litz, B.T. (2009). Mental health treatments in the wake of disaster. In Y. Neria, S. Galea, & F. Norris (Eds.). *Mental health and disasters* (pp. 321–335). New York, NY: Cambridge University Press.

Bryant, R.A., Clarke, B., Coghlan, A., Creamer, M., Eustace, G., Gordon, R., . . . Wallace, C. (Advisory Committee to Australian Red Cross). (2010). *Psychological first aid: An Australian guide*. Australian Red Cross and Australian Psychological Society. Sydney, Australia. Available at http://www.psychology.org.au/Assets/Files/Red-Cross-Psychological-First-Aid-Book.pdf. Accessed June 9, 2013.

Brymer, M., Jacobs, A., Layne, C., Pynoos, R., Ruzek, J., Steinberg, A., . . . Watson, P. (2006). *Psychological first aid: Field operations guide* (2nd ed.). National Center for PTSD and National Child Traumatic Stress Network: UCLA, Los Angeles, CA. Available at: http://www.nctsn.org/content/psychological-first-aid. Accessed June 9, 2013.

Center for the Study of Traumatic Stress. Psychological First Aid. (2007). *How you can support well-being in disaster victims*. Disaster Response Education and Training Project, Center for the Study of Traumatic Stress. Retrieved from: http://www.cstsonline.org/psychological-first-aid/. Accessed June 9, 2013.

Disaster Mental Health Subcommittee. (2009). *Disaster mental health recommendations: Report of the disaster mental health subcommittee of the National Biodefense Science Board*. Retrieved from: http://www.phe.gov/Preparedness/legal/boards/nbsb/Documents/nsbs-dmhreport-final.pdf. Accessed June 9, 2013.

Farberow, N.L. (1978) *Field manual for human service workers in major disasters: Adult psychological first aid*. DHHS Publication No. ADM 78–537. Rockville, MD: National Institute of Mental Health.

Forbes, D., Lewis, V., Varker, T., Phelps, A., O'Donnell, M., Wade, D.J., . . . Creamer, M. (2011). Psychological first aid following trauma: implementation and evaluation framework for high-risk organizations. *Psychiatry, 74*, 224–239. PMID:21916629.

Fox, J.H., Burkle, F.M., Jr., Bass, J., Pia, F.A., Epstein, J.L., & Markenson, D. (2012). The effectiveness of psychological first aid as a disaster intervention tool: Research analysis of peer-reviewed literature from 1990–2010. *Disaster Medicine and Public Health Preparedness, 6*, 247–252. PMID:23077267; http://dx.doi.org/10.1001/dmp.2012.39

Gist, R., Watson, P., Taylor, V., & Elvander, E. (2013). *Curbside manner: Stress first aid for the street* (Student Manual). National Fallen Firefighters Association. Retrieved from: http://www.fireherolearningnetwork.com/Training_Programs/Curbside_Manner__Stress_First_Aid_for_the_Street.aspx. Accessed June 9, 2013.

Hobfoll, S.E., Watson, P., Bell, C.C., Bryant, R.A., Brymer, M.J., Friedman, M.J., . . . Ursano, R.J. (2007). Five essential elements of immediate and mid-term mass trauma intervention: Empirical evidence. *Psychiatry, 70*, 283–369. PMID:18181708; http://dx.doi.org/10.1521/psyc.2007.70.4.283

Inter-Agency Standing Committee (IASC). (2007). *IASC guidelines on mental health and psychosocial support in emergency settings*. Retrieved from: http://www.humanitarianinfo.org/iasc/content/products. Accessed June 9, 2013.

International Federation of Red Cross and Red Crescent Societies. (2009). *Psychosocial interventions: A handbook*. IFRC: Reference Centre for Psychosocial Support. Copenhagen, Denmark. Retrieved from: http://pspdrk.dk/sw40688.asp. Accessed June 9, 2013.

Kelly, C.M., Jorm, A.F., & Kitchener, B.A. (2010). Development of mental health first aid guidelines on how a member of the public can support a person affected by a traumatic event: A Delphi study. *BMC Psychiatry, 10*, 49. http://www.biomedcentral.com/1471–244X/10/49. PMID:20565918; http://dx.doi.org/10.1186/1471–244X-10–49

Lindemann, E. (1944). Symptomatology and management of acute grief. *American Journal of Psychiatry, 101*, 141–148.

National Commission on Children and Disasters. (2010). *National commission on children and disasters: 2010 report to the president and congress*. Retrieved from: http://www.childrenanddisasters.acf.hhs.gov. Accessed June 9, 2013.

National Institute of Mental Health. (2002). *Mental health and mass violence: Evidence-based early psychological intervention for victims/survivors of mass violence: A workshop to reach consensus on best practices*. NIH Publication No. 02–5138. Washington DC: US Government Printing Office. Retrieved from: http://www.nimh.nih.gov/health/publications/massviolence.pdf. Accessed June 9, 2013.

Ng, A.T., & Kantor, E.M. (2010). Psychological first aid. In F. J. Stoddard, C.L. Katz, J.P. Merlino, & M.A. Sudbury (Eds.), *Hidden impact: What you need to know for the next disaster: A practical mental health guide for clinicians* (pp. 115–122). Woodbury, MA: Jones, & Bartlett.

Raphael B. (1977). Preventive intervention with the recently bereaved. *Archives of General Psychiatry, 34*, 1450–1454.

Schafer, A., Snider, L., & van Ommeren, M. (2010). Psychological first aid pilot: Haiti emergency response. *Intervention (Amstelveen), 8*, 245–254. http://dx.doi.org/10.1097/WTF.0b013e32834134cb

Schneiderman, E.S., Farberow, N.L., & Litman, R.E. (eds.). (1970). *The psychology of suicide*. New York, NY: Science House.

Shultz, J.M., & Forbes, D. (2013). Psychological first aid: Rapid proliferation and the search for evidence. *Disaster Health, 1*(2), 1–10.

Substance Abuse and Mental Health Services Administration (SAMHSA). (2005). *Psychological first aid—A guide for emergency and disaster response workers* (fact sheet). US Department of Health and Human Services, Washington, DC, USA. Available at: http://store.samhsa.gov/product/Psychological-First-Aid-for-First-Responders/NMH05–0210. Accessed June 9, 2013.

van Ommeren, M., Snider, L., & Schafer, A. (World Health Organization, War Trauma Foundation and World Vision International). (2011). *Psychological first aid: Guide for field workers.* World Health Organization. Geneva, Switzerland. Retrieved from: http://whqlibdoc.who.int/publications/2011/9789241548205_eng.pdf. Accessed June 9, 2013.

Vernberg, E.M., Steinberg, A.M., Jacobs, A.K., Brymer, M.J., Watson, P.J., Osofsky, J.D., ... Ruzek, J.I. (2008). Innovations in disaster mental health: Psychological first aid. *Professional Psychology Research and Practice, 39*, 381–388. http://dx.doi.org/10.1037/a0012663

Wooding, S., & Raphael, B. (2010). *Psychological first aid—Level 1 intervention following mass disaster.* University of Western Sydney, Australia. Retrieved from: http://www.health.nsw.gov.au/emergency_preparedness/mental/Documents/Handbook_2_PFA_July_2012.pdf. Accessed on February 1, 2014.

6

HOW DO WE UNDERSTAND DISASTER-RELATED VICARIOUS TRAUMA, SECONDARY TRAUMATIC STRESS, AND COMPASSION FATIGUE?

April Naturale

This chapter will discuss the phenomena of vicarious traumatization and secondary traumatic stress with a brief reference and comparison to compassion fatigue and burnout as they are related to the experience of disaster mental health responders and their exposure to disaster material. This exposure may come in the following forms: (1) connection to victims and/or survivors; (2) listening to others share eyewitness accounts; (3) observing television, radio, and print media reports; (4) responding with Psychological First Aid, crisis counseling, or in later stages, formal treatment; and (5) the experience of shared trauma, that is, being both a survivor and a responder (Tosone et al., 2003). The US Federal Disaster Behavioral Health response model currently in use will also be presented in relation to the implementation of vicarious and secondary traumatic stress mitigation efforts.

Traditionally, *disaster responders* referred to emergency management, fire and rescue workers, law enforcement, emergency technicians, ambulance staff, and other health care crisis management staff. After the domestic terrorist act in Oklahoma City and even more so after the events of September 11, 2001, increasing attention has been paid to the broader description of responders, which now includes mental health, faith-based, and substance abuse responders, as well as the National Voluntary Agencies Active in Disasters (N-VOAD) cadre of workers who provide a myriad of supportive response activities.

The large-scale events of 9/11 and Hurricanes Katrina, Gustav, and Ike; as well as the BP Oil Spill in the US, the tsunamis in Indonesia and Japan, the earthquakes and transportation accidents in Europe, and the repeated terrorist events throughout the world; as well as the rising number of veterans returning from the Iraq and Afghanistan wars have prompted an increase in research that can help inform both fields of the direct effects of traumatic events and the experience of vicarious traumatization. Because of the significant increase in weather-related disasters, human-caused accidents, incidents of terrorism, mass violence, and armed conflict over the past decade, there is a need for a larger pool of well-trained disaster behavioral health responders. Responders are being called for multiple deployments both within and outside their own communities. For example, as was seen in the experience of responders in the Aurora shooting in Colorado, addressing the longer term needs of the community after the shooting, then shortly after, deploying to the areas devastated by the Rocky Mountain fires, followed by responding to the flooding in several communities just after the anniversary of the shooting event. These responders need the knowledge and skills to address acute distress, assist survivors to use their coping skills, and support the innate resilience of individuals and communities in post-disaster situations. It is also imperative that responders manage their own emotional responses and attempt to mitigate the development of vicarious trauma due to continuously hearing distressing details and caring for traumatized survivors.

Disasters are events distinct from personal traumatic events such as motor vehicle accidents (one of the most commonly occurring traumatic events in the US); and domestic violence, including physical and psychological abuse, rape, and other types of sexual assault. Individually occurring events are limited in scope and may or may not cause the type of traumatic responses seen in disaster survivors. The term *trauma* has its roots in the medical world, but with the further development and honing of acute and posttraumatic stress disorder diagnoses, the emotional aspects of traumatic events are now included in the references to trauma and identified as traumatic stress. Research by the US Veterans Administration's National Center for Posttraumatic Stress Disorder has previously defined a disaster as "*a sudden event that has the potential to terrify, horrify or engender substantial losses for many people simultaneously*" (Norris, 2002). But in the most recent issue of the *PTSD Research Quarterly*, Norris and Slone (2013) report that the DSM-V has abandoned the A2 criterion (terror, horror, and helplessness) as the research showed these to have little influence on the diagnosis of PTSD (p. 2). Thus the definition of a disaster from a psychological viewpoint may also change as we learn more about the characteristics that assist in both the prevention of the development of negative mental health outcomes after trauma and the paths to recovery that support the natural resilience of the human race.

Disasters are characterized by type, size, and scope. They are generally identified as one of three types: (1) naturally occurring events such as floods, tornados, hurricanes, and other weather-related incidents; (2) human-caused accidents such as transportation crashes, explosions, and industrial incidents; and (3) intentionally caused traumatic incidents of mass violence and terrorism. The size of a disaster refers to the physical geography of the space that was affected by the event and the number of people within the area, whether it is a small, less-populated rural town verses a large landmass and/or densely populated area. Scope covers several indicators including how many people were killed or injured, how many homes and other physical structures were damaged or destroyed, and unique characteristics of the event that might have a high impact regardless of size. For example, it depends whether children were hurt or killed (as in the case of the Newtown, CT, shooting where the death of 20 children had an expansive scope of effect on the nation), the symbolism of the event (such as the destruction of the Twin Towers during 9/11, a symbol of the financial strength not only of New York City, but the nation), or a combination (as in the bombing of the Alfred P. Murrah Building in Oklahoma City where 19 babies were killed *and* the target of a federal building was meant to demean and diminish the strength and reputation of the US government). Evaluating the type, size, and scope of disasters can assist disaster behavioral health responders in planning their response and strategizing about how and where to conduct their outreach activities, who may be at higher risk for developing negative mental health outcomes and what type of interventions may mitigate these outcomes in addition to enhancing their current strengths and opening paths to resilience.

Typical and Atypical Responses Post Disaster

The characteristics of a disaster influence the types of responses to the events themselves. Natural disasters are generally accepted as part of the course of nature and while the effects can be devastating regardless of their occurring naturally, as in a hurricane or tsunami, the human response remains within common domains. These domains include the behavioral, cognitive, emotional, and physical. Additionally, some cultures view natural events from a spiritual perspective often in response to whether a religious deity or the earth itself is requiring a "righting" of environmental circumstances. As will be discussed later in this chapter, the spiritual domain is often where survivors and responders search for meaning related to the effects of disasters and their personal views of the world.

Most of the responses noted here are common in the acute phase (0–14 days) of the event in the general population exposed to a disaster as well as the responders themselves. If symptoms continue after the immediate phase (15–30 days) or become worse, a formal assessment is recommended as a serious mental health problem may be identified.

Common responses to disasters are identified in those exposed both directly and indirectly to the event and/or loved one affected by the event (see Table 6.1). Human-caused incidents can create, in addition to the common responses to traumatic events, added components related to anger and blaming as a result of human error, negligence, or criminal acts. This was clearly exemplified in the April 2010 BP Oil Spill disaster in the Gulf of Mexico where 11 workers were killed and the contamination of the environment created an economic and health crisis in an area of the country that was just beginning to recover from the devastation of Hurricanes Katrina, Rita, and Gustav (IOM, 2010). The event caused so much frustration and other psychological distress in addition to the

TABLE 6.1 Domains of the Human Responses to Disaster

Behavioral
Increase or decrease in activity level
Substance use or abuse (alcohol or drugs)
Difficulty communicating or listening
Irritability, outbursts of anger, frequent arguments
Inability to rest or relax
Decline in job performance; absenteeism
Frequent crying
Hyper-vigilance or excessive worry
Avoidance of activities or places that trigger memories
Becoming accident prone

Cognitive
Memory problems
Disorientation and confusion
Slow thought processes; lack of concentration
Difficulty setting priorities or making decisions
Loss of objectivity

Emotional
Feeling heroic, euphoric, or invulnerable
Denial
Anxiety or fear
Depression
Guilt
Apathy
Grief
Isolation
Blaming
Difficulty in giving or accepting support or help
Inability to experience pleasure or have fun

Physical
Gastrointestinal problems
Headaches, other aches and pains
Visual disturbances
Weight loss or gain
Sweating or chills
Tremors or muscle twitching
Being easily startled
Chronic fatigue or sleep disturbances
Immune system disorders

Spiritual
Questioning one's previously held beliefs
Anger at a perceived higher power
Loss of a sense of safety
Inability to find meaning

---

environmental contamination and economic decline that British Petroleum (BP) set up both medical claims and economic/property damage claims processes for directly affected survivors and small business owners respectively. Calls to the

Substance Abuse and Mental Health Service Administration Oil Spill Distress Helpline were overwhelmingly focused on persons trying to cope with the stress and frustration at the resulting effects of this human-caused event.

Terrorism and Mass Violence

Incidents of terrorism and mass violence cause distress symptoms in survivors (both direct and indirect) that make it more difficult to understand the meaning of the event and can prolong the experience of shock, grief, and trauma, complicating the recovery trajectory (Norris, Friedman, & Watson, 2002). Nowhere in US history has this been more evident than in the aftermath of the terrorist attacks of September 11, 2001. These events introduced complex variables, including individual and community perceptions of the attackers, culture, religion, and politics.

Both natural and human-caused disasters that result in a large-scale loss of life and economic disruptions also result in increased psychiatric disorders (Brewin, Andrews, & Valentine, 2000; Norris et al., 2002). As with any event that affects the social order of the community, culture plays a significant role in how the survivors view the meaning of the event and their role in the recovery process. In individuals and cultures where blaming is the norm, reliance on outside influences may impede natural coping and other abilities that people have to help themselves move more smoothly and quickly to adaptation and a return to their routine activities. In situations where there are tight community bonds and a sense of self-efficacy, the survivors' sense of responsibility and cohesive rebuilding activities are likely to enhance their assignment of positive meaning and their self-reliance.

Disaster Mental Health Principles

A commonly accepted disaster principle tells us that no one who sees a disaster is untouched by it. This does not imply the development of a diagnosable or serious emotional disorder, but rather some kind of an effect in all who are exposed, whether it is in manner or functionality post-disaster or a change in the perspective of one's life and the lives of those around, however significant or minor. Overall, the percentage of people who develop a diagnosable mental illness after a disaster, specifically posttraumatic stress disorder, is no higher than the percentage of the disorder in the general population (Norris et al., 2002; Kessler, Sonnega, Bromet, Hughes, & Nelson, 1995). Each situation, of course, varies depending on the circumstances of the disaster as well as the characteristics of the individual and/or community affected.

The trauma of disaster, like most human experiences, is about perception and each person brings their strengths, challenges, prior experiences, cultural affiliation, history, and current view of the world into the mix of shaping their perceptions. As a result, although we have an understanding of the typical types of human responses to disasters that are seen in various ethnicities and cultures across the globe, each person experiences the event as it happened to them, their family, their home, their community. This results in their seeing the disaster as a unique experience from anyone else's, regardless of how similar the characteristics of the event may be to prior events throughout history.

Another principle tells us that there are direct and indirect victims or survivors. Direct victims are those who have been involved in the event in some way such as witnessing the event firsthand, experiencing physical harm, escaping harm by rapid flight from the site of the event, or being so close to the event as to perceive a threat to their own physical safety. Indirect victims are those who lose a friend or loved one through the event, or have a close association such as narrowly escaping being directly involved by happenstance. Another example of indirect victims are those who are part of a community experiencing a trauma such as those parents in Newtown, CT, whose children were not in the school where the shooting occurred. And the third primary principle is that there are at least two types of trauma in disasters: (1) individual trauma, which includes personal stress and grief reactions and (2) collective or community trauma, which has the potential to damage the bonds and social fabric of the community either by the physical devastation of the community and/or the psyche and connectedness of its members (e.g., the effects that could be observed in the last two major disasters in the US: (1) the terrorist attacks of 9/11, which led to a change in US policies regarding privacy and torture that created a deep divide within states; and (2) the poor response to Hurricanes Katrina and Rita, which exemplified class differences not only in the affected areas, but nationally as well).

As the study of the effects of trauma work on trauma counselors evolves along with the research on posttraumatic stress disorder, the differentiation between vicarious trauma, compassion fatigue, and secondary traumatic stress is becoming more defined. Stamm (personal communication, July 2013) identifies compassion fatigue as having two components: (1) the fatigue and sense of not being able to help or not being effective in the work that is seen in burnout, which is noted to be a fairly common state and increases with time in the field; and then (2) secondary traumatic stress, which is much less common and more serious as it is the development of the same symptoms of posttraumatic stress that are seen in those directly affected. She then goes on to describe vicarious trauma effects as also having two components—the first being negative changes in the way the trauma counselor views the world, their role in it, and their sense of personal safety; and second, vicarious transformation that creates positive changes in how

TABLE 6.2 Timeframe of Disaster Behavioral Health Response Work

Phase 1	0–4 weeks	Acute and Immediate Response Work
Phase 2	30 days to anniversary	Intermediate Response Work
Phase 3	One year follow on	Long-Term Response Work

a trauma counselor sees themselves, others around them, and the world as a result of their vicarious trauma experience. These descriptions are based on research that looks at trauma counselors working with many survivors of child abuse, domestic violence, and other personal assaults such as rape (Jenkins & Baird, 2002; Adams, Matto, & Harrington, 2001; Iliffe & Steed, 2000; Pearlman 1999; Pearlman & Mac Ian, 1995; McCann & Pearlman, 1990).

There is little research that identifies disaster workers as experiencing the same levels of burnout and compassion fatigue as trauma counselors who work with victims of abuse and assault. Overall, more research, especially longitudinal data, are necessary to inform the field of the effects of working with different types of trauma (Collins & Long, 2003). While there is more anecdotal information than formal research, a small base of evidence tells us that disaster workers describe great satisfaction from a sense of meaning and the ability to do something to help in their communities that is derived from their disaster work (Lounsbury, 2006; Lemieux, Plummer, Richardson, Simon, & Al, 2010). This is a different experience from counselors who are trying to assist individuals with long-standing histories of traumatic experiences such as child abuse or neglect, domestic violence, or others situations in a client's past that cannot be altered regardless of the individual or counselor's efforts. Thus, the picture of the types of responses that disaster responders may experience follows more closely the phases of the disaster and the emotional states that the survivors and the community experience. Figure 6.1 provides an example of the moving timeline of the disaster responder's potential responses.

There is potential at any point for the disaster response worker to suffer with Secondary Traumatic Stress if they are exposed to the graphic material of victims, family members, and other survivors and are vulnerable to the negative impact of hearing their stories. This can happen with one incident rather than an accumulation of hearing many stories of trauma over time. Examples of this are described in case histories from 9/11, Hurricane Katrina, and a school shooting by Naturale (2007), and from the Oklahoma City bombing by Wee and Myers (2002).

Compassion Fatigue can develop during disaster work more likely in phase two as some time has passed and the worker may have been in the field for several weeks or longer (See Table 6.2). The honeymoon phase has passed for the community and struggles in recovery are evident (i.e., lack of supports or funding, development of infighting as disparities become apparent) that impact the effectiveness of the disaster response work.

Alternately, responders more often find a great sense of compassion satisfaction from the meaningful interactions with survivors. Positive outcomes of their work become apparent as the community moves through the recovery process, conditions improve, physical reconstruction continues, and a sense of normalcy returns. Compassion satisfaction is the experience of many disaster behavioral health responders (Lemieux et al., 2010; Adams, Boscarino, & Figley, 2006).

Vicarious traumatization occurs over time as responders are exposed to story after story of the losses and grief of victims' families and survivors. Disaster behavioral

Typical Disaster Behavioral Health Response Table for Survivors and Responders

Phase 1: 0-4 weeks Acute and Immediate Response Work	Phase 2: 30 days to anniversary Intermediate Response Work	Phase 3: One year follow-on Long Term Response Work
Short term mild distress: sadness, shock, grief are common and expected in *most* survivors and responders.	Continuing sadness, grief, fatigue in survivors but reports of experiencing a slow steady decline in symptoms. Physical and emotional fatigue in responders, but Compassion Satisfaction is often the more common experience reported.	Emotional recovery continues for survivors as reconstruction occurs and there is a return to routine activities. Responders report a continued sense of meaning and satisfaction in the work as the community recovers and services are integrated by the locality. Compassion Satisfaction and/or Vicarious Transformation are commonly reported in responders.
Or	Or	Or
Short term severe distress: Acute Stress Disorder in Survivors; Secondary Traumatic Stress in disaster behavioral health responders. *Small percentages of each.*	Development of Depression or Posttraumatic Stress in survivors. Increasing distress and both physical and emotional fatigue in responders: Compassion Fatigue or Secondary Traumatic Stress.	Emotional distress remains or increases –risk of PTSD in small percentage of survivors-when symptoms are unattended and anniversary timeframes create anticipatory anxiety and trigger events (media images and news reports, anniversary planning, etc.) Responders express frustration and a continued sense of dissatisfaction in the work as slow progress in reconstruction and fewer services to survivors are evident along with an increase in exposure to struggling survivors without help or hope. Compassion Fatigue, Secondary Traumatic Stress and/or Vicarious Trauma and burnout are risks for the responder population.

FIGURE 6.1 Typical Disaster Behavioral Health Response Table for Survivors and Responders

health responders may stay in the field for a week, a month, or longer, as what happened after Hurricane Katrina where responders (many of whom were survivors themselves experiencing shared trauma) remained for as long as two years after the event helping survivors who were displaced or living in partially destroyed homes and routine community services had not been restored (LaJoie, Sprang, &

McKinney, 2010). The buildup of frustration and a sense of one's inability to help can contribute to the development of vicarious traumatization in responders working in such situations. They may lose their faith within the system they are working in, or in a society that forgets about suffering disaster survivors once the next event hits the media. Their perception of themselves and those around them can change and become increasingly negative.

Again, alternately, more disaster responders report experiencing a vicarious transformation that changes their view of others and the world around them in a positive way (Lemieux et al., 2010). Responders report that survivors often are quite self-sacrificing and suggest that someone else is helped before themselves, often conducting heroic acts for strangers in the danger of the event and continuing to care for others throughout their own struggles for recovery. Community members often show self-reliance and the spirit of resilience is heartwarming to witness (Benight et al., 2000). Vicarious transformation is a gift to many responders who conduct disaster behavioral health services looking to find meaning in their work.

Resilience

While this chapter itself is not focused on resilience, it is important to address this concept as it continues to emerge for disaster behavioral response workers and it relates directly to vicarious traumatization. Human beings have an innate ability to manage the stress of traumatic events, and as research indicates, the majority of survivors are able to recover from the shock, fear, grief, and pain and resume the activities of their lives pre-disaster (Galea et al., 2002, 2005). People have strived toward recovery from the beginning of our existence. There is a self-healing process that begins after a trauma due to humans being hardwired to survive (Hanson & Mendius, 2009). The most recent evidence of this is in the wounded survivors of the Boston Marathon Bombing in April of 2013. Many survivors of the bomb blast lost one or both legs or feet and within three months of the event are seen in the media working intensely in rehabilitation efforts and discussing strategies for resuming their lives, even planning to participate in more marathon events (Boston Globe, 2013). Just as striking were the attitudes and the perspective of the responders who were exposed to some of the most gruesome images, including serious bodily harm and dismemberment, and having to handle body parts as one of their tasks during the day of the disaster. They willingly addressed their risk of traumatization two weeks after the event and worked through the pain of identifying their experiences and the horror they felt. These responders reported high levels of satisfaction and meaning not only due to their own work, but in witnessing the positive attitudes of the injured survivors and in the way the community managed the event as a whole. The "Boston Strong" tagline that was used as part of the recovery campaign sums up the feeling of resilience that permeated the city.

Resilience researcher Bonanno (2009) tells us that this positive attitude and ability to adapt to such adversity is "not extraordinary," and this is supported by the data that tell us the number of people who develop serious mental disorders such as posttraumatic stress disorder and depression after a trauma is generally in the 5%–10% range, with gender accounting for much of the variation (Kessler, Sonnega, Bromet, Hughes & Nelson, 2005; Norris, Friedman & Watson, 2002). As the Adverse Childhood Experiences study reports, most individuals have experienced a traumatic event by the age of 18 and most adults have experienced or witnessed multiple traumas (Centers for Disease Control, 1997, 2010). Still, many perceive resilience as not only extraordinary, but even heroic.

An important note here is that much of the post-trauma research is conducted measuring diagnosable illnesses such as posttraumatic stress, other anxiety-related diagnoses and major depressive disorder. If we are looking only at clinical diagnoses, then the resilience and recovery statements hold. However, it is equally important for us to consider those survivors and responders who experience many distressing symptoms but do not report impairment at work or home, thus are considered sub-clinical or non-diagnosable (Marshall, Galea, & Kilpatrick, 2002). These are people who continue to hold a job, have relationships, take care of their family, and attend to their everyday responsibilities, but do so with a diminished quality of emotional life. This is evidenced by the general rates of alcohol and other substance misuse, domestic violence, and increasing number of attempted as well as completed suicides in our communities across the country including those who respond to disasters and armed conflict (Substance Abuse and Mental Health Services Administration, 2008; American Association of Suicidology, 2013; Bacharach, Bamberger, & Doveh, 2008).

The disaster behavioral health response community needs to make sure that we are not only looking at the natural course of resilience to address all the needs of survivors and responders, but rather integrate what we know about both direct and indirect responses to trauma such as secondary traumatic stress and vicarious traumatization. Currently, this means that in addition to assessing those who exhibit serious psychological symptoms and monitoring those at highest risk for the development of a diagnosable mental illness post disaster, we need to (1) help restore a sense of safety and connectedness to family, friends, and community and find ways to enhance resilience in survivors and responders; (2) provide components of crisis intervention (i.e., having a compassionate presence; engaging in deep listening; providing psychoeducation, encouraging the use of known, effective coping activities; reestablishing social supports that can assist those who do experience serious distress, including responders); and finally (3) attempt to mitigate the development of serious emotional distress in the affected community, again including responders, through public messaging that provides a sense of hope and faith in the recovery process (National Child Traumatic Stress Network and National Center for PTSD, 2005; Hobfoll et al., 2007).

Responders who are also survivors themselves have the added stress of concern for their own and their family's safety and personal losses, making this group a high-risk population for negative mental health outcomes. Whether in the shared trauma experience or in the secondary traumatic exposure situation of the responders, the efforts identified above can assist survivors, loved ones of victims and responders in the post-disaster environment.

The Federal Disaster Behavioral Health Response Model

In the event that a disaster is so large as to overwhelm the ability of localities to adequately respond, a US state, territory, or tribe may request that the president declare the area a federal disaster in an effort to allow access to the supports that the Stafford Act, the federal legislation addressing disasters, allows. This act addresses the needs of a disaster focusing primarily on the physical destruction and public infrastructure needs, but when individual assistance is granted, the mental health response is generally granted, historically approximately 1% of the total budget. The funding for mental health response activities are provided through the state's mental health authority in the form of the Federal Emergency Management Agency (FEMA) disaster response model, the Crisis Counseling Assistance and Training Program or what is commonly known as the CCP (SAMHSA DTAC, 2013).

After the September 11, 2001, terrorist attacks, the state of New York launched the largest mental health response in the history of the country. The amount of $154.2 million totaled more money than had been awarded to all the CCPs in the history of the program combined. Project Liberty, as the program was called, hired close to 5,000 crisis counselors who worked out of approximately 160 provider agencies throughout the five boroughs of New York City (where the largest number of counselors worked) and the additional nine surrounding counties declared disaster areas. The program ran for three years logging over 1.2 million individual contacts in addition to tens of thousands of group contacts and public education sessions, and it delivered over 20,000 pieces of educational material in over 12 languages. By the first anniversary of the 9/11 attacks, many staff had been providing outreach and crisis counseling services almost continuously, first as a part of their natural response to the incident and then as part of Project Liberty. They began expressing their fatigue, and in many agencies, the supervisors and managers who were simultaneously keeping routine services going for their pre-9/11 clients and also pushing themselves to deliver disaster response services, expressed difficulty in providing the type of support and stress management that the crisis counselors required.

The Substance Abuse and Mental Health Services Administration (SAMHSA) who administers the CCP on behalf of FEMA began to recommend compassion fatigue and stress management consultants that the state then hired to provide supports to the crisis counselors and other agency staff participating in Project Liberty service delivery. These supports as well as additional in-service and training events were provided to help staff learn how to plan and implement self-care activities such as massage, acupuncture, meditation, and mindfulness. Self-care and stress management education and training events continued to be offered to the program staff throughout the life of the grant program.

After Project Liberty, CCP, FEMA, and SAMHSA mandated that all future crisis counseling programs include training and support services around stress management, compassion fatigue, and secondary traumatic stress mitigation for the crisis counseling program staff. Currently, stress management and self-care education and training events are included as part of a comprehensive training plan for CCP programs. The CCP recommends that staff attend training events that specifically address the risks of developing negative mental health outcomes and ways to mitigate the development of responder stress such as compassion fatigue, secondary traumatic stress, and vicarious traumatization (SAMHSA DTAC, 2013). These education and training supports are provided along with mandated Core Content, Transition, Anniversaries, Phase Down, and Close Out events.

Although the program is usually implemented after the acute phase (post 14 days) of the event, Psychological First Aid (PFA) is also one of the interventions supported by the CCP and many staff are asked to access the online PFA training module prior to joining the response programs. It is expected that staff apply only those components of PFA that are still applicable to the survivors needs in the post-acute phase of the disaster. Depending on the type, size, and scope of the disaster, intermediate skills training may also be recommended for the response staff to build competence in addressing the distress that may linger past the immediate phase of the event (Gibson et al., 2006). These recommendations are offered for the crisis counselors, outreach workers, and mental health professionals who are working with family members of victims, survivors, and their loved ones as well as other disaster responders.

Training has become an important part of the prevention and mitigation plan for disaster responders. There is a small base of research which indicates that training and preparation as well as the availability of appropriate resources can help decrease disaster responder stress (Bacharach et al., 2008; Young, Ruzek, Wong, Salzer, & Naturale, 2006). The research by Bacharach et al. (2008) also describe risk factors such as length of deployment and the combined effects of multiple events which is supported by Marmar et al. (1999) as well as Ursano, Fullerton, and McCaughey (1994). These risks are part of a larger pool of risk categories for the general population that include gender, levels of exposure, and individual characteristics such as trauma history, social supports, ethnic minority, and low socioeconomic status (Norris et al., 2002; National Center for PTSD, 2011).

Prevention and Mitigation

The primary goal of disaster behavioral health response programs is to mitigate the development of mental health disorders in the affected population. This includes the incidence of vicarious trauma and secondary traumatic stress in the responder population who, as we have indicated earlier in this chapter, are often a high-risk group especially if they are survivors as well as responders who have a shared trauma experience with those they are helping. Organizational management staff has a responsibility to assure that responders have the education, training, and resources necessary to carry out their tasks (Munroe, 1999; Myers & Wee, 2005; Young et al., 2006). Supervisors need to monitor caseloads, the length of time responders spend in the field, especially time spent in direct contact with victims, survivors, and victim's loved ones. It is up to supervisors and managers to plan and implement stress management supports including debriefing, case reviews, and problem-solving activities on a routine basis both individually and with homogenous responder groups (e.g., individuals who have had the same exposure to the event and engage in similar type response activities).

While there remains a dearth of empirical literature on the psychological impact of disaster work on the responder population specifically, the existing research is informative and should be utilized as well as built upon. We know enough that can inform as to how to begin efforts at prevention and mitigation of both secondary traumatic stress and vicarious traumatization in a population that is increasingly called upon to assist our communities in disaster response activities. In the past decade and a half, there has been a 40% increase in natural disasters in the United States and 90% worldwide (Holmes, 2008; FEMA, 2013). These numbers do not even take into account the number of human-caused events like accidents and incidents of mass violence. Our responder population is being called to serve in multiple disaster response assignments here in the US and many abroad, where armed conflict and terrorism are commonplace. If we are to continue to rely on the efforts of our emergency responders, crisis counselors, faith-based and volunteer sector support services, it is in the best interest not only of the responder population, but our communities as well, to support our disaster workers through policies and planning that require attention to the needs of the responders before, during, and after their disaster assignments. The disaster management field has the responsibility to make every effort to prevent and mitigate the development of vicarious traumatization and secondary traumatic stress.

References

Adams, K. B., Matto, H. C., & Harrington, D. (2001). The Traumatic Stress Institute Belief Scale as a measure of vicarious trauma in a national sample of clinical social workers. *Families in Society, 82*(4), 363–371.

Adams, R.E., Boscarino, J.A., & Figley, C.R. (2006). Compassion fatigue and psychological distress among social workers: A validation study. *American Journal of Orthopsychiatry, 76*(1), 103–108.

American Association of Suicidology (2013). Facts and statistics. Retrieved from: http://www.suicidology.org/resources/facts-statistics.

Bacharach, Bamberger, & Doveh, E. (2008). Firefighters, critical incidents, and drinking to cope: The adequacy of unit-level performance resources as a source of vulnerability and protection. *Journal of Applied Psychology, 93*, 155–169.

Benight, C.C., Freyaldenhoven, R.W., Hughes, J., Ruiz, J.M., Zoschke, T.A., & Lovallo, W.R. (2000). Coping self-efficacy and psychological distress following the Oklahoma City bombing. *Journal of Applied Social Psychology, 30*, 1331–1344.

Bonanno, G.A. (2009). Loss, trauma, and human resilience: Have we underestimated the human capacity to thrive after extremely aversive events? *Psychological Trauma: Theory, Research, Practice, and Policy, Vol. S* (1), 101–113.

Boston Globe. (2013). Terror at the Marathon. *Boston Globe.* Retrieved from: http://www.bos tonglobe.com/metro/specials/boston-marathon-explosions. Accessed August 25, 2013.

Brewin, C.R., Andrews, B., & Valentine, J.D. (2000). Meta-analysis of risk factors for post-traumatic stress disorder in trauma-exposed adults. *Journal of Consulting and Clinical Psychology, 68*, 748–766.

Centers for Disease Control. (1997). Adverse childhood experiences. Retrieved from: http://www.cdc.gov/ace/. Accessed August 29, 2013.

Centers for Disease Control. (2010). Adverse childhood experiences reported by adults-five states, 2009. Retrieved from: http://www.cdc.gov/ace/. Accessed August 29, 2013.

Collins, S., & Long, A. (2003). Working with the psychological effects of trauma: Consequences for mental health care workers-a literature review. *Journal of Psychiatric and Mental Health Nursing, 10*, 417–424.

Federal Emergency Management Agency. (2013). Disaster declarations by year. Retrieved from: https://www.fema.gov/disasters/grid/year. Accessed September 5, 2013.

Galea, S., Ahern, J., Resnick, H., Kilpatrick, D., Mucuvalas, M., & Gold, J. (2002). Psychological sequelae of the September 11 terrorist attacks in New York City. *New England Journal of Medicine, 346*(13), 982–987.

Galea, S., Nandi, A., Stuber, J., Gold, J., Acierno, R., Best, C.L., . . . Resnick, H. (2005). Participant reactions to survey research in the general population after terrorist attacks. *Journal of Traumatic Stress, 18*(5), 461–465.

Gibson, L.E. Ruzek, J.I., Naturale, A.J., Watson, P.J., Bryant, R.A., Rynearson, P., . . . Hamblen, J.L. (2006). Interventions for individuals after mass violence and disasters: Recommendations from the roundtable on screening and assessment, outreach and intervention for mental health and substance abuse needs following disasters and mass violence. *Journal of Trauma Practice, 5*(4), 1–28.

Hanson, R., & Mendius, R. (2009). *Buddha's brain: The practical neuroscience of happiness, love and wisdom.* Oakland, CA: New Harbinger Publications.

Hobfoll, S.E., Watson, P., Bell, C.C., Bryant, R.A., Brymer, M.J., Friedman, M.J., . . . Ursano, R.J. (2007). Five essential elements of immediate and mid–term mass trauma intervention: Empirical evidence. *Psychiatry: Interpersonal & Biological Processes, 70*(4), 283–315. doi: 10.1521/psyc.2007.70.4.283

Holmes, J. (2008). More help now, please: How to tackle tomorrow's disasters. *Economist, November 19*, 110.

Iliffe, G., & Steed, L. G. (2000). Exploring the counselor's experience of working with perpetrators and survivors of domestic violence. *Journal of Interpersonal Violence, 15*(4), 393–412.

IOM (Institute of Medicine). (2010). *Assessing the effects of the Gulf of Mexico oil spill on human health: A summary of the June 2010 workshop.* Washington, DC: National Academies Press.

Jenkins, S. R., & Baird, S. (2002). Secondary traumatic stress and vicarious trauma: A validational study. *Journal of Traumatic Stress, 15*(5), 423–432.

Kessler, R.C., Sonnega, A., Bromet, E., Hughes, M., & Nelson, C.B. (1995). Posttraumatic Stress Disorder in the National Comorbidity Survey. *Archives of General Psychiatry, 52*, 1048–1060.

LaJoie, A.S., Sprang, G., & McKinney, W.P. (2010). Long-term effects of Hurricane Katrina on the psychological well-being of evacuees. *Disasters, 34*(4), 1,031–1,044. doi:10.1111/j.1467–7717.2010.01181.x

Lemieux, C.M., Plummer, C.A., Richardson, R., Simon, C.E., & Al, A.L. (2010). Mental health, substance abuse, and adaptive coping among social work students in the aftermath of Hurricanes Katrina and Rita. *Journal of Social Work Education, 46*(3), 391–410. doi: 10.5175/JSWE.2010.200900004

Lounsbury, C. (2006). Risk and protective factors of secondary traumatic stress in crisis counselors. Dissertation Abstracts International Section A: Humanities and Social Sciences. UMI 3220694.

Marmar, C.R., Weiss, D.S., Metzler, T.J., Delucchi, K.L., Best, S.R., & Wentworth, K.A. (1999). Longitudinal course and predictors of continuing distress following critical incident exposure in emergency services personnel. *Journal of Nervous and Mental Disease, 187*(1), 15–22.

Marshall, R.D., Galea, S. & Kilpatrick, D. (2002). Psychiatric consequences of September 11. *Journal of American Medical Association, 288*(21), 2683–2689.

McCann, L. & Pearlman, L. A. (1990). Vicarious traumatization: A framework for understanding the psychological effects of working with victims. *Journal of Traumatic Stress, 3*(1), 131–149.

Myers, D., & Wee, D.F. (2005). *Disaster mental health services.* New York, NY: Brunner and Routledge.

Munroe, J.F. (1999). Ethical issues associated with secondary trauma in therapists. In B.H. Stamm (Ed.) *Secondary traumatic stress self care issues for clinicians, researchers and educators* (2nd ed., pp. 211–230). Baltimore: Sidran Press.

National Center for PTDS. (2011). Research on Trauma and PTSD. PTSD Monthly. Retrieved from: http://www.ptsd.va.gov/public/PTSD-overview/basics/how-common-is-ptsd.asp.

National Child Traumatic Stress Network and National Center for PTSD. (2005). *Psychological First Aid: Field operations guide.* Updated May 2011. Retrieved from: http://www.ptsd.va.gov/professional/materials/manuals/psych-first-aid.asp.

Naturale, A. (2007). Secondary traumatic stress in social workers: Reports from the field. *Clinical Social Work Journal, 35*, 173–181.

Norris, F. (2002). Psychological consequences of disasters. *National Center for PTSD Research Quarterly 13*(2), 1–3.

Norris, F.H., Friedman, M.J., & Watson, P.J. (2002). 60,000 disaster victims speak: Part II. Summary and implications of the disaster mental health research. *Psychiatry: Interpersonal and Biological Processes, 65*(3), 240–260.

Norris, F. & Slone, L. (2013). Understanding research on the epidemiology of trauma and PTSD. *National Center for PTSD Research Quarterly 24*(2–3), 1–5.

Pearlman, L. A. (1999). Self care for trauma therapists: Ameliorating vicarious traumatization. In B. S. Staumm (Ed.), *Secondary traumatic stress self-care issues for clinicians, researchers and educators* (2nd ed.; pp. 51–64). Baltimore, MD: Sidran Press.

Pearlman, L.A., & MacIan, P. (1995). Vicarious traumatization: An empirical study of the effects of trauma work on trauma therapists. *Professional Psychology: Research and Practice, 26*(6), 558–565.

Substance Abuse and Mental Health Services Administration. (2008). *Results from the 2007 National Survey on Drug Use and Health: National findings* (Office of Applied

Studies, NSDUH Series H-34, DHHS Publication No. SMA 08–4343). Rockville, MD. Retrieved from: http://ww.oas.samhsa.gov/msduh/2k6nsduh/2k6Results.cfm#TOC. Accessed September 5, 2013.

Substance Abuse and Mental Health Services Administration Disaster Technical Assistance Center. (2013). Federal Emergency Management Agency Crisis Counseling Assistance and Training Program Guidance. Retrieved from: http://media.samhsa.gov/DTAC-CCPToolkit/docs/gettingstarted/3_CCP_Program_Guidance_Revisions_FINAL_508.pdf. Accessed September 5, 2013.

Tosone, C., Bialkin, L., Campell, M., Charters, M., Gieri, K., Gross, S., . . . Stefan, A. (2003). Shared trauma: Group reflections on the September 11 disaster. *Psychoanalytic Social Work, 10*(1), 57–75.

Ursano, R.J., Fullerton, C.S., & McCaughey, B.G. (1994). Trauma and disaster. In R.J. Ursano, C.S. Fullerton, & B.G. McCaughey (Eds.), *Individual and community response to trauma and disaster: The structure of human chaos* (pp. 3–27). Cambridge, UK: Cambridge University Press.

Wee, D.F., & Myers, D. (2002). Stress response of mental health workers following disaster: The Oklahoma City Bombing. In C.R. Figley (Ed.), *Treating compassion fatigue* (pp. 57–81). New York, NY: Brunner-Routledge.

Young, B.H., Ruzek, J.I., Wong, M., Salzer, M.S., & Naturale, A.J. (2006). Disaster mental health training: Guidelines, considerations and recommendations. In E.C. Ritchie, P.J. Watson, & M.J. Friedman (Eds.), *Interventions following mass violence and disaster* (pp. 55–79). New York, NY: Guildford Press.

PERSONAL REFLECTIONS

When Sandy Struck Us

Ever since Irene sensitized us in coastal Brooklyn to hurricanes, weather reports about a tropical system making its way up the East Coast unerringly increased my heart rate. It wasn't different when Sandy began her unprecedented march and news reports and the Mayor's press conferences gradually grew in volume and significance. I am a community psychiatrist working with drug dependent war veterans in a therapeutic community that day of the week. None of us were strangers to posttraumatic stress.

As the day and the weekend went by, my heart slowly sinking, my stomach in knots, I could neither eat nor sleep well. A paradoxical mixture of hypervigilance and emotional numbness weighed me down. Living in Brooklyn in Flood Zone A, too familiar to us were the initial preparedness suggestions that then became mandatory evacuation orders. The gallon jugs of bottled water sitting unused for over a year suddenly found new purpose. My partner made a "go-bag" as recommended. The usual procession of events followed: neighbors with families left after battening down the hatches using whatever was the remedy of the moment (sandbags and taped windows last year; elevating all electronics, checking sump pumps this year), local bars filled up with dissenters like us who stayed, neighbors touched base across the street: "Shout if you need anything ok?" "Yes, and you do likewise." Under a daylong drizzle the water in New York Harbor rose inexorably and people disobeyed orders not to get too close to take pictures with their phones.

And then the waiting. And wondering.

At 8 p.m. Monday night, as we tried to push a tarp under the refrigerator, the lights flickered a few times. They went out and came back on and then went out again. Water seeped in under the front door. In seconds it grew to jets gushing in from either side of the door. And then the door blew in off its hinges. We fled the water and ran upstairs. All we heard was the crashing of glass and furniture and the alarms of parked cars as they drowned. The night watched the ocean surge down our street, swollen to chest height, dragging front doors and windows. Seawater swirled in backyards. We worried about where we would take shelter if a window were smashed by the wind.

The recovery followed. Mud everywhere, masonry walls pushed over. Government agency acronyms filled trailers in the park. Volunteers, utilities, and men in military fatigues handing out rations from armored vehicles, swarmed the neighborhood. Neighbors became good friends and good friends jumped in to help. City agencies came to the rescue. But, we lived without electricity for three weeks, and proper heat for three months. Anxiety about the future jolted me awake every morning, demanding that I churn my brain for solutions. Uncertainty never left me alone. Sandy was so much bigger than me and my mindfulness skills. The recovery, both physical and emotional, is still in progress.

Yeshwant Chitalkar, MD
Psychiatrist
Project Renewal
NYC

SECTION III

Understanding Vicarious Resilience

7

WHAT IS VICARIOUS RESILIENCE?

Charles Nelson and Kate St. Cyr

> In order to succeed, people need a sense of self-efficacy, to struggle together
> with resilience to meet the inevitable obstacles and inequities of life.
>
> —Albert Bandura

When an infant cries, its mother rouses and attends to the needs of her child. Having then been held, nourished, and made comfortable, the child and the mother return to rest. The child learns there is a predictable pattern of assistance for his or her needs, and the mother learns that through her instrumental efforts she can alleviate any distress that her child may face. During our earliest formative years, we are socialized to communicate our distress to others around us. The evolutionary advantage of being able to communicate in an organized social structure has provided humans a superior edge. The experiencing of and suffering from traumatic events also requires a communication and acceptance of that person's reality. Insofar as the event is shared and processed to a receptive individual who engenders competence, suffering is alleviated and there is a strong potential for both the victim and the competent listener to grow and flourish.

Vicarious resilience becomes possible through this dynamic—the victim and the helper interact, and through this interaction the shared experience meets with a positive outcome. Self-efficacy is enhanced because competence was challenged, and with a successful outcome, mastery leads to growth. This phenomenon predates the treatment of posttraumatic stress disorder and is foundational to all effective forms of psychotherapy. What becomes special about trauma is the magnitude of suffering. When a person suffers so and shares their experience there is a risk that the receiver can also become distressed. This is the germ that leads to vicarious trauma and compassion fatigue. However, when competence is bolstered by successfully navigating through the mire and muck of trauma, and the victim demonstrates a return to adaptive functioning, the listener/helper can attain a higher level of mastery, and perhaps even a higher level of self-awareness. In this regard, the helper knows they can tolerate learning of others' distress, and even more so, they are in fact effective at bringing them back to health. With this exposure and then mastery, vicarious resilience can lead to posttraumatic growth for the victim and the therapist.

Despite the age-old process of challenge leading to mastery, the literature on vicarious resilience is new, even though the nuts and bolts of how this occurs has been well-studied. Bandura and Schunk (1981) in fact focused on this process during the last portion of their life-long research on vicarious learning. Today, greater numbers of clinical examples are being studied and emerging methodologies are being employed to systematically evaluate the process.

This section focuses on the phenomenon of resilience in victims and among those who treat them. It also considers those known factors associated with vicarious resilience, as well as the positive effects of working with victims of trauma. Finally, the section concludes with case examples and opportunities for observing vicarious resilience in everyday practice.

What Is Vicarious Resilience?

A review of some of the overlapping and sometimes confounding terms associated with trauma and therapy are in order. *Resilience* is most generally conceptualized as a process in which various resources or strengths engage and interact to shield an individual, family, or community from negative outcomes despite significant risks or trauma (Kragh & Huber, 2002). *Vicarious resilience* is often used synonymously with posttraumatic growth, and further work needs to be done within the field to develop a clear construct definition that can be used with consistency and meaningfulness. At present, vicarious resilience could be used to express the process of recovering from an experience of vicarious trauma. It could also be used to describe a unique process, by which a clinician experiences resilience vicariously through witnessing his or her own clients' demonstrations of resilience, and benefitting from doing so. For the purposes of this review, we follow Hernandez and colleagues' construct of vicarious resilience, which suggests that vicarious resilience occurs through a process by which clinicians experience positive transformation and empowerment through their empathic engagement with clients (Hernandez, Gangsei, & Engstrom, 2007). Our review of vicarious resilience, or VR, will frame the bulk of our analysis of this unique and beneficial treatment effect.

Prior to delving into VR, however, there is merit in briefly exploring the corollary of *vicarious trauma*, or VT. Typically, the terms compassion fatigue, vicarious trauma, secondary trauma, and secondary traumatic stress are used interchangeably. Figley (1995) defined vicarious trauma as the natural, consequent behaviors and emotions resulting from knowledge about a traumatizing event experienced by another, and the stress resulting from helping or wanting to help a traumatized or suffering person. McCann and Pearlman (1990) describe vicarious trauma as the changes in an individual's "inner experience as a result of empathic engagement with survivor clients and their trauma material" (p. 25). Both challenge our ability to remain objectively compassionate. The therapeutic emphasis on empathy and authenticity in validating another's suffering may inadvertently render the therapist vulnerable. Once again, there may be a distinct role for mastery, or in the case of VT, diminished mastery in the genesis and maintenance of VT.

Suppose for a minute that as a well-intentioned therapist, you endeavor to aid individuals in the sharing and processing of their traumatic experiences. After all, in many cases attending to your clients' struggles with their suffering within a genuine, authentic, and non-judgmental framework yields improvements in symptom reduction due to improved validation and acceptance. This is the foundation of humanistic psychology. However, unlike normal grieving, for instance, in which the events are self-limiting and the expression of grief allows most individuals to process the loss and move on, with the sheer intensity and often horror associated with traumatic experiences, the clinician is ill-prepared to both facilitate empathic listening and simultaneously process the traumatic material. Bad things happening to innocent people have rendered the helper helpless to improve the outcome. The discrete event has come and gone and the victim remains symptomatic; the retelling of the event evoking as much fear and anxiety as the event itself.

In this regard, vicarious trauma is the unintended consequence of being a compassionate therapist.

References

Bandura, A., & Schunk, D.H. (1981). Cultivating competence, self-efficacy, and intrinsic interest through proximal self-motivation. *Journal of Personality and Social Psychology, 41*(3), 586–598.

Figley, C.R. (1995). Compassion fatigue as secondary traumatic stress disorder: An overview. In C. Figley (Ed.), *Compassion fatigue: Coping with secondary traumatic stress disorder in those who treat the traumatized* (pp. 1–20). New York, NY: Brunner/Mazel.

Hernandez, P., Gangsei, D., & Engstrom, D. (2007). Vicarious resilience: A new concept in work with those who survive trauma. *Family Process, 46*(2), 229–241.

Kragh, J., & Huber, C. (2002). Family resilience and domestic violence: Panacea or pragmatic therapeutic perspective? *Journal of Individual Psychology, 58*(3), 290.

McCann, I., & Pearlman, L.A. (1990). Vicarious traumatization: A framework for understanding the psychological effects of working with victims. *Journal of Traumatic Stress, 3*(1), 131–149.

PERSONAL REFLECTIONS

On September 11, 2001, I was in my seventh year as the medical director of a psychiatric day treatment program at St. Vincent's Hospital Manhattan. The window outside my office faced south, the dominant sight being the twin towers of the World Trade Center, just twenty blocks away. This was a view I loved. As I tried to finish some work before a 9:00 a.m. meeting, a psychologist I worked with informed me that he heard a bomb went off at the World Trade Center. We rushed toward the window; I was fearful of what I might see. I remember the large hole, fire, and smoke emanating from one of the towers—I remember thinking this had to be more than a bomb. I called the director of the psychiatry department to inform him of what I had witnessed, anticipating a direction to respond to what we were quickly realizing was a disaster. In the subsequent minutes, I stood by that window with other staff and some patients we were treating.

I do not remember seeing the plane strike the second tower. However, one of my patients informed me that we saw the second plane approach and I repeatedly stated, "Oh my God, oh my God." I suppose I experienced the amnesia that sometimes occurs when witnessing a traumatic event. While some patients in the day treatment program suffered from disorders where there is a loss of reality, this particular patient was not one of them, and I believe his account. In fact, people with serious psychiatric problems often remarkably mobilize themselves when faced with crises and tragedies. Most of the patients in the day treatment program that day, plagued by the most severe and chronic psychiatric illnesses, coped with this situation as well as [the] staff. I had always known this from seeing how my patients reacted when faced with serious medical illnesses; the events of 9/11 just confirmed that belief.

That particular patient and I spoke about the terror attacks for years afterwards, right up until he died of cancer. I recall both patients and staff reacting to the horror and news that was coming in on the radio (our offices at St. Vincent's did not yet have computers). Someone mentioned hearing that the Pentagon was attacked and that Washington was being evacuated. I remember feeling something terrible and unprecedented was happening, and fearing worse was to come. Quickly, we mobilized—I made sure patients who were to be seen that day had their prescriptions, other staff personnel stayed with patients in the day treatment program, and then I went across the street to a meeting in the main hospital building where the leadership was preparing for how we would deal with this disaster. I tried, without full success, to call family and important people in my life. I wanted to confirm their safety, tell them that I was okay, and let them know that as a doctor at St. Vincent's, the closest hospital to the World Trade Center, I would be very busy.

Tragically, many of the people who sought assistance at St. Vincent's Hospital only required our psychiatric services, as the injured we expected in the ER never arrived, perishing with the fallen towers. In the following years, I participated in newly formed programs to treat people affected by 9/11, many with posttraumatic stress. I was the psychiatrist on call two nights after the attack, September 13, 2001, when ABC News interviewed me for a segment that would precede the prayer service at the National Cathedral the following morning. Only a couple of minutes appeared on the air, but I was surprised at how inarticulate my comments were. Images of national ceremonies and panned shots of grieving families were shown, and there I was, stammering about people needing to be with others at such times. I later realized, especially when St. Vincent's closed in 2010, how important those comments actually were. All we could do in those weeks following 9/11 was be together—as a hospital, as a community, and as a country.

In 2012, after completing my first day on jury duty, I decided to take a walk from the courthouse to see the new 9/11 Memorial at the site of the twin towers. I was disappointed that I could not get in without tickets obtained in advance online. I was struck by the bustling activity and height of the new One World Trade Center tower, just one week away from once again becoming the tallest building in New York City. Things seemed so different than they were 11 years ago. As I tried to feel good about the rebuilding, an enormous sadness came over me and I had to leave quickly. I remembered the horrific deaths that were met on that very spot. While so many people were traumatized on that day, I still cannot imagine—or even bear to think—what those who died went through before their deaths, what their loved ones experienced on that day, and what they will continue to live with for the rest of their lives.

Jeffrey B. Freedman, MD
Chief of Psychosomatic Medicine
Roosevelt Hospital
St. Luke's-Roosevelt Hospital Center
New York, NY

8

WHAT FACTORS ARE ASSOCIATED WITH VICARIOUS RESILIENCE?

Charles Nelson and Kate St. Cyr

Factors Associated with Vicarious Resilience

Positive Perception of Self and Abilities

Can mastery in generating therapeutic outcomes influence vicarious resilience? What would happen if during your empathic interaction with your client, you generated a favorable outcome? What if this desired treatment response was consistent and predictable? Could this offset your "inner experience," as Pearlman and Mac Ian (1995) describe it?

Research on levels of therapist experience that use empirically supported treatments for posttraumatic stress disorder (PTSD) tends to support this hypothesis. Cunningham (2003) found that vicarious traumatization was more likely to occur in clinicians new to trauma work. He also found that those who work primarily with sexual abuse clients and those with a personal history of sexual abuse were especially prone to vicarious trauma (VT). This last finding was confirmed by Pearlman and Mac Ian (1995) who noted significantly more vicarious trauma symptoms in 60% of the therapists they surveyed who had reported a personal history of trauma.

But regardless of personal history, if you knew that clinical trials of empirically supported treatments were actually found to improve the lives of people with PTSD, you may also actually begin to relate to their trauma stories somewhat differently. By example, I engage in Prolonged Exposure Therapy with a veteran who witnessed multiple deaths of his peers by improvised explosive devices while in theatre of war. The literature unequivocally supports 50%–80% symptom remission by using this procedure (Resick, Nishith, Weaver, Astin, & Feuer, 2002; Hembree, Rauch, & Foa, 2003). I undertake the protocol and learn of my client's horrific experiences in exquisite detail.

I hear his experiences and reflect on his shock, disgust, and moral apprehensiveness with these profound losses. I may be moved by these events, but I also know that the exposure-based treatment I am providing is most often helpful in ameliorating his suffering and improving his functionality. I may then regard his experiences not only through a compassionate lens, but also through a fulcrum of realistic hope that he can recover. Despair shifts to hope, and each time we meet I can connect the data points . . . the improved behavioral and mental avoidance, the gradual re-immersion into functional roles, and the reduction in anxiety and depressive symptoms. I have living proof that by empathically listening and helping someone process their troubling experiences, they can get better; even grow more experientially. Quite remarkably, so can I.

By using a well-validated treatment protocol with appropriate supervision and experience, clinicians are far less likely to develop VT or compassion fatigue, and even more likely to see evidence of VR or compassion satisfaction on a regular basis (Craig & Sprang, 2010). As remarkable as this may seem, there are several sound treatment protocols to choose from; including cognitive processing therapy (Creamer, Burgess, & Pattison, 1992; Monson et al., 2006), and eye movement and desensitization reprocessing (EMDR; Shapiro, 1989). With continued treatment delivery exposure, and the balance of averages in favor of positive outcomes, the clinician is well-poised to be open to the developmental growth that comes from VR. Additionally, there may be wisdom in the adage that "confidence breeds confidence." A confident therapist may be able to transcend the specific atrocities suffered in favor of the long-view resilience of the human condition (Pearlman & Mac Ian, 1995). One can even look forward to learning of a client's troubling experience in order to be the calming voice that inspires hope.

Positive Acceptance of Changes to Self

Working with victims of trauma, whose deeply held moral beliefs may have been shattered as a result of their traumatic experiences, may bring about changes in the clinician's own views of the world. For example, a clinician working with abused children may find him- or herself feeling angry, hopeless, powerless, or overwhelmed; and questioning how we, as a society, could allow such atrocities to occur. In doing so, the treating clinician may experience changes in his or her own self-identity, spiritual beliefs, and overall psychosocial functioning (McCann & Pearlman, 1990). However, a positive acceptance of these changes in attitude may go a long way, in terms of traumatic resilience.

A qualitative study by Hernandez and colleagues (2007) indicated that the therapeutic relationship between the clinician and victim of trauma allows for both parties to grow and adapt their perspectives of themselves, their attitudes, and their environments. If a clinician is able to embrace these fundamental changes, they may be more likely to experience vicarious resilience. In the same study, it was reported that some therapists, after working with victims of trauma, found their definition of what a "big problem" was changed. For example, after witnessing someone cope with a particularly stressful situation, such as a kidnapping, clinicians were able to better reassess the significance of their own problems—and something that previously seemed like a significant issue, like forgetting to pay a bill on time, no longer seemed so highly stressful. By accepting these changes in attitude with an open heart and open mind, clinicians may be able to manage their own daily stressors in a more calm and resourceful manner. This, in turn, may help foster vicarious resilience.

Clinicians who are able to accept the changes that occur to their views of the world and of themselves as a result of working with victims of trauma often express experiencing sentiments of empowerment. Along with supporting the process of vicarious resilience, this feeling of empowerment may subsequently lead to reinvigoration for their work, and a renewed sense of hope for the future (Richardson, 2001). Another study by Arnold and colleagues (2005) found that clinicians who embraced changes resulting from their work as trauma clinicians experienced increased sensitivity, tolerance, compassion, and insight.

Though it has not been extensively researched, it does appear, from a number of qualitative studies, that positive acceptance of changes that result from working with victims of trauma may lend itself to vicarious resilience or, at the very least, an improved outlook on one's work as a trauma clinician.

Organizational Support

Much of the academic research examining factors that promote vicarious resilience among mental health professionals have explored the role of organizational support. A number of these studies have highlighted the importance of supervision and consultation with other mental health workers (Brady, Guy, Poelstra, & Brokaw, 1999; Follette & Batten, 2000). One-on-one supervision not only provides an opportunity to oversee caseload management and to discuss particularly challenging cases, but also provides a venue for the development and maintenance of a self-care plan (Palm, Polusny, & Follette, 2004). Additionally, raising awareness of the concepts of vicarious trauma and vicarious resilience in a supervision or training session may further assist in the development of a self-care plan.

Consultation with colleagues provides additional opportunities to seek input on difficult cases, and may help strengthen communication between colleagues while fostering a sense of self-efficacy. A clinician participating in a research study led by Hernandez and colleagues (2007) stated that searching out and modeling "a person or a group of people who showed balance in approaching their interactions in difficult situations" helped him learn how to better manage his own challenging situations (p. 236). Other researchers suggest that consultation with colleagues and supervisors may help reduce sentiments of isolation and increase feelings of efficacy (Figley, 1995; Pearlman & Saakvitne, 1995).

Other organizational factors that may help promote vicarious resilience include caseload management, and the provision of training or continuing education opportunities. A substantial number of research studies have found that caseloads with high numbers of trauma victims are associated with increased likelihood of experiencing vicarious trauma or secondary traumatic stress (Brady et al., 1999; Chrestman, 1999; Creamer & Liddle, 2005; Devilly, Wright, & Varker, 2009; Kassam-Adams, 1999; Lind, 2000). By ensuring caseloads are balanced, especially for early-career mental health professionals, organizations may help reduce the likelihood of developing vicarious trauma and may also help clinicians adhere to their self-care plans.

Involvement with Family, Peers, and Leisure Activities

Research findings suggest that mental health professionals who are unable to distance themselves from the personal accounts of trauma of their clients may be more likely to experience negative outcomes than their colleagues who engage in positive coping strategies, such as spending time with others and asking for support when needed (Palm et al., 2004). In fact, a number of research studies have found that trauma workers who use various forms of social support report fewer symptoms of vicarious trauma than those who do not (i.e., Brady et al., 1999; Devilly et al., 2009; Lerias & Byrne, 2003; Schauben & Frazier, 1995).

Previous studies have examined the role of marital status as a predictor of vicarious trauma, with mixed results. Some studies (i.e., Creamer & Liddle, 2005) found that marital status was not significantly associated with risk of developing vicarious trauma; while other studies, such as Adams, Figley, and Boscarino (2008), found a slight association between marital status and the psychological well-being of mental health providers. In all likelihood, marital status is not a strong predictor of vicarious trauma or resilience—after all, one can be unhappily married or very happily single—and it is unlikely that these differences have been taken into account in much of the published research available to date.

However, experts also suggest mental health professionals experiencing symptoms of vicarious trauma attempt to pay attention to the non-professional roles in their lives (i.e., their roles as parents, partners, friends, etc.; Palm et al., 2004). By engaging in pleasant activities outside the workplace, these individuals are able to access a variety of social support networks while simultaneously engaging in important self-care activities. A study by Bober and Regehr (2006) found that a sample of mental health professionals reported believing that vacation, time spent with family, and participation in physical activity/other hobbies could be helpful with dealing with the demands of providing mental health services to victims of trauma. However, the authors of this study found that there was no association between this belief and the amount of time actually spent on self-care in the form of leisure activities. This finding is important, as it indicates that practicing mental health professionals are typically in agreement with published research about the benefit of engaging in leisure activity but that they do not often translate it to their own practice. It therefore may be beneficial to emphasize the importance of including leisure activities when developing a self-care plan.

Religion and Spirituality

Pearlman and Saakvitne (1995) suggest that vicarious traumatization can adversely affect one's attitudes toward spirituality in a variety of ways. For example, clinicians may feel isolated and rejected, while others begin to question their spiritual beliefs (i.e., How could their God let such terrible things happen to innocent people? Does a God truly exist?). Still others respond with cynicism and distrust, while some may find themselves believing that evil exists in the hearts of humans, including themselves (Laidig & Speakman, 2009).

Academic research involving the analysis of religiosity and/or spirituality as a statistical predictor of vicarious traumatization and vicarious resilience has yielded mixed results, with good reason. Spirituality is conceptualized differently by each person, and it may be hard to assess quantitatively. Nevertheless, some studies have found that an association between self-reported religiosity/spirituality and symptoms of vicarious trauma (Quitangon et al., see Chapter 2 in this book; Adams et al, 2008), while others had failed to find an association of significance (Creamer & Liddle, 2005).

Of particular interest is a previous study which found that openness to religious change may be a significant predictor of posttraumatic growth (Calhoun, Cann, Tedeschi, & McMillan, 2000). While it was not clear in that particular study whether openness to religious experiences was a cause of posttraumatic growth or an effect of it, it is possible that, with posttraumatic growth, comes spiritual change. Laidig and Speakman (2009) suggest that when tightly held spiritual beliefs and assumptions are broken, broader spiritual perspectives may be gained. For example, a clinician who was raised to find peace in attending weekly church services may find that, through her own unique path to healing after experiencing vicarious trauma, she can now experience spirituality through other life experiences, such as exploring nature trails. Laidig and Speakman also suggest that experiencing trauma indirectly may help form deeper universal connections to humanity, opening up another avenue for posttraumatic growth. It is possible that simply being open to changes in one's spiritual and religious beliefs, and embracing the new spiritual attitudes that replace them, promote vicarious resilience.

References

Adams, R.E., Figley, C.R., & Boscarino, J.A. (2008). The Compassion Fatigue Scale: Its use with social workers following urban disaster. *Social Work Research and Practice, 18*(3), 238–250.

Arnold, D., Calhoun, L.G., Tedeschi, R., & Cann, A. (2005). Vicarious posttraumatic growth in psychotherapy. *Journal of Humanistic Psychology, 45*(2), 239–263.

Bober, T., & Regehr, C. (2006). Strategies for reducing secondary or vicarious trauma: do they work? *Brief Treatment and Crisis Intervention, 6*(1), 1–9.

Brady, J.L., Guy, J.D., Poelstra, P.L., & Brokaw, B.F. (1999). Vicarious traumatization, spirituality, and the treatment of sexual abuse survivors: A national survey of women psychotherapists. *Professional Psychology: Research and Practice, 30*, 386–393.

Calhoun, L.G., Cann, A., Tedeschi, R.G., & McMillan, J. (2000). A correlational test of the relationship between posttraumatic growth, religion, and cognitive processing. *Journal of Traumatic Stress, 13*(3), 521–527.

Chrestman, K.R. (1999). Secondary exposure to trauma and self-reported distress among therapists. In B.H. Stamm (Ed.), *Secondary traumatic stress: Self care issues for clinicians, researchers, and educators* (2nd ed., pp. 29–36). Baltimore, MD: Sidran Press.

Craig, C.D., & Sprang, G. (2010). Compassion satisfaction, compassion fatigue, and burnout in a national sample of trauma treatment therapists. *Anxiety, Stress, & Coping, 23*(3), 319–339.

Creamer, M., Burgess, P., & Pattison, P. (1992). Reaction to trauma: A cognitive processing model. *Journal of Abnormal Psychology, 101*(3), 452–459.

Creamer, T.L., & Liddle, B.J. (2005). Secondary traumatic stress among disaster mental health workers responding to the September 11 attacks. *Journal of Traumatic Stress, 18*(1), 89–96.

Cunningham, M. (2003). Impact of trauma work on social work clinicians: Empirical findings. *Social Work, 48*(4), 451–460.

Devilly G.J., Wright, R., & Varker, T. (2009). Vicarious trauma, secondary traumatic stress, or simply burnout? Effect of trauma therapy on mental health professionals. *Australian and New Zealand Journal of Psychiatry, 43*, 373–389.

Figley, C.R. (1995). Compassion fatigue as secondary traumatic stress disorder: An overview. In C. Figley (Ed.), *Compassion fatigue: Coping with secondary traumatic stress disorder in those who treat the traumatized* (pp. 1–20). New York, NY: Brunner/Mazel.

Follette, V.M., & Batten, S.V. (2000). The role of emotion in psychotherapy supervision: A contextual behavioral analysis. *Cognitive and Behavioral Practice, 7*, 306–312.

Hembree, E., Rauch, S., & Foa, E. (2003). Beyond the manual: The insider's guide to prolonged exposure therapy for PTSD. *Cognitive and Behavioral Practice, 10*(1), 22–30.

Hernandez, P., Gangsei, D., & Engstrom, D. (2007). Vicarious resilience: a new concept in work with those who survive trauma. *Family Process, 46*(2), 229–241.

Kassam-Adams, N. (1999). The risks of treating sexual trauma: Stress and secondary trauma in psychotherapists. In B.H. Stamm (Ed.), *Secondary traumatic stress: Self-care issues for clinicians, researchers, and educators* (2nd ed., pp. 37–48). Baltimore, MD: Sidran Press.

Laidig, J., & Speakman, D. (2009). The role of spirituality in understanding and coping with traumatic stress in humanitarian aid workers. Retrieved from http://www.headington-institute.org/Portals/32/Resources/Spirituality,%20traumatic%20stress,%20and%20humanitarian%20workers_CE%20Module%20PDF.pdf. Accessed on July 16, 2013.

Lerias, D., & Byrne, M.K. (2003). Vicarious traumatization: symptoms and predictors. *Stress and Health, 19*(3), 129–138.

Lind, E.W. (2000). Secondary traumatic stress: Predictors in psychologists. *Dissertation Abstracts International, 61*, 3283.

McCann, I. & Pearlman, L.A. (1990). Vicarious traumatization: A framework for understanding the psychological effects of working with victims. *Journal of Traumatic Stress, 3*(1), 131–149.

Monson, C.M., Schnurr, P.P., Resick, P.A., Friedman, M.J., Young-Xu, Y., & Stevens, S.P. (2006). Cognitive processing therapy for veterans with military-related posttraumatic stress disorder. *Journal of Consulting and Clinical Psychology, 74*(5), 898–907.

Palm, K.M., Polusny, M.A., & Follette, V.M. (2004). Vicarious traumatization: Potential hazards and interventions for disaster and trauma workers. *Prehospital and Disaster Medicine, 19*(1), 73–78.

Pearlman, L.A., & Mac Ian, P.S. (1995). Vicarious traumatization: An empirical study of the effects of trauma work on trauma therapists. *Professional Psychology: Research and Practice, 26*, 558–565.

Pearlman, L.A., & Saakvitne, K.W. (1995). Treating therapists with vicarious traumatization and secondary traumatic stress disorders. In C. Figley (Ed.), *Compassion fatigue: Coping with secondary traumatic stress disorder in those who treat the traumatized* (pp. 150–177). New York, NY: Brunner/Mazel.

Rauch, S.M., Defever, E., Favorite, T., Duroe, A., Garrity, C., Martis, B., & Liberzon, I. (2009). Prolonged exposure for PTSD in a Veterans Health Administration PTSD clinic. *Journal of Traumatic Stress, 22*, 60–64.

Resick, P., Nishith, P., Weaver, T., Astin, M., & Feuer C. (2002). A comparison of cognitive-processing therapy with prolonged exposure and a waiting condition for the treatment of chronic posttraumatic stress disorder in female rape victims. *Journal of Consulting and Clinical Psychology, 70*(4), 867–879.

Richardson, J.I. (2001). *Guidebook on vicarious trauma: Recommended solutions for anti-violence workers*. Ottawa, ON: National Clearinghouse on Family Violence.

Rothbaum, B.O., Astin, M.C., & Marsteller, F. (2005). Prolonged exposure versus eye movement desensitization and reprocessing (EMDR) for PTSD rape victims. *Journal of Traumatic Stress, 18*(6), 607–616.

Schauben, L.J., & Frazier, P.A. (1995). Vicarious trauma: The effects on female counselors of working with sexual violence survivors. *Psychology of Women Quarterly, 19*, 49–54.

Shapiro, F. (1989). Efficacy of the eye movement desensitization procedure in the treatment of traumatic memories. *Journal of Traumatic Stress, 2*, 199–223.

9

WHAT ARE THE POSITIVE EFFECTS OF WORKING WITH VICTIMS OF TRAUMA?

Charles Nelson and Kate St. Cyr

Clinicians who work with victims of trauma often find their work challenging, yet incredibly rewarding. While the positive effects of working with victims of trauma are perhaps less likely to be highlighted than the potential detrimental effects, it is important to reiterate that benefits to the clinician do exist.

Positive Attitudes Toward Work

Previous qualitative and quantitative research suggests that many clinicians report experiencing positive attitudes towards their work with victims of trauma; and a study by Eidelson, D'Alessio, and Eidelson (2003) found that over half of the mental health professionals who participated in their study reported an increase in their positive feelings towards work as a result of working with victims of the September 11, 2001 attacks at the World Trade Center. Some of the reasons provided for this increase in positivity toward their work included feeling as though they were making a significant contribution to their clients, and lending themselves to their country in a time of need. Others valued the widespread recognition for their profession that resulted from their work with victims of 9/11.

Others find positivity knowing that the work they do is life-changing. Richardson (2001) recounts the story of a children's advocate who was inspired after a former client told her how much he remembered the time he spent in a shelter she had previously worked in. The children's advocate explained that those words are with her every time she watches another family leave the shelter.

Ability to Reframe Negative Experiences

Mental health professionals who work with victims of trauma may also find that they are better equipped to address negative experiences in a resourceful manner as a result of their work experiences. Another counselor, this one employed at a women's shelter, states that whenever she is having a tough day, she watches the children or speaks with the women who live at the shelter. Their courage is inspiring to her, and she states that she can then revisit her problem, taking it on using the skills she teaches to her clients (Richardson, 2001). Another mental health professional stated that working with victims of trauma changes how you define a problem, and forces you to become less fearful and more resourceful when facing your own problems (Hernandez, Gangsei, & Engstrom, 2007). It appears that the process of working with victims of trauma and observing them overcome seemingly insurmountable problems, whether tangible (such as loss of family or friends) or not (loss of innocence or world beliefs), helps the clinician reframe his or her idea of the significance of everyday stressors.

Vicarious Learning from Stories of Courage

Mental health professionals and others who provide services to victims of trauma may find motivation to continue engaging in their trauma work as a result of their professional experiences. For example, Eidelson and colleagues (2003) reported that a number of the mental health professionals included in their study found a renewed sense of purpose in their work as a result of working with individuals affected by the attacks of 9/11. Other clinicians may find motivation in the courage of their clients to overcome their difficulties and move forward with their lives (Hernandez et al., 2007).

Hope for Future

Perhaps one of the most important outcomes of providing services to victims of trauma is that of hope for future. The clinician who struggled to understand a world in which a child could be abused may find that witnessing first-hand the capacity of humans to heal emotionally and psychologically lends itself to yet another view of the world; one of hope, one of strength (Hernandez et al., 2007). It is perhaps through this newly formed view of the world that clinicians are better able to find satisfaction and value in their work; and to continue to have hope for the future.

Case Examples

Case 1: Military trauma

"John" is a 29-year-old Canadian Forces veteran who returned home from deployment in the theater of war in Afghanistan in 2007. He was deployed for six-and-a-half months and had no prior deployment history. He was a member of the army for five years and was trained in logistics and transport. There is no major premorbid history of trauma or abuse, and he otherwise had a positive developmental history.

While abroad, John witnessed the accidental death of a close peer by friendly fire. He also learned of the suffering and abuse of children for which he was unable to intervene. John was also involved in numerous fire-fights with the enemy and witnessed repeated casualties. These incidents occurred in the context of chronic stress associated with being amidst hostile groups and the uncertainty associated with a high probability for violence to occur specifically while he was being attacked.

Upon returning home, he took a parental leave and soon after noticed dramatic changes in his mood and reactivity with normal domestic and childrearing tasks. He experienced hallmark features of posttraumatic stress disorder, including re-experiencing, nightmares, hyperarousal, and avoidance of most social interactions. He spent most of his time self-isolating in his basement, and feared that his partner would soon leave him because of his lack of interest in intimacy and very limited emotional expressiveness, other than irritability and anger.

John sought individual psychotherapy in 2009 in order to improve his increasing symptoms and functional impairments. He had taken to using marijuana to "relax," and found that he still had prominent insomnia and daytime fatigue. He disliked using prescribed antidepressants and felt that his inability to recover was indirectly a sign of weakness.

John embarked on prolonged exposure therapy (PE) at a specialized outpatient mental health clinic and reluctantly began to share specific details of his trauma-related experiences. John had an experienced therapist who was familiar with military trauma, as well as the events known to occur in 2006–2007 in Afghanistan. The therapist had previously helped similar soldiers who were deployed over this time-period. The therapist treated and discharged several members from this cohort and had previous knowledge of the well-publicized events in Afghanistan including the accidental air-strike on Canadian soldiers meant for the Taliban.

John required 15 treatment sessions of PE for his symptoms of re-experiencing to abate, and gains were also seen in returns to social activities, including public outings with his family. At the close of focal treatment for his PTSD symptoms, he was considering vocational retraining as a finishing carpenter. The therapist felt satisfied with John's treatment progress and agreed to bridge therapeutic involvement to specialized resources that could aid in the transition back to work.

The therapist enjoyed his work with John and did not endorse any troubles with VT. He shared the successful outcome with his colleagues and in fact corresponded with a former supervisor of his PE training about how well the protocol had worked. The therapist reported feeling "buoyed" by John's courage and indomitable spirit. He reflected how this facet of the human condition gives hope to anyone who has suffered needlessly at the hands of others.

Case 1 Deconstruction

The traumatic experiences suffered by John were of a high magnitude in terms of intensity of horror suffered. The details of the events were also of a universal nature and many parallels could be made about how others suffer in everyday aspects of their lives domestically and in theater of war. Specifically, one could easily see the parallel about losing a close friend to accidental death. Child abuse too continues even in well-socialized communities in North America, and there are reports of gun violence happening on North American soil. So the events suffered were readily relatable and possibly transferrable to the therapist's personal worldview.

So why would the therapist report feeling "'buoyed' by the indomitable spirit of the human condition"? Table 9.1 may help illustrate. Although there are numerous risk factors associated with developing VT in this case, the therapist also had a number of protective factors that likely promoted VR. In isolation, the risk factors alone give potential to an adverse course of over-identification and internalization of the traumatic material by the therapist. Certainly, if an individual shared this account of their traumatic injury with a peer, the peer would recoil at the sheer level of distress encountered. What makes the therapist different? Essentially, the therapist is as vulnerable as a "non-trained" peer when it comes to VT, especially if they're unaware of the risk and protective factors.

The therapist has developed specific self-efficacy with trauma from his or her experiences training and successfully administering therapy. In the desire to act empathically, he or she is mindful of not over-identifying with the unique features of his or her client's history. This is likely supported by not also having a personal trauma history, but even if this were the case, such therapists who have worked through their own mental health issues are more likely to be spared the impact of association in their own lives.

TABLE 9.1 Case 1 Protective and Risk Factors for Vicarious Resilience and Vicarious Trauma

Protective Factors Promoting VR	Risk Factors for Developing VT
• Experienced therapist. • Selection and use of Empirically Validated Treatment (EVT). • Therapist had training and supervision in EVT. • No personal trauma history. • Therapist was familiar with known details of the geopolitical war. • Therapist had experienced previous successful treatment outcomes among this population. • Therapist demonstrated significant aspects of having trait resilience.	• High intensity traumatic material. • Relatable universal themes of human suffering. • Initial high symptomatic presentation of client, including complicating factors of marijuana use. • Client's family was initially at risk of dissolution. • Client was initially reluctant to engage in treatment and offer details of the traumatic events. • Client initially felt strongly that his suffering was intractable (i.e. that he was hopeless).

While it seems obvious that clinicians should have worked through any residual influence of trauma in their past in order to optimize their positive influence in therapy, this too is controversial. Macaskill (1988) found that personal therapy in the early stages of training may have a deleterious effect on the therapist's work with patients: 15%–40% of therapists reported unsatisfactory outcomes or negative effects from their own therapy on subsequent relations with clients. No evidence was found to support the view that personal therapy significantly enhanced therapeutic effectiveness. Once again, Pearlman and Mac Ian (1995) noted significantly more vicarious trauma symptoms in 60% of the therapists they surveyed who had reported a personal history of trauma. So, minimally, care must be taken when embarking on trauma therapy if the therapist has a trauma history—with or without a course of personal treatment.

Finally, the therapist believed that he was fundamentally "resilient" in nature. He attributed this core belief to having a repertoire of bouncing back from adversity and practical challenges over his lifespan. He reflected and savored memories of having met the challenges of graduate school, as well as family and child-rearing responsibilities. This is consistent with recent modeling research by Bensimon (2012) in which participants with varied trauma exposure levels completed measures of resilience, trauma history, PTSD, and posttraumatic growth. Results of structural equation modeling showed that trauma increased PTSD and growth levels, whereas resilience was associated positively with growth and negatively with PTSD. It was concluded that salutogenic and pathological responses to trauma show differential associations with trait resilience. *Salutogenic* in this case is a term borrowed from medical sociology describing an approach focusing on factors that support human health and well-being, rather than on factors that cause disease. Engendering an overall competency with resilience is very likely protective and positively related to VR.

Case 2: Civilian Trauma

"Sarah" is a 33-year-old married mother of two children who was raped by a not formerly known assailant. She had also been sexually abused between the ages of 9 and 11 by an older brother. The details of the recent index trauma were graphic, and she required facial reconstructive surgery as a result of the violent attack. She continues to have chronic pain, as well as the typical PTSD symptoms of avoidance, hyperarousal, and nightmares. Despite this, she had testified against the assailant, and he was convicted of sexual assault and is now in prison. She is eager to commence treatment in order to get her life back on track. She expressed a belief that she was a strong person who was capable of overcoming adversity, and she in fact felt proud of how she worked through her prior child sexual abuse.

The therapist was assigned to Sarah as part of a criminal injury compensation package. The therapist is well-trained in family systems psychology but has little experience with adult sexual trauma. She has not been abused or traumatized herself, and otherwise is an adaptive coper with routine life stressors. She is intrigued by the victim's symptoms and contracts for an open-ended course of supportive psychotherapy. They meet regularly and based on the supporting police and medical reports the therapist learns of the severe beating and sexual violation; the client is reluctant to share details of the assault fully and completely and the therapist supports her decision by focusing on positives since the attack.

Sarah begins to deteriorate as treatment progresses. She has become more distant from her children and husband, and has sharply increased her alcohol consumption. In therapy, there appears to be transient dissociative periods when she reports on the stressful impact of the assault. The therapist feels they are at a recovery plateau and she is at a loss to improve her symptoms. The therapist finds herself thinking a great deal about what it must have been like to suffer the assault; conversely, she has begun to dread meeting with her client as she finds the interchanges exceptionally draining. She feels guilt and self-reproach for backing away from her usual level of compassionate and empathic therapeutic engagement. She also has become generally avoidant of other aspects of her work role, and it now takes extraordinary effort for her to complete reports and liaise with other staff. She has also been avoiding some aspects of sexual intimacy with her boyfriend.

Case 2 Deconstruction

The therapist has begun to experience caregiver burnout and is also showing symptoms of VT related to the trauma material. It has impacted related aspects of her professional work role as well as intimacy with her own partner. She feels powerless to help her client and this leads to global feelings of incompetence. She is bewildered as to why her usual supportive and compassionate therapeutic approach is not effective. She has helped many other individuals in her usual role as therapist, but is not fully aware why her current PTSD client is languishing. She is also unable to see the connection between her own recent intimacy issues and the trauma material, as well as her self-doubt as a professional therapist.

Table 9.2 overviews the imbalance of risk and protective factors for Case 2. In Case 2, there were reliable indicators that the client and therapist could in fact thrive in their therapeutic relationship. Prognostically, there were clinical factors to support a recovery, and the therapist was eager to undertake the assignment. However, her limited history of working productively with this specialized clinical population did emerge as a principal factor in both the client failing to ameliorate her symptoms, and her own VT impact on her professional and personal roles. The therapist's lack of efficacy in influencing change began to clash with her previous level of confidence and perceived competence. This, as well as the specific trauma material, ultimately combined to adversely influence her own sexual intimacy.

Apart from reducing the known risk factors in this case example, the therapist may have additionally benefited from ongoing supervision. A colleague more

TABLE 9.2 Case 2 Protective and Risk Factors for Vicarious Resilience and Vicarious Trauma

Protective Factors Promoting VR	Risk Factors for Developing VT
• Experienced therapist. • No personal trauma history. • Therapist had experienced previous successful treatment outcomes (although not among this population). • Therapist was familiar with known details of the trauma from collateral information. • Client was initially eager to engage in treatment. • Client initially felt that she was a strong person capable of overcoming adversity. • Justice was served in prosecuting the offender.	• High-intensity traumatic material. • Relatable universal themes of human suffering. • Initial high symptomatic presentation of client, including complicating factors of alcohol use. • Did *not* select and use an Empirically Validated Treatment (EVT). • Therapist did *not* have training and supervision in (EVT).

familiar with the treatment of trauma would likely have been able to point out the risk factors. Additionally, they may have also acted with influence in normalizing the response to plateaus in recovery. In fact, an initial increase in symptom acuity is a known treatment effect of exposure-based trauma therapy. Foreknowledge in this area may have circumvented increased self-doubt and perceptions of incompetence.

Case 3: Mass Trauma

"Ross" is a 54-year-old married man, who earns his living as a farmer outside of a small town in a rural area. In 2011, the region was struck by an F4 tornado that resulted in the death of several members of his community, including Ross's brother and a young girl who attended Ross's church, and severe injury to a number of others. Ross lost many of his livestock when the roof of his barn collapsed during the tornado, and experienced significant damage to his home; such that he and his wife "Charlotte" needed to seek alternative living arrangements until their home could be repaired several months later.

As a volunteer firefighter, Ross spent the days initially following the tornado assisting in the search for missing persons, clearing debris from homes and roadways, and working in the temporary shelter that was established at the local high school for those who could not return to their homes. During this time, Ross was exposed to the graphic injuries of people that he knew and helped rescue, as well as the destruction of many of the homes and buildings in his community.

In the weeks that followed, Charlotte noticed that Ross was becoming socially withdrawn and increasingly irritable. He often had nightmares related to his role with the recovery effort, and stopped attending church on weekends, stating that he had trouble believing that a higher being could impart such destruction on the good people of his community. After a great deal of urging from Charlotte, Ross agreed to speak to a therapist in a neighboring community about his anger and frequent flashbacks of the tornado.

The therapist in the neighboring community was one of the few experienced mental health professionals in the rural area affected by the tornado. While his own community was not directly affected by the tornado and he was lucky enough to be spared any personal loss, he too knew a number of individuals who had been affected by the tornado and had since been providing services to several other members of Ross's community.

Ross was reluctant to engage in the therapeutic process. He felt that, as a volunteer firefighter and farmer who has seen the impact of nature over the years, he should be strong enough to move on without talking about his feelings and experiences related to the tornado. He refused to discuss the events he witnessed as part of the recovery effort in therapy, instead wanting to focus on his anger, guilt for escaping some of the hardships fallen on his neighbors, and the displacement of his previously firmly held spiritual beliefs.

Case 3 Deconstruction

The therapist feels frustrated at Ross's reluctance to engage in therapy, as he strongly feels that Ross would benefit from a course of trauma-focused therapy. As one of the few mental health practitioners in the area, the therapist turns to some of his peers from the trauma-focused therapy training program he participated in several years ago for consultation. Despite feeling slightly overwhelmed by the sudden increase in his caseload following the tornado, the therapist decides to offer Ross a time-limited contract of supportive therapy with the objective of moving on to a course of protocol-driven trauma-focused therapy if Ross so chooses when his supportive therapy contract comes to an end. He is optimistic that he can build enough of a therapeutic relationship over the time-limited course of supportive therapy to encourage Ross to try trauma-focused therapy. The risk and protective factors for this case are covered in Table 9.3.

There are a number of protective factors in Case 3 that promote VR and suggest that a successful therapeutic relationship could exist. The therapist was optimistic that the client could achieve recovery following a course of trauma-focused therapy, something that he had a substantial amount of experience with, and had access to peers with similar training for consultation when necessary. The client, while not initially interested in therapy, was willing to discuss aspects of his reaction to the trauma and to work on select outcomes (e.g., anger management). The client also had the support of his family.

However, the therapist himself was indirectly affected by the traumatic event in question and lacked consistent opportunities for professional support with a supervisor or colleagues. These factors, combined with the recent increase in the therapist's caseload as well as the graphic material of the trauma, may increase the therapist's risk of experiencing VT.

TABLE 9.3 Case 3 Protective and Risk Factors for Vicarious Resilience and Vicarious Trauma

Protective Factors Promoting VR	Risk Factors for Developing VT
• Experienced therapist. • Therapist was familiar with the details of the traumatic event. • Therapist had access to peers for consultation. • Therapist had training in trauma-focused therapies. • Therapist was optimistic of his abilities to create a therapeutic alliance. • Client was willing to work on some aspects related to his experience (e.g., anger). • Client's spouse was supportive of him seeking therapy.	• High-intensity traumatic material. • Relatable universal themes of human suffering. • Therapist was experiencing a sudden increase in his caseload. • Therapist was indirectly affected by the traumatic event in question. • Therapist lacked consistent professional and organizational support (e.g., from colleagues or a supervisor). • Client was reluctant to engage in trauma-focused therapy.

Summary

Vicarious resilience (VR) occurs through a process by which clinicians experience positive transformation and empowerment through their empathic engagement with clients. This happens despite the specific nature of the trauma material, and is more centrally related to self-efficacy and demonstrated competence with achieving desired treatment outcomes. Many factors enhance the likelihood of VR, including the following:

• holding a positive perception of self and abilities
• having a positive acceptance of changes to self
• having organizational support and clinical supervision
• benefiting from involvement with family, peers, and leisure activities
• openness to spiritual change (growth)
• possessing positive attitudes toward work
• ability to reframe negative experiences
• enhanced motivation from vicarious learning from stories of courage
• holding beliefs of hope for future (trait resilience)

While the above-noted list is not likely exclusive or exhaustive, the nine known factors that increase the likelihood of promoting VR have met a critical threshold of acceptance in the literature. Conversely, known factors, to a greater or lesser extent, are related to VT and caregiver burnout. Briefly, the following factors may impede VR and curtail positive therapist experiences and jeopardize patient outcomes for individuals suffering from trauma exposure:

• High-intensity traumatic material; magnitude of suffering is salient
   Many mental health professionals who work with victims of trauma may be exposed to highly graphic details of the traumatic event in question, which

may increase the likelihood of experiencing vicarious traumatization reactions. These reactions may also be intensified when working with victims of mass trauma (e.g., 9/11 attacks in New York City) as the clinician may experience an increase in the number of trauma cases making up his or her caseload. The clinician working with victims of mass trauma will also be faced with dealing with the same traumatic content in consecutive cases. All of these factors may contribute to an increase in the likelihood of experiencing vicarious trauma (Pearlman & Saakvitne, 1995; Palm, Polusny, & Follette, 2004). It is worth noting that similar results have been reported in other populations: studies have found that war journalists were more likely to experience symptoms of traumatic stress and depression than their peers who had never covered war stories (Feinstein, Owen, & Blair, 2002; Pyevich, Newman, & Daleiden, 2003).

- Relatable universal themes of human suffering; violation of "just world" internal schema
  Figley (1995b) suggests that empathizing with clients' traumatic stories renders the clinician susceptible to being traumatized by the event as well. This may be particularly likely in the event that the traumatic event is a relatable event involving human suffering—for example, the kidnapping and subsequent murder of a child may cause the clinician to experience disruptions in his or her cognitive schema more so than he or she might upon hearing details of a veteran's war-related traumatic experience. Significant disruptions in the clinician's previously held beliefs may thereby increase his or her likelihood of experiencing a vicarious trauma reaction.

- Complex symptom presentation of the client, including comorbid conditions
  While published research to date has not appeared to investigate the role of complex symptom presentation of the client, anecdotal evidence suggests that there may be an association between case presentation and vicarious traumatization, particularly if the clinician in question has a high caseload of clients with complex presentations. Comorbid conditions are typically more difficult to treat effectively, especially if substance or alcohol misuse is involved (Ouimette, Moos & Brown, 2003); and the challenges associated with such cases may adversely affect the treating clinician, particularly if the clinician is lacking specific trauma-focused training or supportive resources.

- Poor selection of therapeutic modality (i.e., usage of treatment that is not well-suited for a trauma population)
  Previous research suggests that not all trauma-specific therapeutic modalities will be appropriate for every client. For example, the utility of Prolonged Exposure (PE) therapy in trauma populations has been well-documented (Foa et al., 2005; Rauch et al., 2009; Rothbaum, Astin, & Marsteller, 2005; etc.). However, a very small number of trauma survivors will experience survivor guilt to such a degree that PE may not be considered the most effective form of psychotherapy (Foa & McNally, 1996). Use of a contraindicated therapy may result in premature treatment dropout or lack of success in meeting treatment goals for the client, and feelings of failure for the clinician.

- Inadequate training, and limited or poor supervision on the part of the clinician
  Previous research indicates that access to clinical supervision and consultation, as well as the provision of training opportunities for early-career clinicians, may help mediate the development of vicarious traumatization (Follette, Polusny, & Milbeck, 1994; Pearlman & Mac Ian, 1995; Chrestman, 1999).
- History of unresolved trauma on the part of the clinician
  A number of research studies have found that a history of previous trauma is associated with an increased risk of experiencing vicarious trauma (e.g., Kassam-Adams, 1995; Pearlman & Mac Ian, 1995). Seeking intervention for previous personal trauma may help reduce the likelihood of experiencing a vicarious traumatization reaction.

Perception and context are critical when understanding the impact of trauma on post-trauma suffering. If the traumatic material is minimally understood and is so far afield from our worldview, a certain level of clinical objectivity may allow for a natural distancing of empathy. While this may at first sound complicated, it is simple logic that dictates that we can't really be affected by something we don't really understand.

Take, for instance, an older war veteran who, decades after losing a peer in battle, continues to have unwanted and intrusive recollections of the event. A therapist can certainly relate to the profound feelings of loss that can accompany the death of a loved one. However, consider further that this World War II vet has also lived a full life of prosperity and dignity, respected by his nation for liberating and protecting his people. With the limited intensity and magnitude of the traumatic event, as well as the post-event lifetime of highly adaptive functioning, it would be highly improbable that a therapist would experience VT or caregiver burnout. Consider, however, that the trauma material occurs in the context of an innocent bystander tragically harmed by a senseless act of violence. In this case, the therapeutic landscape is ripe with opportunity for over-identification and philosophical and perhaps spiritual conflicts with how so much hurt and devastation can befall anyone without rhyme or reason. "Anyone" in this case can also be the therapist. A war veteran who commits to a life of service has surely entertained the possibility of death occurring while in theater of war. When we learn of the very real possibility of harm occurring to the innocent, our internal beliefs or schemas are shifted to the real possibility of serious harm happening to us. If we are resistant to accommodating this new worldview into our belief structure, we are at risk of VT and burnout.

The notion of accommodation of self that promotes growth was first espoused by Hernandez and colleagues in relation to therapists working with victims of political violence, in which they interviewed therapists who "learned something about overcoming adversity" through their work with torture survivors. The authors describe VR as positively analogous to vicarious traumatization. Here's their summary:

[a] complex array of elements contributing to the empowerment of therapists through interaction with clients' stories of resilience: . . . witnessing and reflecting on human beings' immense capacity to heal; reassessing
the significance of the therapists' own problems; incorporating spirituality
as a valuable dimension in treatment; developing hope and commitment;
articulating personal and professional positions regarding political violence;
articulating frameworks for healing; developing tolerance to frustration;
developing time, setting, and intervention boundaries that fit therapeutic
interventions in context; using community interventions; and developing
the use of self in therapy.

(Hernandez et al., 2007)

VR may have some elements that are dispositional, such as trait resilience or engendering a certain openness to change and growth, but other factors can be learned
and integrated into our practices to optimize the likelihood of positive treatment
experiences with our clients. Seeking clinical supervision and organizational support can increase our self-confidence and also serve to "share the wealth" so to
speak when we debrief and decompress after learning of a poignant and truly sad
retelling of traumatic events. Selecting empirically sound modalities of psychotherapy further optimize the chances of treatment recovery. This makes us feel good,
and capable, and efficacious. Not everyone may be suited for conducting trauma
therapy, but for those who seek a deeper understanding into their own strengths
and vulnerabilities there is the possibility of a rich and impactful career helping others re-learn that the world does offer safe and responsible allies who genuinely care.

Definitions

Compassion fatigue, sometimes referred to as secondary traumatic stress and often
used interchangeably with caregiver burnout, refers to a clinician's increase in
reactivity with the clinical content within the therapeutic relationship that results
in a diminished capacity for empathy and general avoidance and/or deterioration
of clinically related activities.

Prolonged exposure therapy (PE) is a type of exposure-based therapy developed by
Edna Foa used to treat PTSD. PE relies on three facets of treatment: (1) in vivo
exposure—real-life efforts to stop mental and behavioral avoidance, and extinguish the cognitive fear network; (2) imaginal exposure—repetitive retelling of
the traumatic event to promote habituation and abate anxious distress; and (3)
cognitive processing—to process and digest the role of the individual in experiencing the traumatic event.

Resilience is a process in which various resources or strengths engage and interact
to shield an individual, family, or community from negative outcomes despite
significant risks or trauma (Kragh & Huber, 2002).

Salutogenic describes an approach focusing on factors that support human health and well-being, rather than on factors that cause disease (Antonovsky, 1979).

Vicarious resilience (VR), often used synonymously with posttraumatic growth, occurs through a process by which clinicians additionally experience positive transformation and empowerment through their empathic engagement with clients.

Vicarious trauma (VT) is the natural, consequent behaviors and emotions resulting from knowledge about a traumatizing event experienced by another, and the stress resulting from helping or wanting to help a traumatized or suffering person (Figley, 1995a).

References

Antonovsky, A. (1979). *Health, stress and coping*. San Francisco, CA: Jossey-Bass Publishers.

Bensimon, M. (2012). Elaboration on the association between trauma, PTSD and post-traumatic growth: The role of trait resilience. *Personality and Individual Differences, 52*(7), 782–787.

Chrestman, K.R. (1999). Secondary exposure to trauma and self-reported distress among therapists. In B.H. Stamm (Ed.), *Secondary traumatic stress: Self care issues for clinicians, researchers, and educators* (2nd ed., pp. 29–36). Baltimore, MD: Sidran Press.

Eidelson, R.J., D'Alessio, G.R., & Eidelson, J.I. (2003). The impact of September 11 on psychologists. *Professional Psychology: Research and Practice, 34*, 144–150.

Feinstein, A., Owen J, & Blair, N. (2002). A hazardous profession: War, journalists, and psychopathology. *American Journal of Psychiatry, 159*, 1570–1575.

Figley, C.R. (1995a). Compassion fatigue as secondary traumatic stress disorder: An overview. In C. Figley (Ed.), *Compassion fatigue: Coping with secondary traumatic stress disorder in those who treat the traumatized* (pp. 1–20). New York, NY: Brunner/Mazel.

Figley, C.R. (1995b). Compassion fatigue: Toward a new understanding of the costs of caring. In B.H. Stamm (Ed.), *Secondary traumatic stress: Self-care issues for clinicians, researchers, and educators* (pp. 3–27). Baltimore, MD: Sidran Press.

Foa, E.B., Hembree, E.A., Cahill, S.P., Rauch, S.A.M., Riggs, D.S., Feeny, N.C., & Yadin, E. (2005). Randomized trial of Prolonged Exposure for PTSD with and without cognitive restructuring: Outcome at academic and community clinics. *Journal of Consulting and Clinical Psychology, 73*, 953–964.

Foa, E.B., & McNally, R.J. (1996). Mechanics of change in exposure therapy. In R.M. Rapee (Ed.), *Current controversies in the anxiety disorders* (pp. 329–343). New York, NY: Guilford Press.

Follette, V.M., Polusny, M.M., & Milbeck, K. (1994). Mental health and law enforcement professionals: Trauma history, psychological symptoms, and impact of providing services to child sexual abuse survivors. *Professional Psychology: Research and Practice, 25*(3), 275–282.

Hernandez, P., Gangsei, D., & Engstrom, D. (2007). Vicarious resilience: A new concept in work with those who survive trauma. *Family Process, 46*(2), 229–241.

Kassam-Adams, N. (1995). The risks of treating sexual trauma: Stress and secondary trauma in psychotherapists. In B.H. Stamm (Ed.), *Secondary traumatic stress: Self-care issues for clinicians, researchers, and educators* (2nd ed., pp. 37–48). Baltimore, MD: Sidran Press.

Kragh, J., & Huber, C. (2002). Family resilience and domestic violence: Panacea or pragmatic therapeutic perspective? *Journal of Individual Psychology, 58*(3), 290.

Macaskill, N.D. (1988). Personal therapy in the training of the psychotherapist: Is it effective? *British Journal of Psychotherapy, 4*, 219–226.

Ouimette, P., Moos, R.H., & Brown, P.H. (2003). Substance use disorder-posttraumatic stress disorder comorbidity: A survey of treatments and proposed practice guidelines. In P. Ouimette & P.J. Brown (Eds.), *Trauma and substance abuse: Causes, consequences, and treatment of comorbid disorders* (pp. 91–110). Washington, DC: American Psychological Association.

Palm, K.M., Polusny, M.A., & Follette, V.M. (2004). Vicarious traumatization: Potential hazards and interventions for disaster and trauma workers. *Prehospital and Disaster Medicine, 19*(1), 73–78.

Pearlman, L.A., & MacIan, P.S. (1995). Vicarious traumatization: An empirical study of the effects of trauma work on trauma therapists. *Professional Psychology: Research and Practice, 26*, 558–565.

Pearlman, L.A., & Saakvitne, K.W. (1995). Treating therapists with vicarious traumatization and secondary traumatic stress disorders. In C. Figley (Ed.), *Compassion Fatigue: Coping with secondary traumatic stress disorder in those who treat the traumatized* (pp. 150–177). New York, NY: Brunner/Mazel.

Pyevich, C.M., Newman, E., & Daleiden, E. (2003). The relationship among cognitive schemas, job-related traumatic exposure, and posttraumatic stress disorder in journalists. *Journal of Traumatic Stress, 16*, 325–328.

Rauch, S.M., Defever, E., Favorite, T., Duroe, A., Garrity, C., Martis, B., & Liberzon, I. (2009). Prolonged Exposure for PTSD in a Veterans Health Administration PTSD clinic. *Journal of Traumatic Stress, 22*, 60–64.

Richardson, J.I. (2001). *Guidebook on vicarious trauma: Recommended solutions for anti-violence workers.* Ottawa, ON: National Clearinghouse on Family Violence.

Rothbaum, B.O., Astin, M.C., & Marsteller, F. (2005). Prolonged exposure versus eye movement desensitization and reprocessing (EMDR) for PTSD rape victims. *Journal of Traumatic Stress, 18*(6), 607–616.

Managing Vicarious Trauma in Disasters

10

HOW DO WE MEASURE VICARIOUS TRAUMA?

Kate St. Cyr

Introduction

There are a number of self-administered tools that assess symptoms of vicarious trauma, secondary traumatic stress, or compassion fatigue available for clinicians. This section of the book provides an overview of a number of existing tools that have been used to measure symptoms of vicarious trauma and similar concepts (e.g., secondary traumatic stress) among mental health professionals who work with victims of trauma. It also provides some information pertaining to the development of the scales and their psychometric properties, whenever possible, as well as their scoring instructions.

A Guideline for Using These Measures

One expert suggests that mental health professionals and others who work with victims of trauma complete a self-assessment tool upon commencement of employment, if possible, and every six months after that (Richardson, 2001). This way, the original assessment scale can be used as a baseline for comparison to follow-up questionnaires.

Some of the tools presented below can be administered by an organization to its employees or they can be self-administered. Many of these tools have also been used in published research, some more psychometrically sound than others. Regardless of the intention behind its use, once a tool is selected, it is best to use the same measure for repeat administrations so that changes in responses can be tracked longitudinally.

Measures of Vicarious Trauma and Similar Concepts

Compassion Fatigue Self-Test

The Compassion Fatigue Self-Test (CFST; Figley, 1995) was one of the first measures developed to measure compassion fatigue, and continues to be one of the most commonly used measures, albeit in a revised form (Bride, Radey, & Figley, 2007). A number of revisions to the scale have been made since its initial development and, as such, several versions of the scale exist. The original version, developed by Charles Figley in 1995, is a 40-item self-report measure consisting of two subscales: compassion fatigue (23 items), which measures secondary traumatic stress; and burnout (17 items). A total score is also calculated. Examples of items assessed in the CFST include "I have flashbacks connected to those I help," "I wish I could avoid working with some people I help," and "I find it difficult separating my personal life from my helper life." Respondents are asked to rate how frequently they experience each item on a scale of 1–5, where 1 = rarely/never and 5 = very often. Compassion fatigue subscale scores of 26 and lower indicate extremely low risk, scores between 27 and 30 suggest low risk, scores between 31 and 35 indicate moderate risk, scores between 36 and 40 indicate high risk, and scores 41 and above indicate extremely high risk. Burnout subscale scores of 36 and lower indicate extremely low risk while scores between 37 and 50 indicate moderate risk, scores between 51 and 75 indicate high risk, and scores 76 and higher indicate extremely high risk (Figley, 1995). Estimates of the internal reliability of the scale and subscales are good to excellent (Cronbach's alpha = 0.84 for the compassion fatigue subscale, 0.83 for the burnout subscale, and 0.90 for the total scale; Jenkins & Baird, 2002); and internal consistency estimates from the subscales and combined scale range from 0.86 to 0.94 (Figley, 1995; Figley & Stamm, 1996).

In 1996, Stamm and Figley adapted the CFST to include a compassion satisfaction subscale. This revised measure consists of 66 items, and includes a number of positively oriented items such as "I feel that I might be positively 'inoculated' by the traumatic stress of those I help" and "I have thoughts that I am a success as a helper" that were not included in the original version. Respondents rate how frequently they experienced each of the items in the past seven days. Higher scores on the compassion fatigue and burnout subscales indicate higher risk of experiencing compassion fatigue or burnout; whereas higher scores on the compassion satisfaction indicate greater potential for compassion satisfaction. The revised CFST demonstrated good internal consistency in study samples (alpha = 0.87 for both the compassion satisfaction and compassion fatigue subscales, and 0.90 for the burnout subscale; Stamm, 2002). Further revisions to this iteration of the measure led to the development of a renamed scale—the Professional Quality of Life (ProQOL) measure, which is discussed in detail later in this chapter.

Another revised version of the CFST—the Compassion Fatigue Scale-Revised (CFS-R)—was developed by Gentry, Baranowsky, and Dunning in 2002. This shortened version of the CFST consists of 22 items measuring compassion fatigue/secondary traumatic stress and another 8 items measuring burnout, for a total of 30 items. Respondents rate how frequently they experience each item using a 10-point scale, where 1 = "Never/Rarely" and 10 = "Very often." Higher scores on the subscales are indicative of increased symptoms of secondary traumatic stress and burnout. Items measured in this scale include "I have difficulty falling or staying asleep" and "I have had first-hand experience with traumatic events in my childhood" (Gentry et al., 2002). However, because of concerns related to the psychometric properties of the CFS-R, it was again revised, this time by Adams, Boscarino, and Figley (2006). The subsequent version, renamed the Compassion Fatigue-Short Scale (CF-Short Scale), is a 13-item measure that measures secondary traumatic stress (8 items) and burnout (5 items) using the same 10-point scale as the CFS-R. Items measuring secondary traumatic stress included in this scale include "I have experienced intrusive thoughts after working with especially difficult clients/patients"; items measuring burnout include "I have a sense of worthlessness, disillusionment, or resentment associated with my work." Internal reliability estimates for the CF-Short Scale were good to excellent (Cronbach's alpha—0.80 for the secondary trauma subscale and 0.90 for both the burnout subscale and the combined total scale; Adams et al., 2006).

Impact of Event Scale

The Impact of Event Scale (IES; Horowitz, Wilner, & Alvarez, 1979) and the Impact of Event Scale—Revised (IES-R; Weiss & Marmar, 1997) are tools that were designed to measure traumatic stress symptomatology related to a specific traumatic experience; however, both have been widely used to assess compassion fatigue among mental health service provides (Bride et al., 2007).

The original 15-item IES consists of two subscales, based loosely on the B and C criteria of a PTSD diagnosis: intrusion and avoidance. The intrusion subscale contains seven items assessing the frequency of intrusive thoughts and images as well as dreams related to the traumatic experience in question. Examples of items included in the intrusion subscale are "Pictures about it popped into my mind," "I had waves of strong feelings about it," and "I thought about it when I didn't mean to." The 8-item avoidance subscale assesses endorsement of concepts such as emotional numbing, engagement in avoidance behaviors, and denial. Items included in the avoidance subscale are "I stayed away from reminders of it," "I was aware that I still had a lot of feelings about it, but I didn't deal with them," and "I felt as if it hadn't happened or wasn't real" (Weiss, 2004). Both subscales use a relatively uncommon scoring system, a 4-point Likert-type scale where 0 = "not at all," 1 = "rarely," 3 = "sometimes," and 5 = "often," to assess frequency of symptoms over the past week. A combined score of 26 or higher was suggested by the authors of the scale as a reasonable cut-off for clinically significant reactions. In the initial report of the measure, test-retest reliability was adequate (0.87 for the intrusion subscale and 0.79 for the avoidance subscale); and data supported the existence of two unique clusters of symptoms (Cronbach's alpha = 0.79 for intrusion and 0.82 for avoidance; Horowitz et al., 1979).

An updated report on the psychometric properties of the original IES was published by Sundin and Horowitz in 2002. Using unweighted averages from 18 published research papers, they found that the alpha coefficient for the intrusion subscale was 0.86 and that for the avoidance subscale was 0.82. The same paper included a review of factor analyses for the original IES. This review found that, of 12 studies, 7 supported the two-factor structure of the scale while 3 found that numbing and avoidance better existed as separate factors, for a total of 3; data from the remaining two studies supported a single-factor scale (Sundin & Horowitz, 2002).

Despite the demonstrated utility of the IES, its failure to assess the third concept of traumatic stress symptomatology, hyperarousal, led to the eventual development of the IES-R (Weiss & Marmar, 1997). Designed to maintain compatibility with the original scale, the IES-R initially used the same scoring system, and only one of the existing items was modified from its original wording (a single item assessing frequency of experiencing difficulty falling or staying asleep was separated into two unique items). In addition, six new items assessing symptoms of hyperarousal, such as anger and irritability, trouble concentrating, and hypervigilance, were created and added to the scale, for a total of 22 items. Examples of items included in the hyperarousal subscale are "I was jumpy and easily startled," "I had trouble falling asleep," and "Reminders of it caused me to have physical reactions, such as sweating, trouble breathing, nausea, or a pounding heart" (Weiss, 2004). After assessing the psychometric properties of the IES, a small number of additional changes were made to the measure: (1) respondents were no longer asked to report how frequently they experienced each of the items, instead they were asked to indicate the degree of distress associated with each item over the past seven days; (2) the scoring scale was revised, so that 0 = "not at all," 1 = "a little bit," 2 = "moderately," 3 = "quite a bit," and 4 = "extremely"; and (3) instead of summing each of the items to obtain a subscale score, the mean of the responses for each subscale was used so that it was presented using the same scoring system as the items. Unlike the original IES, no cutoff scores of clinical significance were established (Weiss & Marmar, 1997).

Internal estimates of consistency for the IES-R, when used for individuals who have directly experienced trauma, are good (0.89 for the intrusion subscale, 0.84 for the avoidance subscale, and 0.82 for the hyperarousal subscale; Weiss, 2004). The IES-R has also been published in a number of languages (e.g., French, Spanish, and Japanese, among others); and the psychometric properties for many of these translated versions support their use. It has also been translated, though not formally published, in Italian and Dutch (Weiss & Marmar, 1997).

Professional Quality of Life Scale

As previously mentioned, the Professional Quality of Life Scale (ProQOL; Stamm, 2010) was developed as a result of revisions made to the CFST, and has continued to be adapted over time. Typically used for research and to monitor or self-monitor professional quality of life, the most recent version, ProQOL Version 5, is a 30-item self-report questionnaire consisting of three subscales, each of which measure distinct constructs: compassion satisfaction, compassion fatigue, and burnout. Each subscale consists of 10 items; respondents are asked to indicate how frequently they have experienced each of the items in the past 30 days using a scale of 1 to 5, where 1 = "Never" and 5 = "Very often." Examples of items included in the compassion fatigue subscale are worded positively and include such statements as "I feel invigorated after working with those I help" and "I believe I can make a difference through my work." Items included in the compassion fatigue scale, which measures secondary traumatic stress or vicarious trauma, include "I feel depressed because of the traumatic experiences of the people I help" and "I avoid certain activities or situations because they remind me of frightening experiences of the people I help." Finally, items assessed in the burnout subscale include "I am not as productive at work because I am losing sleep over traumatic experiences of a person I help" and "I feel overwhelmed because my case [work] load seems endless" (Stamm, 2010).

Each of the subscales is scored separately; there is no total score. Subscale totals are derived by summing each item; five items on the burnout subscale must be reverse-scored before calculating the subscale total (Bride et al., 2007). The Pro-QOL uses percentiles to establish potential for compassion satisfaction and risk for compassion fatigue and burnout, using a mean of 50 and a standard deviation of 10 for each of the scales. On the compassion satisfaction subscale, a score of 57 is considered the 75th percentile, and indicates that the respondent likely achieves a good amount of satisfaction from his or her professional role. A score of 43 is considered the 25th percentile, and scores lower than 40 are indicative of low satisfaction. Similarly, scores of 57 and 43 are the 75th and 25th percentiles, respectively, for the compassion fatigue and burnout subscales; however, for both of the subscales, lower scores indicate lower risk. Internal reliability estimates for the three subscales range from adequate to good (Cronbach's alpha = 0.75 for the burnout subscale, 0.81 for the compassion fatigue subscale, and 0.88 for the compassion satisfaction subscale); and good construct validity, as evidenced by over 200 published research papers (Stamm, 2010).

Secondary Traumatic Stress

The Secondary Traumatic Stress Scale (STSS; Bride, Robinson, Yegidis, & Figley, 2004) has been used in a number of research studies to assess symptoms of vicarious trauma in mental health professionals. It is a self-report scale consisting of 17 items which measure past-seven-day symptoms associated with indirect exposure to traumatic events, using the following DSM-IV symptom clusters: intrusion (criterion B), avoidance (criterion C), and arousal (criterion D; American Psychiatric Association, 2004). Examples of items included in the intrusion subscale include "I thought about my work with clients when I didn't intend to," "I had disturbing dreams about my work with clients," and "It seemed as if I was reliving the trauma(s) experienced by my client(s)." Some items included on the avoidance subscale are "I felt emotionally numb," "I noticed gaps in my memory about client sessions," and "I avoided people, places, or things that reminded me of my work with clients." Finally, the arousal subscale was comprised of items such as "I had trouble sleeping," "I was easily annoyed," and "I expected something bad to happen" (Bride et al., 2004). Respondents rate their responses to each item using a 5-point Likert-type scale, where 1 = "never" and 5 = "very often." Subscale scores are calculated by summing the scores of each of the items in that particular subscale; a total score is calculated by summing the scores of all items (Bride et al., 2007).

Similarly to the ProQOL, users of the STSS may choose to utilize percentiles to interpret scores. A score at or below the 50th percentile indicates little or no secondary traumatic stress; whereas scores in the 51st to 75th percentile suggest mild secondary traumatic stress. Scores between the 76th and 90th percentiles are considered indicative of moderate secondary traumatic stress. A score between the 91st and 95th percentile is interpreted as high secondary traumatic stress, and a score at or above the 96th percentile are considered to be severe secondary traumatic stress. Alternatively, users of the STSS may opt to use a cutoff score identified by the creators of the scale to interpret their results. By this scoring method, a score of 38 or greater indicates some degree of secondary traumatic stress, and that further consideration should be given to address potential issues. Finally, an algorithm can be used to identify vicarious trauma using the STSS. In this approach to scoring the STSS, the respondent may be experiencing secondary traumatic stress if he or she endorses at least one item on the intrusion subscale, at least three items on the avoidance subscale, and at least two items on the arousal subscale. Items are only considered to be endorsed, for the purposes of the algorithmic scoring, if the respondent rates the items at a "3" or higher (Bride, 2007).

Self-Care Assessment Scale

The Self-Care Assessment Scale was developed by Saakvitne and Pearlman in 1996 to help care providers assess how well they are meeting their own self-care needs. Respondents are asked to rate how frequently they engage in a number of self-care behaviors using a five-point Likert-type scale, where 5 = "always" and 1 = "it never occurred to me." Items are divided among six domains of self-care: physical (14 items), psychological (12 items), emotional (10 items), spiritual (16 items), workplace or professional (11 items), and balance (two items). Examples of the types of items included in the physical self-care scale are "Eat regularly (e.g., breakfast, lunch, and dinner)," "Get regular medical care for prevention," and "Dance, swim, walk, run, play sports, sing, or do some other physical activity that is fun." The psychological self-care domain includes items such as "Make time for self-reflection," "Have your own personal psychotherapy," and "Notice your inner experience—listen to your thoughts, judgments, beliefs, attitudes, and feelings"; while items on the emotional subscale include "Stay in contact with important people in your life," "Identify comforting activities, objects, people, relationships, places, and seek them out," and "Allow yourself to cry." Items in the spiritual self-care domain include "Spend time with nature," "Be open to inspiration," and "Identify what is meaningful to you and notice its place in your life." The workplace and professional self-care subscale consists of items such as "Balance your caseload so no one day or part of a day is 'too much,'" "Get regular supervision or consultation," and "Identify projects or tasks that are exciting and rewarding"; while the two items included in the balance subscale are "Strive for balance within your work life and work day" and "Strive for balance among work, family, relationships, play, and rest" (Saakvitne & Pearlman, 1996). Unlike many of the other scales used in the assessment of vicarious trauma or compassion fatigue, the tool is used to identify domains of self-care where the respondent is excelling or doing well (as indicated by a large number of higher scores assigned to individual items within that domain); and to identify areas of self-care for further improvement (as indicated by a large number of lower scores assigned to individual items within that domain).

Traumatic Stress Institute Belief Scale and the Trauma and Attachment Belief Scale

The Traumatic Stress Institute Belief Scale (TSI; Pearlman, 1996), which was origin-ally published in 1996, existed in a number of forms (e.g., TSI Revision L, TSI Revision M, etc.) before evolving into and being published as the Trauma and Attachment Belief Scale (TABS; Pearlman, 2003). Early versions of the TSI consist of approximately 80 items, though there is some variation between versions, and measure cognitive disruptions resulting from psychological trauma in five hypoth-esized areas of psychological need: safety, trust, intimacy, esteem, and power/con-trol. Two subscales for each domain exist; one for self and for others, for a total of 10 subscales. Respondents rate items using a 6-point scale, where 1 = "strongly disagree" and 6 = "strongly agree" (Pearlman, 1996). A total score is also available, with higher scores suggesting increased cognitive disturbance.

The original TSI scale was developed for use among adults who had experi-enced a traumatic event, but has been used to assess vicarious trauma in a number of research studies. The psychometric properties of the original TSI were reported as acceptable to excellent (Cronbach's alpha = 0.77 for the other-control subscale to 0.98 for the total scale; Pearlman, 1996); however, a study by Jenkins and Baird (2002) demonstrated slightly lower values in terms of internal reliability (Cron-bach's alpha = 0.62 to 0.83).

The primary difference between the original versions of the TSI and the Trauma and Attachment Belief Scale (TABS; Pearlman, 2003) is that the TABS underwent some wording changes to make it user-friendly for younger populations (i.e., ado-lescents aged 9–18). Other minor changes include the addition of four new items, and the replacement of some items with lower item-scale correlations with items that are better related to the subscale in question. The TABS consists of the same subscales as the TSI and uses the same scoring system. Examples of items included in the TABS include "When I am alone, I don't feel safe" and "The important people in my life are in danger" from the safety subscales, "I can trust my own judgment" and "You can't trust anyone" from the trust subscales, "I don't feel like I deserve much" and "People are wonderful" from the esteem subscales, and "I hate to be alone" from the intimacy subscale (Pearlman, 2003).

The psychometric properties of the TABS are freely available on the National Child Traumatic Stress Network website (http://www.nctsn.org/content/trauma-and-attachment-belief-scale). Estimates of test-retest reliability were acceptable (Pearson's $r = 0.60$ to 0.79 for the subscales and 0.75 for the total scale); as were estimates of internal consistency (Cronbach's alpha $= 0.67$ to 0.96 for the subscales and 0.96 for the total scale; Pearlman, 2003). Construct validity has been provided by some studies (e.g., Jenkins & Baird, 2002) but other studies (e.g., Adams, Matto, & Harrington, 2001) have found less support for the construct validity of the TABS.

Use for Monitoring or Self-assessment

Compassion Fatigue Self-Test

CFST (Figley, 1995) would be an acceptable tool to use in the monitoring or self-assessment of adverse symptoms related to working with victims of trauma. The psychometric properties of the CFST indicate that it is a stable measure; therefore, it would allow for changes to be tracked over time.

Impact of Event Scale

Similar to other measures available, the authors of IES-R (Horowitz et al., 1979) emphasize that it is not meant to be used as a diagnostic tool; rather, it should be used to raise awareness of one's current symptomatic status and to track changes in symptomatology over time.

Professional Quality of Life Scale

Because there is no summary score, the ProQOL Version 5 manual (Stamm, 2010) provides guidance for interpreting various combinations of the subscale scores, which may be very useful for mental health professionals and organizations using the tool as a self-assessment measure. For example, an individual who receives a high score on the secondary traumatic stress subscale and low scores on the compassion satisfaction and burnout subscales, upon consulting the manual, will learn that this combination of scores is usually associated with a negative work experience characterized by fear. The manual also provides suggestions for addressing the unique combinations of subscale scores; using the example provided above (i.e., a high level of secondary traumatic stress symptoms), the recommendations include seeking treatment for the secondary traumatic stress and introducing changes to the work environment, such as revising one's caseload (Stamm, 2010).

It is important to note that the authors of the ProQOL emphasize that it should not be used as a diagnostic tool. It is, instead, intended to raise awareness of potential issues that could be explored further with diagnostic testing; and to shed additional light on the balance of positive and negative experiences related to an individual's professional quality of life.

Secondary Traumatic Stress Scale

Unlike some of the other tools that were created to assess symptoms relating to direct experiences of trauma but that have been used to assess the presence and severity of secondary traumatic stress symptoms, the STSS (Bride et al., 2004) was designed specifically to measure symptoms of secondary traumatic stress among mental health professionals. However, similar to many of the other tools included in this review, the authors of the STSS emphasize that, while certainly a useful screening tool, the STSS is not a diagnostic tool and should not replace a clinical interview if high levels of secondary traumatic stress are suspected.

Self-Care Assessment Scale

The authors recommend using the Self-Care Assessment scale (Saakvitne & Pearlman, 1996) at regular intervals, so that changes over time can be monitored and early intervention, if needed, can be arranged.

Traumatic Stress Institute Belief Scale and the Trauma and Attachment Belief Scale

Previous research supports the use of the TSI (Pearlman, 1996) or TABS (Pearlman, 2003) for mental health professionals who may be at risk of vicarious traumatization. However, because of the relative length of these measures, mental health professionals and other care providers may prefer to use a shorter tool if they plan on completing it at regular intervals.

Use for Research Purposes

Compassion Fatigue Self-Test

Both the CFST (Figley, 1995) and CF-Short Scale (Adams et al., 2006) have demonstrated psychometric properties that would be considered acceptable for use in research studies. In fact, the CFST has previously been used in a number of research studies to assess the impact of working with victims of trauma with satisfactory results.

Impact of Event Scale

Despite the promising psychometrics of the IES-R (Horowitz, et al., 1979) in trauma samples, the psychometric properties of the IES-R when used to assess compassion fatigue or secondary traumatic stress have not yet been fully established (Bride et al., 2007). Despite the lack of formal data, the IES-R may be an acceptable tool to use in research studies evaluating the presence of vicarious trauma among mental health professionals and/or other care providers.

Professional Quality of Life Scale

The ProQOL Version 5 and its predecessors (earlier versions of the CFST) is one of the most widely utilized tools in research studies assessing compassion fatigue, secondary traumatic stress, or burnout (Stamm, 2010). Moreover, use of the ProQOL for evaluating symptoms of vicarious traumatization, compassion fatigue, or burnout is not limited to mental health professionals, but can be used in a number of other populations (e.g., teachers, lawyers, humanitarian workers, etc.) for research purposes, and to assess compassion satisfaction and job burnout. Additionally, the ProQOL is a stable measure and can be used to track changes across time, making it a particularly attractive tool for research purposes.

Secondary Traumatic Stress Scale

The psychometric properties of the STSS (Bride et al., 2004) support its use for assessing symptoms of vicarious trauma among mental health professionals in research. Internal consistency estimates in the scale development sample were good (Cronbach's alpha = 0.80, 0.87, 0.83, and 0.93 for the intrusion, avoidance, arousal, and total scores, respectively). Confirmatory factor analysis was used to establish the factorial validity of the scale; the results of this analysis indicated that the factor structure of the STSS was also acceptable (Bride et al., 2004).

Self-Care Assessment

The Self-Care Assessment Scale (Saakvitne & Pearlman, 1996) has not been widely used in quantitative or mixed methods research; as such, no psychometric properties appear to be available at this point in time.

Traumatic Stress Institute Belief and the Trauma and Attachment Belief Scale

The TSI (Pearlman, 1996) and TABS (Pearlman, 2003) have been used in previous research studies assessing the effect of vicarious traumatization on mental health professionals. The psychometric properties of these measures are acceptable, though not ideal, and would be considered acceptable for use in future research studies.

Summary

The aim of this chapter was to provide a list of tools that clinicians may find acceptable for measuring the presence and severity of symptoms of vicarious trauma associated with working with victims of trauma. Though certainly not an exhaustive list, many of the more commonly used tools are presented here as well as some of the considerations for their use in either monitoring or research capacities. None of these tools are meant to replace diagnostic testing or interviews, and therefore results should be interpreted cautiously. However, the use of one of these tools at regular intervals may help with the early identification of a potential problem and can certainly be used as a "flag" for further investigation and intervention, if warranted.

References

Adams, R.E., Boscarino, J.A., & Figley, C.R. (2006). Compassion fatigue and psychological distress among social workers: a validation study. *American Journal Orthopsychiatry, 76*, 103–108.

Adams, K.B., Matto, H.C., & Harrington, D. (2001). The Traumatic Stress Institute Belief Scale as a measure of vicarious trauma in a national sample of clinical social workers. *Families in Society, 8*, 363–371.

American Psychiatric Association. (2004) *American Psychiatric Association diagnostic and statistical manual of mental disorders 4th edition* (DSM-IV). Washington DC: Author.

Bride, B.E. (2007). Secondary traumatic stress among social workers. *Social Work, 52*, 63–70.

Bride, B.E., Radey, M., & Figley, C.R. (2007). Measuring compassion fatigue. *Clinical Social Work Journal, 35*, 155–163.

Bride, B., Robinson, M.R., Yegidis, B., & Figley, C.R. (2004). Development and validation of the Secondary Traumatic Stress Scale. *Research on Social Work Practice, 14*, 27–35.

Figley, C.R. (1995). *Compassion fatigue: Coping with secondary traumatic stress disorder.* New York, NY: Brunner/Mazel.

Figley, C.R., & Stamm, B.H. (1996). Psychometric review of the compassion fatigue self test. In B.H. Stamm (Ed.), *Measurement of stress, trauma, & adaptation.* Lutherville, MD: Sidran Press.

Gentry, J.E., Baranowsky, A.B., & Dunning, K. (2002). ARP: The accelerated recovery program (ARP) for compassion fatigue. In C.R. Figley (Ed.) *Treating compassion fatigue* (pp. 123–137). New York, NY: Brunner-Routledge.

Horowitz, M.J., Wilner, N., & Alvarez, W. (1979). Impact of Event Scale: A measure of subjective stress. *Psychosomatic Medicine, 41*, 209–218.

Jenkins, S.R., & Baird, S. (2002). Secondary traumatic stress and vicarious trauma: A validational study. *Journal of Traumatic Stress, 15*, 423–432.

Pearlman, L.A. (1996). Psychometric review of TSI Belief Scale, revision L. In B.H. Stamm (Ed.), *Measurement of stress, trauma, and adaptation* (pp. 415–417). Lutherville, MD: Sidran Press.

Pearlman, L.A. (2003). *Trauma and attachment belief scale.* Los Angeles, CA: Western Psychological Services.

Richardson, J.I. (2001). Guidebook on vicarious trauma: Recommended solutions for anti-violence workers. Health Canada. Retrieved from: http://www.mollydragiewicz.com/VTguidebook.pdf. Accessed on June 14, 2013.

Saakvitne, K.W., & Pearlman, L.A. (1996). *Transforming the pain: A workbook on vicarious traumatization*. New York, NY: Norton.

Stamm, B.H. (2002). Measuring compassion satisfaction as well as fatigue: Developmental history of the Compassion Satisfaction and Fatigue Test. In C.R. Figley (Ed.), *Treating compassion fatigue* (pp. 107–119). New York, NY: Brunner-Routledge.

Stamm, B.H. (2010). *The concise ProQol manual* (2nd ed.). Pocatello, ID: ProQOL.org.

Sundin, E.C., & Horowitz, M.J. (2002). Impact of Event Scale: Psychometric properties. *British Journal of Psychiatry, 180*, 205–209.

Weiss, D.S. (2004). The impact of event scale—Revised. In J.P. Wilson & T.M. Keane (Eds.), *Assessing psychological trauma and PTSD*, (2nd ed., pp. 168–189). New York, NY: Guilford Press.

Weiss, D.S. & Marmar, C.R. (1997). The Impact of Event Scale—Revised. In J.P. Wilson & T.M. Keane (Eds.), *Assessing psychological trauma and PTSD* (pp. 399–411). New York, NY: Guilford Press.

11

HOW CAN WE RESCUE OURSELVES FROM VICARIOUS TRAUMA?

Danielle Kaplan

Introduction

Mel is a social worker employed in a city hospital's outpatient clinic. When a hurricane unexpectedly strikes the city in which he works, Mel and his family are forced to evacuate their home and move in with relatives an hour away. Their house sustains a good deal of damage in the storm, and it is unclear when they will be able to return. The move is disruptive for Mel's young children, who begin having nightmares about the hurricane and are irritable due to the change in their routine. Mel and his wife are sleeping on a couch in the den and have little space or time to themselves. Many of Mel's ongoing clients are in similar circumstances, and the content of their therapy sessions deals with their sense of dislocation, powerlessness, and frustration at not knowing when life will return to normal. Mel, who typically approaches his clinical work with a sense of optimism, is often at a loss for what to say when his clients are in need of comfort and hope.

Mel is very close to one of his coworkers, Norma, whose clients' lives have been similarly disrupted by the storm. Mel and Norma arrange to have a weekly lunch together during which they discuss the cases that are affecting them most deeply. At Norma's suggestion, Mel asks his supervisor if any new case assignments can be limited to clients who were not affected by the hurricane until he and his family return home. Mel, his wife, and children begin taking nightly family walks in their new neighborhood, which provides them with both a sense of familiarity with their new surroundings and a welcome opportunity to reconnect at the end of the day. Mel and his wife also volunteer to cook dinner for the entire extended family once a week, an activity that they enjoyed in their early days as a couple that also gives them some time alone together in the kitchen.

Mel is frequently tired from his long commute and concerned about the impact of the hurricane on his children, but is able to remain present with his clients as they share their own stories of loss and dislocation. He is grateful for the support of his family and, in turn, is able to act as a support to his wife and children as they ride out the aftermath of the storm together.

Psychotherapy is an endeavor replete with unique rewards. The opportunity to enter into the intimate space of a client's history and affective experience is one afforded in few other professional contexts. However, it is this very gift—the act of empathic engagement that drives the therapeutic process—that may also place the self of the psychotherapist at particular risk. It is by now a well-documented phenomenon that therapists who feel overloaded by their work with complicated or difficult clients may be vulnerable to burnout (Figley, 2002; Trippany, Kress, & Wilcoxon, 2004). Burnout, "a state of physical, mental, and emotional exhaustion caused by long-term involvement in emotionally demanding situations" (Pines & Aronson, 1988, p.9), may occur among mental health practitioners in any setting, and indeed among members of any profession where the work demands are complex and unrelenting (McCann & Pearlman, 1990).

Practitioners who specialize in work with trauma survivors are equally vulnerable to experiencing burnout. Due to the specific content of the therapeutic material to which they are exposed, however, trauma therapists are additionally susceptible to the development of vicarious traumatization (VT). There is significant overlap in the presentations of therapists experiencing burnout and those suffering from vicarious traumatization; both may present with physical and emotional symptoms, work-related issues, and interpersonal problems (Trippany et al., 2004). In addition, therapists experiencing both burnout and vicarious traumatization may experience a decrease in their ability to empathize with and be fully present with their clients, which may compromise the quality of the care that they provide (Raquepaw & Miller, 1989).

Therapists experiencing the effects of vicarious traumatization, however, are specifically vulnerable to changes in their cognitive schemas or overall world view. Because vicarious traumatization is a reaction not to the difficulty of working with traumatized clients but to the traumatic material itself (Trippany et al., 2004), therapists may experience cognitive and affective disruptions similar to those experienced by the clients who were exposed to the original trauma. These disruptions may occur in the domains of trust of self and others, self and other esteem, safety, intimacy, perceived control, and spirituality (see Pearlman & Mac Ian, 1995; and Pearlman & Saakvitne, 1995, for a comprehensive discussion of these issues). The erosion—or, at times, the sudden transformation—of previously held assumptions in these domains may leave the trauma therapists vulnerable to alienation and despair in their personal lives, and to ethical lapses and a decrease in clinical efficacy in their professional lives (Herman, 1992).

Among the subset of mental health professionals who work with trauma survivors, those who specialize either by choice or by circumstance in the treatment of trauma following a disaster may find themselves confronted with particular challenges to their worldview and sense of well-being. In contrast to practitioners who work with survivors of traumas at the individual level, such as sexual abuse or assault, practitioners working with disaster survivors may find themselves exposed abruptly and repeatedly to frequent retellings of traumatic contact related to the same event (Palm, Polusny, & Follette, 2004). Media coverage of the disaster, which has been shown to be related to an increase in PTSD symptoms among individuals directly affected by a trauma (Ahern et al., 2002), may also exacerbate providers' exposure to traumatic content. Finally, depending on the setting in which services are provided, disaster-relief workers may be in the unique position of attempting to provide care to others while their own safety or that of their loved ones is in jeopardy (Eidelson, D'Alessio, & Eidelson, 2003).

Efforts have been made in the conceptual literature to identify self-care strategies that may be helpful in mitigating the effects of vicarious traumatization. However, the efficacy of these interventions remains unclear. A recent study by Bober and Regehr (2006) measured the degree to which therapists and hospital workers working with traumatized populations endorsed the utility of self-care strategies, the frequency with which they engaged in them, and the relationship between the use of these strategies and therapists' self report of vicarious trauma and secondary traumatization.

The majority of participants surveyed rated engaging in leisure activities and engaging in self-care as helpful for reducing vicarious trauma; however, no significant association was found between respondents' stated belief in the utility of these strategies and the amount of time that they dedicated to engaging in them (Bober & Regehr, 2006). Most relevant to the current discussion, however, was the authors' finding that there was no significant relationship between the time participants spent engaging in self-care and leisure activities, supervision, and research and development and the severity of their vicarious traumatization as measured by the Impact of Events Scale.

It is striking that self-care strategies that have such unanimous conceptual endorsement in the literature do not seem to have substantial empirical support. One possible explanation for this is that self-care strategies, like the therapeutic interventions we use in working with traumatized individuals, are not one size fits all. Prescribing leisure activities or peer consultation as an intervention for all trauma therapists might be akin to constructing the same exposure hierarchy for decreasing avoidance in all trauma survivors. Although all the strategies identified in the literature as potentially helpful for reducing vicarious traumatization will undoubtedly prove helpful to some providers at some points in their professional lives, none are likely to be helpful for all therapists all the time. Just as it is clinically and ethically imperative, then, to provide traumatized clients with state-of-the-art, empirically supported interventions to alleviate their suffering, it behooves us as a field to identify strategies that are equally effective in mitigating the effects of vicarious traumatization in those who seek to help them.

Pearlman and Saakvitne (1995) conceptualize the changes in the therapist's inner world that occur as a result of vicarious traumatization through the lens

TABLE 11.1 Domains Affected by VT with Suggested Individual and Organizational Strategies

Domain Affected by VT	Suggested Individual Strategies	Suggested Organizational Strategies
Safety	Establishing routine Limiting media exposure Mindfulness practice	Specific training in disaster relief work Adequate preparation for deployment
Control	Balancing trauma and non-trauma caseload Advocacy and volunteerism "Mastering the possible" (Walsh, 2007)	Decreasing chronic occupational stress Providing adequate administrative support
Esteem	Balancing trauma and non-trauma caseload Balancing therapy with other professional activities	Respecting cultural and individual differences Providing adequate financial compensation Conveying respect and trust
Trust and Intimacy	Utilizing peer supervision Accessing social support Creating family rituals and shared meaning	Providing mental and physical health services Providing support services during and after a deployment

of Constructivist Self-Development Theory (CSDT). CSDT posits that trauma results in a disruption in development that requires the trauma survivor to assimilate new information about self, world, and others and to change one's schemas to accommodate heretofore unimagined information about the world. When this new information cannot be assimilated, disruptions in key areas of cognition and functioning can result. In the pages that follow, several of the core schemas that are most vulnerable to disruption through vicarious traumatization will be identified and interventions that have conceptual and empirical support for addressing these disruptions will be discussed. It is hoped that rather than selecting from among a preset menu of self-care options, clinicians will be able to identify the specific areas in which they are most vulnerable and employ self-care strategies that are targeted at building resilience in these areas, as shown in Table 11.1.

Safety

Lillian is a new doctor with an international medical relief corps, whose job involves providing emergency medical care to inhabitants of areas struck by natural disasters. Lillian and her coworkers often find themselves living and working in conditions that mirror those of the populations they serve, with intermittent electricity and poor sanitation. She is stunned by the intensity of suffering that she sees around her and finds herself worrying that she will fall sick or be injured during her deployment due to her unsafe working conditions. At times she is so anxious that she questions her ability to make decisions in the moment about her patients' medical care. Lillian decides to begin and end each day with a simple following-the-breath exercise, and to take mindfulness breaks during her clinic day. After several days, she notices that she is less anxious and physically on edge, and is able to be more fully present with her patients.

By definition, a traumatic event is one in which the safety of the trauma survivor or someone close to them is threatened. As witnesses after the fact to events that threaten the safety and well-being of their clients, trauma therapists are vulnerable to disruption in their schemas around predictability and safety. Just as it is critical for therapists to help their clients engage in activities and rituals that restore their sense of safety, trauma therapists should be mindful of the importance of incorporating such activities in their own lives. Daily routines that promote a sense of predictability are as important for the therapist as they are for the clients they serve. These might include the development and maintenance of individual or family rituals or consistent activities that bookend the work day and mark the transition from the therapeutic space into one's daily life.

The sudden and far-reaching nature of disasters may mean that achieving in-the-moment predictability may be particularly challenging for disaster-relief workers. For those working at the site of a disaster, the ability to maintain basic safety may be in question until the immediate threat subsides. Disaster-relief workers who are unable to create immediate zones of safety and predictability during their work with traumatized populations should be mindful of limiting their exposure to media coverage related to the disaster when not directly necessary for their professional activities. Further, they might find it beneficial to consider a "planned sabbatical" from trauma work as soon as is practical (Pearlman & Saakvitne, 1995, p. 169).

A regular mindfulness practice may also be helpful in providing the therapist with a sense of grounding and safety in their everyday surroundings, and in addressing the disruptions to the memory system that often accompany vicarious traumatization. A full discussion of the benefits of mindfulness practice is beyond the scope of this chapter. However, there is growing empirical support for the notion that mindfulness-based intervention can play a role in increasing well-being among care providers.

Jon Kabat-Zinn (2003) defines mindfulness as "the awareness that emerges through paying attention, on purpose, in the present moment, and non-judgmentally to the unfolding of experience moment by moment" (p.145). During a typical mindfulness practice, "attention rests with various stimuli, including breath, bodily sensations, perceptions (sights, sounds), as well as cognitions and emotions" (Irving, Dobkin, & Park, 2009, p. 62). Mindfulness exercises may be self-guided, but are often initially guided through audio recordings for use in at-home practice. Participants are encouraged to hold an attitude of active engagement, and to engage in the process without expectation of specific outcomes, such as relaxation or a reduction in physical symptoms (Kabat-Zinn, 2003).

The utility of mindfulness practice as an intervention for health-care providers is well-documented. A regular mindfulness practice has been shown to be associated with a decrease in emotional exhaustion and depersonalization and an increase in personal accomplishment among nurses (Cohen-Katz, Astin, Bishop, & Cordova, 2005), and a decrease in stress and an increase in self-compassion and perceived quality of life in a multidisciplinary group of health-care professionals (Shapiro, Astin, Bishop, & Cordova, 2005). Participants in both qualitative and quantitative studies of mindfulness interventions report a decrease in symptoms of burnout and mood disturbance and an increase in positive outcomes such as increased self-care, improved interpersonal interactions, and coping with stress (Irving et al., 2009).

Recent neuroimaging studies provide further support for the benefits of mindfulness training in reducing vulnerability to vicarious traumatization. For example, Hölzel and colleagues reported that "stressed but otherwise healthy individuals" who underwent an 8-week mindfulness-based stress reduction intervention reported both a subjective decrease in perceived stress and a corresponding decrease in gray matter density in the right basolateral amygdala (Hölzel et al., 2010, p. 11). Similarly, Taylor et al. (2011) identified decreased activity in the left amygdala in response to emotional pictures among participants with no prior meditation or yoga experience who practiced meditation for 20 minutes a day in the 7 days prior to the fMRI experiment, reflecting decreased reactivity during emotional processing. Given the growing understanding of the role of the amygdalic system in the development and maintenance of PTSD (e.g., Liberzon et al., 1999; Armony, Corbo, Clément, & Brunet, 2005), an intervention that directly impacts amygdalic arousal and the associated experience of fear or anxiety seems to hold particular promise.

The nature of mindfulness practice itself holds several compelling advantages for disaster-relief workers. It is portable, allowing relief workers to engage in self-care even while deployed away from home. Any activity, from walking to brushing one's teeth, can be practiced mindfully. Thus, the practice of mindfulness does not require additional time or resources under circumstances in which both may be in short supply. Finally, clinicians who are mindfully engaged in the work of therapy itself may be both more present with their clients and better attuned to and more accepting of their own reactions in the moment (Segal, 2010), benefits that directly mitigate the detachment, compassion fatigue, and negative countertransferential reactions that are often early indicators of vicarious traumatization.

Disaster relief workers' sense of physical and psychological safety can also be increased through adequate training and preparation for their job responsibilities. Providers working with traumatized populations would benefit from organizations' investment in their professional development and preparation for doing trauma work. For example, a psychoeducational intervention designed in part to increase knowledge about trauma in infants and young children among nurses in an area of Israel affected by war (Berger & Gelkopf, 2011) was demonstrated to increase nurses' sense of professional self-efficacy and reduce their symptoms of vicarious traumatization. Similarly, Brondolo et al. (2008) stress the importance of information sessions, technical drills, skills training, and education about medical and psychological sequelae to traumatic events in decreasing vulnerability to vicarious traumatization among responders to mass fatality incidents. This call for trauma-specific and disaster-specific training echoes the recommendation by Pearlman and Saakvitne (1995) that providers seek out specialized education in traumatology before working with traumatized populations.

It should be noted, however, that requiring care providers to obtain education in trauma- and disaster-specific interventions is distinct from providing them with on-the-job training and dedicated time in which to pursue it. In fact, child welfare workers surveyed by Regehr and her colleagues (2004) noted that the requirement to attend job trainings was a factor contributing to their chronic levels of work stress. Organizations must take care, then, to ensure that training and education are integrated into their employee's schedules and that the onus for seeking out and making time for educational opportunities is on the organization rather than the employee.

Control

Francesca is an intern working in the mental health division of a disaster relief organization. Although she was initially delighted to be placed with the organization, whose focus on serving dislocated populations with multiple trauma mirrors her own professional with multiple trauma values, Francesca's supervisors report that her initial enthusiasm has waned and she often seems checked out and angry. When she is asked about this directly, Francesca reports feeling powerless in the face of the extreme need her clients experience and the intensity of the traumas they have suffered. "It's like there's no point," she says. "They can start again and rebuild, and their lives will still be impossibly hard and there could always be another earthquake. There's nothing I can do to change any of this—and there's nothing they can do, either. What's the point of their coming to therapy at all? It isn't going to change anything."

After discussing her concerns with her supervisor and in her own therapy, Francesca arranges to spend part of her internship rotating through the policy and fundraising divisions of the organization. She begins to become increasingly informed about resources available to her displaced clients and about the channels for advocating for their well-being on a systemic level. In the spring of her training year, Francesca runs in a 5K race with other employees of the organization, through which she helps raise money to support the organization's mission. Although she is still saddened at the multiple hardships that her clients face, Francesca begins to identify a role for therapy in helping her clients cope with and at times improve their challenging life circumstances.

The desire to make a difference is a common motivation for those entering the helping professions. In the face of repeated exposure to clients' trauma narratives, therapists may be confronted with the genuine limitations of their ability to be helpful. Although understanding the realistic parameters of our ability to change our clients' histories and current circumstances is key to the maintenance of appropriate therapeutic boundaries, therapists working with traumatized clients risk having this realistic appraisal of their limitations transform into an overall feeling of helplessness and powerlessness. This may be particularly true of therapists who work with disaster survivors, who may be confronted with their very real powerlessness to prevent cataclysmic events such as earthquakes, tsunamis, or acts of terrorism.

Therapists experiencing the effects of vicarious traumatization may find their clinical effectiveness and their personal sense of control hampered by a "heightened awareness of the illusory nature of control over capricious or unexpected life events" (McCann & Pearlman, 1990, p. 139). At its worst, this awareness may be experienced as "helplessness, depression, and despair about the uncontrollable forces of nature or human violence" (McCann & Pearlman, 1990, p. 139).

There is a large body of literature that supports a dose-response relationship between working with trauma-exposed individuals and the development of VT (Baird & Kracen, 2006; Brady, Guy, Poelstra, & Brokaw, 1999; Cornille & Meyers, 1999; Marmar et al., 1999; Ortlepp & Friedman, 2002). Thus, maintaining a clinical caseload that is balanced between trauma survivors and other clinical populations may be helpful in counteracting clinicians' all-or-nothing thinking about the controllability of events and the efficacy of therapeutic intervention in helping clients to change their life circumstances. Relatedly, practitioners should be mindful of the timing and spacing of therapy sessions with traumatized clients. Clinicians should also be cautioned not to overcompensate for their feelings of powerlessness by relaxing their professional boundaries with clients. Maintaining professional boundaries, including limiting availability to clients between sessions, was identified as an important protective factor in a survey of peer-nominated master therapists who worked with traumatized clients (Harrison & Westwood, 2009).

In addition to the suggestions above, which may be useful for regaining a sense of control in one's professional life, it is important for clinicians to continue to engage in activities that provide them with a sense of control and efficacy in their personal lives. For some, this may mean engaging in activities that provide a sense of mastery, such as learning a new skill or setting and working towards a goal outside of a professional context, such as training for a race. Advocacy and volunteerism, whether directly related to mental health issues or not, may also provide a means of combating the feelings of personal and professional powerlessness that are often a component of vicarious traumatization. For example, a therapist working with survivors of Hurricane Sandy found it meaningful to volunteer at an animal shelter taking care of pets that were displaced after the storm. This idea of "mastering the possible" (Walsh, 2007) by engaging in activities that promote a sense of efficacy is crucial in helping trauma workers balance realistic acceptance of forces beyond their control with belief in their ability to be a force for healing and growth.

Organizations that employ trauma counselors can also play a part in helping their employees to regain a sense of control. In a 2004 study of factors contributing to the development of vicarious traumatization among child welfare workers (Regehr, Hemsworth, Leslie, Howe, & Chau, 2004), the greatest predictor of post-traumatic distress was the organizational environment, including the ongoing, chronic stressors that accompanied direct clinical work. These included workload, paperwork requirements, travel, changing policies, conflict with coworkers and supervisors, and public or media scrutiny. Similar findings have been reported by Mitani et al. (2006) in their study of burnout and PTSD symptoms among firefighters, in which they reported a direct relationship between chronic job stress and the experience of burnout. One interpretation of these findings is that vicarious traumatization may be the final step in a pathway in which care providers who are already taxed through chronic exposure to stress are exposed to critical incidents after their coping resources have been exhausted. The daily lack of control that often accompanies work in a high-demand, low-resource environment may increase trauma workers' perceptions that they have little ability to impact their own day to day well-being or those of their clients.

Organizational factors involved in reducing occupational stress may include streamlining and reducing paperwork demands, ensuring adequate vacation time, and providing employees with administrative support for and recognition for the value of their work. As has been repeatedly noted in the literature, a significant source of workplace stress among trauma workers is the number or percentage of traumatized clients on their caseloads. Thus, a key component in the reduction of occupational stress is the assignment of work duties that ensure some balance between trauma and non-trauma patients. In cases where this is not possible, such as when an organization exclusively serves traumatized populations, supervisors should be mindful of balancing their employees' clinical work with non-clinical activities that enable them to achieve some measure of balance in their professional responsibilities.

During or immediately after a disaster, it might be unrealistic for an organization to ensure balance or attend to chronic stressors that may affect an employee's vulnerability to vicarious traumatization. When relief workers are directly deployed to the site of a disaster, employers should aim whenever possible to provide their employees with timely rotation out of the affected area and consider relaxing their duties upon the end of their deployment (Bilal, Rana, Rahim, & Ali, 2007). Organizations that provide services in the aftermath of a disaster or at a site removed from the location of the original traumatic event, however, are in a better position to be mindful of chronic occupational stressors among their employees and address them wherever possible.

Esteem

Ursula is a social worker who returned to school to get her MSW after having worked in advertising. Though she enjoyed the creative aspects of her first career, it is a point of pride for her that she is now dedicating her professional life to helping others. Ursula lives and works in a city that has a large population of Haitian immigrants, many of whom left Haiti after the earthquake in 2010. Recently, many of these families have come to the clinic where Ursula works in search of therapy for themselves and their children. Ursula quickly finds herself overwhelmed by their stories and often becomes tearful in sessions as her clients describe the destruction of their homes and the losses they have suffered. During a meeting with her supervisor, Ursula confesses that she feels ill-equipped to help her clients in any meaningful way. She begins to question her competence as a therapist and wonders whether she has anything useful to offer them in the face of all they have suffered. Ursula begins to speculate about whether she made a mistake in leaving her first career. "I may not have been saving the world when I worked in advertising," she tells her supervisor, "But it's not like I'm any good at this either."

Korman (1970, p. 32) defines self-esteem as "the degree to which the individual sees him [or her]self as a competent, needs-satisfying individual." Survivors of a disaster, regardless of its nature, are likely to be faced with disruptions and needs in areas far beyond the capacity of any single relief worker to address. It is understandable, then, that even the most skilled professional might be confronted with concerns about his or her own adequacy and ability to be of use to a population with such a breadth of needs. Therapists whose personal identities are closely tied to their ability to be helpful to others may experience a threat to their self-concept as they increasingly view themselves as powerless and their efforts as futile.

Helping professionals may find that the strategies that are useful in restoring a sense of control, such as balancing one's caseload between traumatized and non-traumatized patients, may also help to restore their sense of personal and professional efficacy. It may also be helpful for practitioners to balance their clinical work with other professional activities that allow them to make an impact on their field or either directly or indirectly on the lives of their clients. Therapy can be balanced with research, teaching, and writing that adds to the body of knowledge in the field. For more experienced therapists, providing supervision to other clinicians may also serve as a counterbalance to trauma work and may increase feelings of professional efficacy and utility.

Organizations that employ disaster-relief workers can be instrumental in preserving their employees' sense of esteem. Practices and working conditions that convey an organization's valuing, support, and respect of its employees are positively correlated with employees' reported sense of self-esteem in an occupational context across cultures and types of employment (Pierce & Gardner, 2004). These practices may take the form of managerial respect for employees, attention to employees' on-the-job training needs, opportunities for employees to engage in self-directed work responsibilities, respect for employees' cultural and individual differences, and adequate financial compensation.

Trust and Intimacy

Sarah is a social worker who was working in New York when the World Trade Center was attacked on 9/11. Many of her patients worked near the World Trade Center, and her caseload became filled with people wanting to process the aftermath of the trauma. Sarah spent much of her time at work helping patients to deal with their guilt at having survived the attack and their pain at having lost coworkers in the Towers. In session after session, Sarah heard about her patients' pain, grief, and anger at organizations that seemed to be more concerned with paperwork and documentation than with providing her clients with help relocating or obtaining disability benefits.

Although she shared in the communal feeling experienced by many New Yorkers immediately after the attacks, Sarah soon became frustrated at how quickly her friends and family were able to return to their daily routines. She often found herself irritated when conversations with her friends turned towards topics that she considered trivial in the aftermath of 9/11. When her friends asked how she was, she was often at a loss for how to respond. "What's the difference?" she often thought. "They don't really want to know how I am. They don't really want to know how anything is." Typically a very social person, Sarah began to turn down most social invitations and spent much of free time at home alone, reading everything she could find online about 9/11 and imagining her patients sitting alone in their apartments reading the same information. She even found herself inexplicably angry at other passengers on the subway, who seemed to be going about their daily routines with no idea that the world had changed forever.

While browsing a listserv for local clinicians, Sarah came across a posting for a peer supervision group for therapists working with 9/11 survivors. She began to attend regularly and was relieved to find herself in a supportive community dealing with similar issues. The other therapists in the group provided Sarah with helpful information about how to help her clients navigate the application process for concrete services, and she began to have greater success in helping her clients understand the systems involved in their care. One of the other group members gave Sarah the name of a more experienced therapist with whom she began to meet for private supervision. Sarah was relieved to find a forum in which to discuss her reactions to her patients' narratives and her frustration with what she saw as her friends' lack of awareness. Gradually, she began to make dinner plans with some of her closest friends, and was able to share some of her recent experiences with them. Although her friends were surprised at how profoundly Sarah was affected by her work, many offered their support and let her know that they were open to discussing her experiences.

Just as trauma survivors often experience a profound sense of alienation from others, therapists who work with survivors of trauma are vulnerable to a sense of separateness and disconnection from friends, family, and even other helping professionals, whom they may view as blissfully ignorant of the depths of suffering that their patients experience. As McCann and Pearlman (1990, p. 141) point out, "this sense of separateness is compounded by the requirement for confidentiality in psychotherapy, which precludes one's ability to reveal the disturbing traumatic material." The ability to connect to others in a meaningful and intimate way may also be disrupted by a fundamental shift in the ability to trust that others are well intentioned and benign. In some cases, this lack of trust may extend beyond the level of the individual, as organizations and systems that are ostensibly meant to be of help can be viewed as impotent, ineffectual, or corrupt.

Peer consultation can be a powerful antidote to the feelings of isolation and disconnection to which trauma therapists are vulnerable. In a survey of peer-identified master clinicians, countering personal and professional isolation was consistently identified as a protective factor against vicarious traumatization (Harrison & Westwood, 2009). In a 1993 survey by Pearlman and MacIan, 85% of trauma counselors reported that peer consultation was their most common mechanism for dealing with vicarious traumatization. Similarly, Catherall (1995) suggests that peer consultation provides trauma therapists with social support and a normalization of their experiences, which in turn lessens the impact of vicarious traumatization. Further, discussing their clinical work with colleagues offers therapists a forum for debriefing in a confidential manner, which may enable them to identify and address the cognitive distortions and countertransferential reactions that may arise in the course of their work with traumatized patients. Peer supervision has also been found to increase counselor objectivity, empathy, and compassion (Lyon, 1993), benefits that may directly ameliorate some of the professional effects of burnout and vicarious traumatization. Relatedly, being able to share one's experiences with others in a supportive and nonjudgmental context may help to restore one's belief in the trustworthiness of some, if not all, individuals.

For providers working in an area with a large concentration of helping professionals, peer supervision groups may be readily available. Even providers in less resource-rich areas, however, may be able to derive some of the benefits of peer consultation through attendance at workshops and conferences, membership in professional organizations, professional listserv discussions, and Internet or telephone-based mentoring programs available through professional organizations.

Although connecting to one's professional community through ongoing consultation and interaction with other trauma professionals is critical to maintaining professional well-being, it is equally crucial for practitioners to employ strategies that help them maintain connectedness to their friends and loved ones. Trauma therapists may experience difficulty integrating the simultaneous realities of the everyday life of their family and community with their patients' narratives and the dramatic changes in their internal worlds. For mental health workers deployed to the site of a disaster, this may be particularly challenging, as their daily experiences differ so dramatically from those of their intimate partners (see Gottman, Gottman, & Atkins, 2011, for a closely related discussion of the challenges in maintaining connection to family among deployed military personnel).

Maintaining intimate connections may involve creating and participating in rituals that are specific to one's family or community, such as a family dinner hour or attendance at religious services. Even in circumstances in which rituals are disrupted due to separation from family or friends, there is often opportunity for the therapist to maintain connectedness. For example, a disaster relief worker whose job involved frequent travel always traveled with copies of the bedtime stories that her children were reading. Whenever possible, she arranged to be near a phone at her children's bedtime so they could read together even in her absence.

Intimacy, particularly with family and romantic partners, may also involve the creation of shared meaning (Gottman et al., 2011). Because this sense of meaning may be disrupted for the partner who is involved in trauma work, it may be helpful for trauma workers to partner with their loved ones in discovering activities that create shared meaning in areas unaffected by the trauma. This may include working toward a common goal, exploring a shared hobby or interest, or setting aside protected time for conversation.

Organizations that employ disaster relief workers can provide their employees with institutional scaffolding that may be useful in combating the sense of isolation to which its employees may be vulnerable. Eriksson et al. (2001) found that although it was not related to the likelihood of developing PTSD during a deployment, support by the sending organizations served as a protective factor for humanitarian aid workers upon their return. In keeping with this finding, confidential mental and physical health services should continue to be made available to disaster relief workers throughout their deployment and beyond. Brondolo and her colleagues (2008) recommend that organizations provide ongoing health screenings for long-term related stress disorders, clarification of mental health coverage and related insurance benefits, and clear policies for facilitating medical leaves of absence when needed. All of these may help disaster-relief workers access venues through which they can discuss and find validation for their experiences and decrease their feelings of isolation. In addition, clear communication from organizations to their employees about the supportive resources available to them and demonstrable efforts to provide employees with those resources may help to maintain relief workers' sense of trust in the organizations for which they work and the benevolence of institutions as a whole.

Other Protective Factors

Spirituality

Jonathan was raised in a Jewish community that emphasized the concept of tikkun olam, *or "repair of the world," which suggests that it is humanity's shared responsibility to heal the parts of the world that are broken. This concept motivated Jonathan to pursue a career in psychology, and eventually to specialize in working with children who had lost family members in terrorist attacks. Although his colleagues saw him as having an innate ability to connect with his clients, Jonathan found himself becoming skeptical about the meaning of his work. His belief that the world could be healed was repeatedly challenged by the narratives of his child patients, and he began to view the world as irreparably broken. Jonathan found himself becoming less creative in his clinical work, and began relying on the same interventions over and over again as he became increasingly doubtful that anything he did would make a difference.*

At his wife's urging, Jonathan began taking his 9-year-old daughter to a small community garden that was in need of volunteers. To his surprise, he found himself enjoying the feeling of the soil between his fingers and the subtle changes in the garden's appearance from week to week. He was also moved by his daughter's gentleness and sense of wonder as she cared for the plants that emerged from the soil. Jonathan began to look forward to his weekend excursions to the garden. As the plants began to flourish, he began to bring clippings from the garden to his office and encouraged his child patients to tend them with him as part of their weekly therapy.

Spirituality may be understood as "the process of searching for the sacred in one's life" (Pargament & Sweeney, 2011, p. 59). It involves a quest for meaning and purpose that goes beyond the self, and may serve as an "animating impulse-a motivating force that is directed to realizing higher-order goals, dreams, and aspirations" (Pargament & Sweeney, 2011, p. 58). Qualities associated with spirituality include purpose and meaning and a sense of interconnectedness—the very qualities that are often directly disrupted as a result of vicarious traumatization.

Pearlman and Saakvitne (1995, p. 153) conceptualize the disruption in spirituality that may arise in vicarious traumatization as distinct from the "soul sadness" that may arise in the work of all mental health service providers. Rather, they characterize the spiritual damage that accompanies vicarious traumatization as a "loss of meaning, connection, and hope" (Pearlman & Saakvitne, 1995, p. 167). Therapists who are able to utilize spirituality as a resource for coping with the effects of trauma work, however, report that it serves a protective function against vicarious traumatization. In a survey of trauma therapists, 44% of trauma therapists reported finding spirituality to be an effective coping mechanism (Pearlman & Mac Ian, 1993). Wittine (1995) suggests that a spiritual life helps trauma therapists to develop increased acceptance of existential realities, which may help them to be more present with their clients in discussing painful material.

Although cultivating one's spiritual life may involve participation in a religious community, spirituality can be bolstered through any avenue that accesses the transcendent. Others avenues for accessing spirituality that have been suggested in the literature include yoga, dance, meditation, art, music, and philosophy. As Pearlman and Saavitke (1995, p. 167) remind us,

> finding a way to restore faith in something larger than oneself, whether by reconnecting with the best of all that is human, with nature, or with a spiritual entity . . . taking risks, loving and being loved, and creating and pursuing joy, wonder, and awe addresses the fundamental disruption in meaning created by vicarious traumatization and is a potent antidote

to the threats to our sense of meaning and purpose that may arise from work with traumatized clients.

Although an organization's ability to effectively address disruptions in its employees' sense of higher meaning and purpose may be limited, there is some suggestion (e.g., Bilal et al., 2007; Cornum, Matthews, & Seligman, 2011) that specific briefing prior to deployment to a trauma-affected area may help relief workers to frame their mission and purpose in helpful ways. Specifically, organizations employing relief workers can provide their employees with information about the larger context in which they will be working and their role as part of a larger community of helping professionals. Additionally, organizations employing relief workers can provide them with education on the concept of post-traumatic growth, the "positive psychological change experienced as the result of the struggle with highly-challenging life circumstances" (Tedeschi & Calhoun, 2004, p. 1). This positive change may result in increased empathy for and connection with others, a greater sense of possibility, and increased engagement with questions of meaning and purpose. Introducing the concept that schematic and relational changes following a trauma can be positive as well as negative may prime relief workers to approach their work with decreased trepidation and increased expectation of positive change.

Psychotherapy

Given the repeated exposure to traumatic material that is an integral part of working with disaster survivors, a shift in worldview among relief workers is unsurprising, if not inevitable. A distinction must be made, however, between changes in helping professionals' view of self, world, and others that can be mitigated through informal self-care and those that result in significant disruption in both cognitive and affective domains. Such disruptions might include intrusive thoughts or images of their clients' narratives, somatic disturbances such as insomnia or hyperarousal, or difficulty managing their own or their clients' affect through non-harmful means (Pearlman & Saakvitne, 1995). When such disturbances occur—and, indeed, whenever naturally existing coping mechanisms and support systems are not sufficient to manage the effects of vicarious traumatization—relief workers should be mindful of the benefits of engaging in their own therapy. In addition, relief workers should make every effort to be aware of their personal areas of vulnerability, such as a history of childhood trauma (Bober & Regehr, 2006), substance abuse, or emotional or behavioral dysregulation, and consider therapy as a proactive component of their self-care.

Directions for Future Research

Although there is a growing body of literature on self-care strategies for professionals working with traumatized clients, little to no empirical research exists on the specific efficacy of these strategies with disaster-relief workers. There are some obvious similarities between the work done with survivors of individual traumas, such as sexual assault or robbery, and that done by disaster-relief workers, and in the potential emotional impact of the work on each. However, some key differences in the predictability, nature, and setting of the work suggest that one must be cautious in assuming that knowledge of effective interventions for one group is readily generalizable to another. For example, mental health professionals typically work with sexual abuse or domestic violence survivors at predictably scheduled times, within the generally consistent frame of a therapy session, and in the familiar setting of their own offices and communities. In contrast, disaster relief workers may find themselves working in traumatogenic circumstances with little notice, in unpredictable working and physical conditions, and removed from the familiar settings and people that might serve a protective function against vicarious traumatization. Even when providing services in familiar settings and within the framework of a standard therapy session, practitioners working with disaster survivors are much more likely to have the content of their therapy sessions mirrored and amplified by media coverage of the traumatic event. Thus, research conducted specifically with this population would be helpful in substantiating the utility of self-care strategies through direct investigation rather than by analogy.

There is a growing recognition that self-care strategies for providers working with traumatized populations must be coupled with organizational and systemic strategies aimed at reducing the burden on the individual provider. However, this conceptual recognition has not, to date, been substantiated with empirical work that identifies which organizational strategies are most helpful for reducing the likelihood of vicarious traumatization. The example of single-session or Critical Incident Stress Debriefing, which seemed conceptually sound as an intervention for preventing the development of PTSD but was in fact demonstrated to be associated with an increase in PTSD symptoms among trauma-exposed individuals receiving the intervention (Rose, Bisson, Churchill, & Wessely, 2002), highlights the importance of relying on empirical validation rather than face validity in selecting intervention strategies for disaster-exposed populations.

Many of the suggested organizational strategies for reducing vicarious traumatization among disaster workers lend themselves easily to empirical exploration and validation. Questions about the optimal frequency with which care providers should be rotated out of direct care responsibilities after a trauma, the most effective form of debriefing after an assignment, and the key concepts to convey in briefing the care provider prior to the intervention can easily be turned into testable research questions and would help advance the current state of knowledge in the field from the conceptual and intuitive to the empirically supported.

Conclusion

According to the International Federation of Red Cross and Red Crescent Societies,

> A disaster is . . . a sudden, calamitous event that seriously disrupts the functioning of a community or society and causes . . . losses that exceed the

community's or society's ability to cope using its own resources . . . *A disaster occurs when a hazard impacts on vulnerable people.*
(International Federation of Red Cross and Red Crescent Societies, 2013)

As a community of health care providers, we aim to reduce vulnerability, bolster resilience, and restore functioning to people whose lives have been disrupted by trauma and tragedy. If we are continue to do so compassionately and effectively, we must take steps to ensure that our own functioning remains intact.

It behooves us, then, to protect ourselves from the impact of vicarious traumatization by attending to our own care and well-being along with that of the communities we serve. If we wish to preserve a sense of purpose in the face of senseless events, we must take care to identify and nurture those activities, experiences, and relationships that lend meaning to our own lives. If we are to support those we serve in remaining present with the vicissitudes of their own experiences, we must ourselves cultivate a sense of mindfulness and acceptance. Similarly, if the systems and organizations within which we work are to be effective in their mission, they must be committed to providing adequate resources and support to those who carry that mission out. As we continue to identify and develop effective means of protecting therapists against vicarious traumatization, we hope that the rewards of our work and our own ability to cope will, increasingly, be greater than the hazards.

References

Ahern, J., Galea, S., Resnick, H., Kilpatrick, D., Bucuvalas, M., Gold, J., & Vlahov, D. (2002). Television images and psychological symptoms after the September 11 terrorist attacks. *Psychiatry: Interpersonal and Biological Processes, 65*(4), 289–300.

Armony, J.L., Corbo, V., Clément, M.H., & Brunet, A. (2005). Amygdala response in patients with acute PTSD to masked and unmasked emotional facial expressions. *American Journal of Psychiatry, 162*(10), 1961–1963.

Baird, K., & Kracen, A.C. (2006). Vicarious traumatization and secondary traumatic stress: A research synthesis. *Counselling Psychology Quarterly, 19*(2), 181–188.

Berger, R., & Gelkopf, M. (2011). An intervention for reducing secondary traumatization and improving professional self-efficacy in well baby clinic nurses following war and terror: A random control group trial. *International Journal of Nursing Studies, 48*(5), 601–610.

Bilal, M.S., Rana, M.H., Rahim, S., & Ali, S. (2007). Psychological trauma in a relief worker: A case report from earthquake-struck areas of north Pakistan. *Prehospital and Disaster Medicine, 22*(5), 458–461.

Bober, T., & Regehr, C. (2006). Strategies for reducing secondary or vicarious trauma: Do they work?. *Brief Treatment and Crisis Intervention, 6*(1), 1–9.

Brady, J.L., Guy, J.D., Poelstra, P.L., & Brokaw, B.F. (1999). Vicarious traumatization, spirituality, and the treatment of sexual abuse survivors: A national survey of women psychotherapists. *Professional Psychology: Research and Practice, 30*(4), 386.

Brondolo, E., Wellington, R., Brady, N., Libby, D., & Brondolo, T.J. (2008). Mechanism and strategies for preventing post-traumatic stress disorder in forensic workers responding to mass fatality incidents. *Journal of Forensic and Legal Medicine, 15*(2), 78–88.

Catherall, D.R. (1995). Coping with secondary traumatic stress: The importance of the therapist's professional peer group. In B. Stamm (Ed.), *Secondary traumatic stress: Self-care issues for clinicians, researchers, and educators* (pp. 80–92). Lutherville, MD: Sidran Press.

Cohen-Katz, J., Wiley, S., Capuano, T., Baker, D.M., Deitrick, L., & Shapiro, S. (2005). The effects of mindfulness-based stress reduction on nurse stress and burnout: A qualitative and quantitative study, part III. *Holistic Nursing Practice, 19*(2), 78–86.

Cornille, T.A., & Meyers, T.W. (1999). Secondary traumatic stress among child protective service workers prevalence, severity and predictive factors. *Traumatology, 5*(1), 15–31.

Cornum, R., Matthews, M.D., & Seligman, M.E. (2011). Comprehensive soldier fitness: Building resilience in a challenging institutional context. *American Psychologist, 66*(1), 4.

Eidelson, R.J., D'Alessio, G.R., & Eidelson, J.I. (2003). The impact of September 11 on psychologists. *Professional Psychology: Research and Practice, 34*(2), 144.

Eriksson, C.B., Kemp, H.V., Gorsuch, R., Hoke, S., & Foy, D.W. (2001). Trauma exposure and PTSD symptoms in international relief and development personnel. *Journal of Traumatic Stress, 14*(1), 205–212.

Figley, C.R. (2002). Compassion fatigue: Psychotherapists' chronic lack of self care. *Journal of Clinical Psychology, 58*(11), 1433–1441.

Gottman, J.M., Gottman, J.S., & Atkins, C.L. (2011). The comprehensive soldier fitness program: Family skills component. *American Psychologist, 66*(1), 52.

Harrison, R.L., & Westwood, M.J. (2009). Preventing vicarious traumatization of mental health therapists: Identifying protective practices. *Psychotherapy: Theory, Research, Practice, Training, 46*(2), 203.

Herman, J.L. (1992). *Trauma and recovery.* New York, NY: Basic Books.

Hölzel, B.K., Carmody, J., Evans, K.C., Hoge, E.A., Dusek, J.A., Morgan, L., Pitman, R.K., & Lazar, S.W. (2010). Stress reduction correlates with structural changes in the amygdala. *Social Cognitive and Affective Neuroscience, 5*(1), 11–17.

International Federation of Red Cross and Red Crescent Societies (2013, December 1.) *What Is A Disaster?* Retrieved from: http://www.ifrc.org. Accessed February 1, 2013.

Irving, J.A., Dobkin, P.L., & Park, J. (2009). Cultivating mindfulness in health care professionals: A review of empirical studies of mindfulness-based stress reduction (MBSR). *Complementary Therapies in Clinical Practice, 15*(2), 61–66.

Kabat-Zinn, J. (2003). Mindfulness-based interventions in context: past, present, and future. *Clinical Psychology: Science and Practice, 10*(2), 144–156.

Korman, A.K. (1970). Toward an hypothesis of work behavior. *Journal of Applied Psychology, 54,* 31–41.

Liberzon, I., Taylor, S.F., Amdur, R., Jung, T.D., Chamberlain, K.R., Minoshima, S., Koeppe, R.A., & Fig, L.M. (1999). Brain activation in PTSD in response to trauma-related stimuli. *Biological Psychiatry, 45*(7), 817–826.

Lyon, E. (1993). Hospital staff reactions to accounts by survivors of childhood abuse. *American Journal of Orthopsychiatry, 63*(3), 410–416.

Marmar, C.R., Weiss, D.S., Metzler, T.J., Delucchi, K.L., Best, S.R., & Wentworth, K.A. (1999). Longitudinal course and predictors of continuing distress following critical incident exposure in emergency services personnel. *Journal of Nervous and Mental Disease, 187*(1), 15–22.

McCann, I.L., & Pearlman, L.A. (1990). Vicarious traumatization: A framework for understanding the psychological effects of working with victims. *Journal of Traumatic Stress, 3*(1), 131–149.

Mitani, S., Fujita, M., Nakata, K., & Shirakawa, T. (2006). Impact of post-traumatic stress disorder and job-related stress on burnout: A study of fire service workers. *Journal of Emergency Medicine, 31*(1), 7–11.

Ortlepp, K., & Friedman, M. (2002). Prevalence and correlates of secondary traumatic stress in workplace lay trauma counselors. *Journal of Traumatic Stress, 15*(3), 213–222.

Palm, K.M., Polusny, M.A., & Follette, V.M. (2004). Vicarious traumatization: Potential hazards and interventions for disaster and trauma workers. *Prehospital and Disaster Medicine, 19*(01), 73–78.

Pargament, K.I., & Sweeney, P.J. (2011). Building spiritual fitness in the Army: An innovative approach to a vital aspect of human development. *American Psychologist, 66*(1), 58.

Pearlman, L.A., & Mac Ian, P.S. (1993). Vicarious traumatization among trauma therapists: Empirical findings on self-care. *Traumatic Stress Points: News for the International Society for Traumatic Stress Studies, 7*(3), 5.

Pearlman, L.A., & MacIan, P.S. (1995). Vicarious traumatization: An empirical study of the effects of trauma work on trauma therapists. *Professional Psychology: Research and Practice, 26*(6), 558.

Pearlman, L.A., & Saakvitne, K.W. (1995). *Trauma and the therapist: Countertransference and vicarious traumatization in psychotherapy with incest survivors.* New York, NY: W.W. Norton & Co.

Pierce, J.L., & Gardner, D.G. (2004). Self-esteem within the work and organizational context: A review of the organization-based self-esteem literature. *Journal of Management, 30*(5), 591–622.

Pines, A., & Aronson, E. (1988). *Career burnout: Causes and cures.* New York, NY: Free press.

Raquepaw, J.M., & Miller, R.S. (1989). Psychotherapist burnout: A componential analysis. *Professional Psychology: Research and Practice, 20*(1), 32.

Regehr, C., Hemsworth, D., Leslie, B., Howe, P., & Chau, S. (2004). Predictors of post-traumatic distress in child welfare workers: A linear structural equation model. *Children and Youth Services Review, 26*(4), 331–346.

Rose, S., Bisson, J., Churchill, R., & Wessely, S. (2002). Psychological debriefing for preventing post traumatic stress disorder (PTSD). *Cochrane Database of Systematic Reviews, 2*(2).

Segal, Z.V. (2010). *Mindfulness and the therapeutic relationship.* S.F. Hick, & T. Bien (Eds.). New York, NY: Guilford Press.

Shapiro, S.L., Astin, J.A., Bishop, S.R., & Cordova, M. (2005). Mindfulness-based stress reduction for health care professionals: Results from a randomized trial. *International Journal of Stress Management, 12*(2), 164.

Taylor, V.A., Grant, J., Daneault, V., Scavone, G., Breton, E., Roffe-Vidal, S., . . . Beauregard, M. (2011). Impact of mindfulness on the neural responses to emotional pictures in experienced and beginner meditators. *NeuroImage, 57*(4), 1524–1533.

Tedeschi, R.G., & Calhoun, L.G. (2004). A clinical approach to posttraumatic growth. In P.A. Linley & S. Joseph (Eds.), *Positive psychology in practice* (pp. 405–419). Hoboken, NJ: Wiley.

Trippany, R.L., Kress, V.E.W., & Wilcoxon, S.A. (2004). Preventing vicarious trauma: What counselors should know when working with trauma survivors. *Journal of Counseling & Development, 82*(1), 31–37.

Walsh, F. (2007). Traumatic loss and major disasters: Strengthening family and community resilience. *Family Process, 46*(2), 207–227.

Wittine, B. (1995). The spiritual self: Its relevance in the development and daily life of the psychotherapist. In M.B. Sussman (Ed.), *A perilous calling: The hazards of psychotherapy practice* (pp. 288–301) Hoboken, NJ: John Wiley and Sons.

PERSONAL REFLECTIONS

Excerpt from a Post–9/11 Grand Rounds

Crisis counseling in the immediate aftermath of a disaster and the later treatment of traumatic anxiety and depression are demanding work. First, the therapist must create a safe and accepting environment to facilitate emotional expression and trauma reconstruction. Then, the therapist must listen and offer encouragement as the terrible truths of the painful and dehumanizing experiences of violent trauma are verbalized.

After 9/11, the staff of Saint Vincent's understood firsthand the patient who commented: "I remember vividly the smell of the burning bodies that spread across the city. That was the most unbearable part." Another therapist emotionally resonated with the patient who lamented: "I still do not feel truly safe anywhere." Imagine treating the patient who described feeling: "a sense of dread, of lack of control that I get. It scares the crap out of me. Some days are fine, some days are good, but some days I feel like my heart is going to burst out of my chest. I decide today is the day the GW will blow and I sit there with my mouth drying up & waiting. I don't say anything. I barely move, and when we reach the Westside Highway I thank god. There is nothing anyone can say that will make me feel better or tell me that it won't blow up, because people said the same thing about the WTC. So I sit and wait."

That therapists themselves develop symptoms as a result of caring for traumatized patients is well documented. Cumulative exposure to victims' accounts can induce negative changes in the therapist's sense of self, others, and the world, especially if the therapists also shared the same traumatic experience. An attending psychiatrist observed: "I have begun to think of St. Vincent's as Ground One, just slightly north of the disaster, but still the epicenter of doctors doing what doctors grew up to do, to help people regardless of personal sacrifice." A resident psychiatrist, more deeply affected, explained: "Listening to the talk about horrific experiences forced me to experience fresh trauma on a regular basis. I had no chance to heal. I was becoming easily frustrated, crying over my feelings of helplessness, and experiencing insomnia because of my anxieties."

In a landmark 1990 paper, Lisa McCann and Laurie Pearlman referred to these disruptive and painful emotions as vicarious traumatization. The concept overlaps with professional burnout by having in common symptoms of depression, cynicism, boredom, loss of compassion, and discouragement. But vicarious traumatization is specific to trauma patients, where its impact is felt most acutely in certain areas: relationships, safety, dependency, trust, and self-efficacy. In a parallel process, therapists find their own world altered in response to the experience of treating trauma patients. Earlier investigations of therapists found the following risk factors for vicarious traumatization:

inexperience; a personal history of trauma; heavy caseload; current level of personal stress; and poor social support. Our study supports and extends these prior findings.

How can clinicians become more effective and more resilient in working with victims of trauma?

The Do's

- take care of yourself physically, psychologically, and spiritually, through healthy living and maintaining a balance in your professional and personal life
- remain connected with family, friends, and community
- be flexible
- seek supervision and professional affirmation
- recognize commonalities between patients and yourself
- reinforce boundaries
- diversify practice
- help trauma victims with their struggle for meaning as they work through guilt and suspicion

The Don'ts

- get too close to cases that touch personal issues: trauma victims, more than any other type of patient, can be just like us
- overwork or feel invulnerable
- ignore signs and symptoms of burnout
- forget that understanding your patients' experiences does *not* require that you actually visualize their traumas or feel their emotions
- lose focus on the essential trauma work of creating a verbal narrative that incorporates mood, behavior, and thought
- become cynical—trauma treatment offers the hope for a positive transformation in the patient's appreciation of life, family, and emotional involvement
- give up—recall that for the patient therapeutic engagement = threat, since treatment constitutes a traumatic reminder. Avoidance is a natural resistance to working through the pain that need not defeat the therapy

Spencer Eth, MD
Associate Chief of Staff for Mental Health
Miami, VA
Professor of Clinical Psychiatry
University of Miami Miller School of Medicine

12

WHAT CAN ORGANIZATIONS DO TO ADDRESS VICARIOUS TRAUMA IN DISASTERS?

Gertie Quitangon and Mark R. Evces

Introduction

This chapter identifies strategies and pragmatic organizational approaches to address vicarious trauma (VT) and build resilience based on the model described in *Employer Practices for Addressing Stress and Building Resilience* released in August 2013 by Partnership for Workplace Mental Health, a program of the American Psychiatric Foundation. The impetus behind the research study was the premise that reduced stress and enhanced resilience results in positive individual and organizational outcomes such as employee satisfaction, recruitment and retention, absence reduction, work engagement, productivity, and financial performance. Studies have shown that stress from excessive work demand affects individual job performance (Motowildo, Packard, & Manning, 1986) as well as team work (Driskell, Salas, & Johnston, 1999). This chapter goes beyond workplace stress and aims to address VT as an occupational hazard in disaster mental health response. It presents a framework to guide individuals and organizations in understanding VT and in taking meaningful action to promote resilience in mental health providers in the workplace.

Worker Health Promotion Versus Occupational Safety and Health

In 1984, the National Institute for Occupational Safety and Health (NIOSH) recommended efforts at integration of occupational safety and health (OSH) and worker health promotion (WHP) in order to achieve a comprehensive risk reduction and improve the health of workers. According to Walsh and colleagues (1991),

there are two types of risk exposures—individual behavioral and personal exposures called "life risks" and "job risks," which are the physical and organizational
exposure in the work environment. Historically, WHP programs focus on reduction of "life risks" or individual risk-related behaviors and promote healthy behaviors such as smoking cessation, weight control, healthy nutrition, physical activity,
influenza vaccination, and seatbelt use. OSH interventions minimize "job risks"
by focusing on workplace safety such as exposures to physical, biological, chemical, ergonomic and psychosocial hazards, and stressful work situations (Levy &
Wegman, 2000).

WHP is best known for wellness programs that have components of
health education, supportive social and physical environments, and linkages
to employee assistance programs, clinical prevention services, disease management programs, and other health benefits (O'Donnell, 2002). Participation of
employers have surged in the last several decades because of incentives that are
good for business including enhanced cost-effectiveness, improved risk management, increased organizational recruitment and retention of staff, as well
as a sense of corporate social responsibility. Because WHP efforts are directed
toward improving individual health-related behaviors, they have been perceived
to shift the burden of health promotion in the workplace from employers to
workers as opposed to the traditional OSH interventions that predominantly
require employers to make changes in the organization and environment to
protect workers and reduce work hazards (Green & Johnson, 1990; DeJoy &
Southern, 1993).

OSH research and practice in the US goes as far back as the start of the
twentieth century when socially progressive occupational physicians called
attention to lead, dust, and other hazards, paving the way for the practice of factory inspections (Hamilton, 1943). Most of the earlier research studies were limited to establishing associations between certain working conditions and worker
illness and injury, thereby providing evidence that reducing hazardous conditions would result in fewer injuries and illnesses. The National Occupational
Research Agenda (NORA) was developed in 1996 to guide OSH research
(Lusk & Raymond, 2002; NIOSH, 1999) and as scientific research grew, the
emphasis shifted from establishing associations for the prevention and ameliora-
tion of hazards to establishing the efficacy and safety of interventions (Roelofs,
Barbeau, Moure-Eraso, & Ellenbecker, 2003).

Worker health and the movement toward integration of WHP and OSH has
received considerable international support (WHO, 1997; 1999; 2000; European Network for Workplace Health Promotion, 1997). Studies have shown
that the wellness programs that not only focus on quitting smoking, losing
weight, and other personal health behaviors but also provide healthy working
conditions and information on health and safety hazards are more effective in
reducing chronic diseases (NIOSH, 2012; Sorensen & Barbeau, 2004). Sorensen

et al. (2004) postulated that workers may be more likely to change their personal health behaviors in response to a WHP if they believe that their employers are protecting them from workplace hazards. In June 2011, the NIOSH launched the Total Worker Health Program to expand the development of research and best practices integrating occupational safety and health protection with health promotion. The Total Worker Health Program built on lessons learned beginning in 2003 from the NIOSH Steps to a Healthier U.S. Workforce and the NIOSH Work Life Initiatives and they drafted a list of a wide range of work-related factors that have the potential to impact health. Early in 2013, an initiative addressing the promotion of mental health and prevention of psychological harm in the workplace was launched in Toronto, Canada. Called the *National Standard of Canada for Psychological Health and Safety in the Workplace or "the Standard"* (Mental Health Commission of Canada, 2013), its goal is to integrate psychological health and safety management with conventional business practices by providing employers with guidelines, resources, and tools. In the US, the American Psychiatric Foundation published a white paper called *Employer Practices for Addressing Stress and Building Resilience* in August 2013. This qualitative research project was a collaboration of groups of professionals from multiple industry sectors representing three organizations—the Disability Management Employer Coalition, the Mid America Coalition on Health Care, and Partnership for Workplace Mental Health. The document identified a number of strategies that employers implement to build coping and resilience skills and decrease the risk of having "troubled employees" who present with frequent absences, disability leaves, and disciplinary difficulties related to or complicated by stress. The strategies were classified into three categories: (1) preventing distress and building organizational resilience; (2) providing screenings, information, resources, and benefits; (3) actively intervening with "troubled employees" (Spangler et al., 2013).

Research studies have indicated that the workplace setting has the capabilities to influence both life risks and job risks through organizational approaches that can reinforce long-term behavioral changes, mobilize peer supports, and use environmental resources (DeJoy & Southern, 1993; Abrams, 1991; Chu, Driscoll, & Dwyer, 1997; Baker, Israel, & Schurman, 1996; Blewett & Shaw, 1995). The components of a comprehensive organizational approach include (1) education and training, (2) modification of the work environment or organization, (3) integration of programs into the organizational structure, and (4) screening and referral (Business for Social Responsibility, 2004). This chapter will familiarize readers with organizational strategies that are consistent with these components and have research evidence proving their effectiveness in workplace health promotion and occupational safety. It is hypothesized that these approaches are also effective when tailored specifically to decrease the risk of VT and promote resilience in mental health providers who respond to disasters either by choice or by circumstance. The strategies are a combination of wellness- and resilience-based interventions adapted from the model described in the *Employer Practices for Addressing Stress and Building Resilience* (Spangler, 2013) and applied to address five psychological domains that are thought to be disrupted in VT (See Table 12.1) throughout the disaster mental health timeline.

The earlier chapters in this book explored the current knowledge base on VT and disaster mental health as well as the limitations and methodological challenges in the research literature (i.e., lack of theoretical framework to guide evaluation and intervention, lack of conceptual clarity, small sample size, non-experimental and cross-sectional study design, outcome measures based solely on self-reports). With that in mind, this chapter proposes a practical framework for systematically addressing VT using the Constructivist Self-Development Theory (CDST) as the theoretical basis, and operationalizing the concept by concentrating on five schemas (safety, esteem, trust, control, and intimacy) postulated to be disrupted in vicarious traumatization (see Table 12.1). The intention is to stimulate further research studies and build a foundation to solidify CDST or otherwise develop a viable alternative theory, and ultimately, to accumulate experiential knowledge and empirical validation demonstrating the effectiveness of organizational approaches addressing VT in the context of disaster work. While it is challenging to conduct research in VT and a chaotic post-disaster setting, the gaps in literature should not impede efforts at promoting the psychological health and safety of mental health providers in their work during disasters.

TABLE 12.1 Cognitive Domains Disrupted in Vicarious Traumatization

SAFETY	Self: *to feel reasonably invulnerable to harm inflicted by oneself or others* Other: *to feel that valued others are reasonably invulnerable to harm inflicted by oneself or others*
ESTEEM	Self: *to feel valued by oneself and others* Other: *to value others*
TRUST	Self: *to have confidence in one's own judgment and ability to meet one's needs* Other: *to have confidence in others to meet one's needs*
CONTROL	Self: *to feel able to manage one's feelings and behaviors in interpersonal situations* Other: *to feel able to manage or exert control over others in interpersonal situations*
INTIMACY	Self: *to feel connected to oneself* Other: *to feel connected to others*

Source: Saakvitne & Pearlman (1996). *Transforming the pain: A workbook on vicarious traumatization*. New York, NY: W.W. Norton & Company.

Organizational Approaches to Address VT and Promote Resilience

Safety

Self: *to feel reasonably invulnerable to harm inflicted by oneself or others*
Other: *to feel that valued others are reasonably invulnerable to harm inflicted by oneself or others*

Strategies

- Development of individual emergency plan
- Supervised implementation of individual emergency plan
- Self-care education and training
- Supportive organizational practices

Jay arrived to work the day after the hospital flooded. The lobby was dark without power, and full of security officers, staff members, and patients with no apparent organization. Jay felt confused and concerned, and his hope that he would arrive to find an organized effort to respond to the flood began to turn to concern for his own safety. He noticed as the week progressed that his exposure to his patients' distress began to exacerbate his fear for his own safety and that of his family. He found himself distracted while working with patients, fearful that the hospital building would collapse, despite its thorough inspection by hospital engineers. He began to consider calling in sick for a week or two in order to avoid the building altogether. On the third week following the flood, he arrived to work to find his department set up a table for orienting staff to the disaster response, including an Employee Assistance Program coordinator who provided Jay with access to a disaster self-care plan via website, mobile application, regular staff assistance meetings, and contact information for an EAP therapist. Jay was able to track his personal response to the disaster through assessment tools and organized meetings with other staff members. Jay's fear lessened as he felt the institutional support of the hospital and as he began to practice the self-care strategies he learned about through the hospital's EAP service. Over time, he developed an increased sense of purpose and mastery as he noticed a feeling of empowerment in the face of an increasing caseload of traumatized patients.

In the pre-disaster phase, preparation for the safety of workers by developing individual and family emergency plans at home and at work can increase the likelihood of their availability to report to work and deliver services in case of a disaster (Myers & Wee, 2005). Mandatory inclusion of self-care education and training for mental health providers in every disaster preparation event is a strategy that can prevent the disruption of the safety domain in VT. The federal government has endorsed this approach by incorporating stress management and self-care education in every comprehensive training plan for all Crisis Counseling Programs (CCP; Chapter 6 this book) based on lessons learned from Project Liberty following the September 11 attacks. Moreover, knowledge of self-care and peer care techniques has been included in the Disaster Mental Health Core Competencies drafted by the Center for Disaster & Extreme

Event Preparedness (DEEP Center; Center for Disaster & Extreme Event Preparedness, 2003). The DEEP Center was developed by the Centers for Public Health Preparedness under the auspices of the Centers for Disease Control and Prevention (CDC) and the American Schools of Public Health, and its mission is to maximize the well-being and increase resilience of both disaster survivors and responders by conducting training and research in disaster science, covering topics from disaster behavioral health principles to support for disaster survivors and the optimal performance of responders. The World Association for Disaster and Emergency Medicine (WADEM) has adopted the DEEP Center's Disaster Mental Health Core Competencies and included the understanding and implementation of self-care in the competencies required in response to a pandemic influenza (Cox, n.d.).

In their survey on therapists and hospital workers, Bober and Regehr (2006) noted that while a majority of the respondents believed that self-care strategies can reduce the risk of VT, very few reported actually practicing the strategies. In the work setting, managers and supervisors can play an important role in developing an individualized self-care plan with each staff and monitoring its implementation when circumstances call for it.

Online self-care planning and other innovative electronic formats such as mobile apps can also increase compliance because of increased access 24/7 and have the advantage of confidentiality particularly when mental health providers are concerned about a negative performance review, or worse, the potential stigma of reporting symptoms of VT and other work-related negative outcomes. The National Child Traumatic Stress Network and the National Center for PTSD, together with the National Center for Telehealth & Technology launched the *PFA Mobile* app designed to familiarize disaster responders with Psychological First Aid (PFA) and it includes sections on provider self-care and self-assessment before, during, and after disaster relief work. SAMHSA released the *Behavioral Health Disaster Response App*, which provides pre- and post-deployment guides, "On-the-Ground" assistance, and a "Readiness Refresher" section for both the behavioral health responder and the supervisor. Another mobile app called *Provider Resilience* provides self-care tools for healthcare professionals who work with military service members, veterans, and their families.

Esteem

> Self: *to feel valued by oneself and others*
> Other: *to value others*

Strategies

- Integration of worker health in organizational mission and vision
- Role modeling
- Strong communication practices

- Supportive organizational culture
- VT risk appraisal and self-assessments

As part of a disaster response preparation plan, Mary's manager introduced self-assessment tools into his monthly meetings with staff. Materials included a description of self-care and employee health as an extension of the Community Mental Health Center's core values of health and wellness for all. Mary felt supported and valued by the Center's administration, and when a storm destroyed much of the town's infrastructure, including much of the Center's main building complex, Mary implemented the assessment plan to monitor her stress level and signs of vicarious traumatization. As she began to see her patients in a temporary office building, she felt less and less effective in the face of highly traumatized patients who were showing up for treatment in greater numbers. She met with her manager who reminded her of the assessment and intervention tools provided to her during previous meetings, and they discussed the challenges of working in a new and less comfortable work site. Mary completed an online VT self-assessment and noticed she was having strong feelings of inadequacy and ineffectiveness at work. During subsequent meetings with her manager, they discussed strategies for taking a restorative break from work, managing her caseload, and assertively seeking support from her coworkers. Over time, her sense of self-esteem improved at work, and she was able to support her colleagues and patients more effectively.

According to the Model of Employer Practices (Spangler, 2013), the primary preventive strategies that build resilience and keep employees as healthy and productive as possible begin with the alignment of an organization's values and mission with the individual worker's goals and values as well as a supportive organizational culture shaped by strong communication, ethical management practices, and visible leadership support. Many corporate boards of directors have incorporated worker health and well-being into their organizations' business plans and key operating principles (NIOSH, 2008). Adoption of the value of personal, family, and work/life balance in organizations helps guide behaviors that promote resilience in the workplace (Spangler, 2013). For example, when an executive manager models positive health practices and advocates work/life balance, it sets the tone and exemplifies the ability to replenish energy for work in healthful ways. Integration of worker health promotion in an organization's mission and vision and role modeling are two approaches that could prevent the disruption of the domain of esteem in VT. Hernandez, Gangsei, and Engstrom (2007) published a study on vicarious resilience supporting the value of having role models at work.

Supervisors and managers are key to integrating, motivating, and communicating with employees (NIOSH, 2008). General strategies for enhancing communication are regular live meetings with executive leaders, frequent formal and informal feedback from supervisors, and performance review practices (Spangler, 2013). During the pre-disaster phase, managers can raise awareness of VT by disseminating available information and resources and communicating widely. Strong communication practices are characterized by clarity, transparency, frequency, consistency, and predictability (Spangler, 2013); and in conjunction with proactive efforts to address the potential negative impact of disaster mental health work, can make employees feel heard and valued and mitigate disruption of the trauma-focused schema of esteem.

Health risk appraisal is a secondary prevention strategy used by many employers to screen workplace stress (Spangler, 2013). Employers ask standard questions about health history, lifestyle habits, levels of stress, and sources of stress to establish a baseline and whenever appropriate, offer invitations to health coaching, stress management, and related programs. Self-assessments and screenings that are made available electronically enhance access, privacy, and consistency (Spangler, 2013) and increase the likelihood of employee participation. In the context of the acute phase of disasters, VT risk appraisals can help establish personal strengths as well as risks and vulnerabilities of mental health clinicians, track VT symptom development, and direct timely interventions as needed. In a related study, Brondolo and colleagues (2008) identified ongoing screenings for stress-related disorders as a workplace intervention strategy that can decrease negative mental health outcomes in forensic workers responding to massive disasters. A number of validated instruments that can be used to measure symptoms of VT were discussed in Chapter 11.

Other examples of a supportive organizational culture that enhance coping and resilience and prevent disruption of the domain of esteem include having a policy on flexible emergency work schedules that allow staff to manage personal post-disaster adversities. Organizations can also improve access to relevant resources by encouraging self-referral, removing co-payments for behavioral health benefits, and offering free counseling sessions through EAPs (Spangler, 2013). Brondolo et al. (2008) also recommends clarification of mental health coverage and related insurance benefits as well as policies for facilitating medical leaves of absence when appropriate.

Trust

> Self: *to have confidence in one's own judgment and ability to meet one's needs*
> Other: *to have confidence in others to meet one's needs*

Strategies

- "Disaster Readiness"
- Education and training on the disaster context
- Education and training on evidence-informed interventions
- Trauma-informed supervision

Carlos began to question his colleagues' ability to function effectively following a flood that resulted in relocation of the entire mental health clinic. After an initial period of helping with setting up the new office, his caseload filled with patients whose homes and workplaces had been destroyed. He began to question his colleagues' and his own ability to treat patients in acute stress. The clinic responded by offering training in Psychological First Aid, and the clinic's trauma clinicians began a trauma-informed open supervision group that met weekly. Carlos became more confident in the clinic's ability to respond effectively as he began to trust his peers' clinical ability to treat traumatized patients. He began to interact with his colleagues more and share his own insecurities about providing effective trauma treatments. A sense of trust began to develop among the staff that allowed for more collaboration and social support in the clinic, which resulted in better outcomes for patients and less distress and impairment among clinicians and staff.

Several studies in the disaster literature have posited the responsibility of organizations to ensure that disaster responders have the appropriate resources and training to perform their roles (Munroe, 1999; Myers & Wee, 2005; Young, Ruzek, Wong, Salzer, & Naturale, 2006). Regardless of formal disaster response roles, it only makes sense that mental health clinicians receive education and training on the disaster context and keep informed on evidence-based disaster specific interventions particularly because these courses are not yet fully integrated in traditional mental health training curricula. "Disaster readiness" in the pre-disaster stage includes an understanding of a mental health clinician's roles, the scope of practice in a disaster setting and an awareness of the limits of one's individual training and knowledge prior to integrating into a disaster response (Kantor & Beckert, 2011). Many disaster response agencies recommend training in Psychological First Aid (PFA) prior to providing basic mental health interventions in major traumatic events (Hobfoll et al., 2007; National Institute of Mental Health [NIMH], 2002; Ng & Kantor, 2010). Organizations can offer these training events to mental health staff to reduce the risk of disrupting the schema of trust and dependency in VT. Such trainings can be in the traditional format of seminars and lectures, and there are also a number of Internet-based trainings and mobile apps that are made available by organizations such as the National Center for PTSD (NCPTSD) and the National Child Traumatic Network (NCTN).

Trauma-informed supervision for mental health providers who respond to disasters is an example of a strategy that modifies the work environment or organization by implementing policies and procedure in support of building resilience, and in this case, specifically addressing the risk of VT. There are a number of studies that have highlighted the importance of trauma-informed supervision in VT (Brady, Guy, Poelstra, & Browkaw, 1999; Follette & Batten, 2000). One-on-one supervision provides a venue to discuss particularly challenging cases, oversee caseload management, raise awareness of VT and vicarious resilience, and develop a self-care plan (Palm, Polusny, & Follette, 2004). In a survey of mental health professionals who provided services to disaster survivors immediately after the September 11 attacks, those who received individual supervision at least once a week had lower intrusion scores on the Impact of Events Scale-revised compared with those who had less frequent supervision (see Chapter 2 in this book).

Control

Self: *to feel able to manage one's feelings and behaviors in interpersonal situations*
Other: *to feel able to manage or exert control over others in interpersonal situations*

Strategies

- Education and training on VT
- Flexible work practices
- Proactive outreach and linkage to resources
- Caseload management

Following an earthquake in a nearby city, an urban medical center implemented an employee response plan designed to empower employees dealing with an influx of traumatized patients. Many employees were directly affected by loss of home, property, and disruption of infrastructure such as transportation and power. Employees were allowed flexible schedules for a period of one month, to be arranged with managers, and caseloads were monitored for size and patient trauma level. E-mails were sent to employees reminding them of educational and training materials they reviewed in previous disaster preparation meetings, and the company's EAP placed representatives at each worksite to coordinate self-care programs and disseminate self-care materials. Employees were notified that EAP mental health clinicians were accessible and available in various areas in town to accommodate employee schedules and locations. The company CEO described their efforts as a way to empower their employees to feel as in control as possible in the face of the great many circumstances beyond their control now emerging after such a devastating disaster.

Interventions in the workplace that educate individuals on worker health have a strong potential to influence both life and job risks. Many large organizations have seminar-type trainings to help employees better understand stress and improve coping skills and attitudes. They can also have an array of wellness practices backed by research evidence, from encouraging healthy lifestyle habits (e.g., exercise, yoga, relaxation, nutrition, sleep) to improving financial knowledge and skills (Quick, Nelson, & Hurrell, 1997; Seligman, Steen, Park, & Peterson, 2005; Van der Klink, Blonk, Schene, & Van Dijk, 2001). There are programs that target specific high-stress work groups, such as burnout prevention for health care providers, typically provided by Employee Assistance Programs (EAPs). Many employers have recognized the importance of EAPs in organizational effectiveness and their roles have expanded. Some examples of what they do are "executive coaching" for more effective communication, facilitating conflict resolution in teams, developing strategies for managing work-related stressors, and addressing work-life issues such as caregiver roles and financial concerns (Spangler, 2013). EAPs more commonly provide on-site education and training on a range of topics, including workplace violence and prevention and suicide awareness training.

Disruption of the schema of control in VT can be mitigated by having educational training events on VT in the pre-disaster stage through EAPs or outside vendors. In the process of learning about VT comes awareness of personal strengths and vulnerabilities, which is essential for the occupational health and safety of mental health providers prior to any disaster. FEMA and SAMHSA have recognized the need to better understand the negative mental health outcomes of disaster work by mandating all CCP programs to include training events and support services on compassion fatigue, secondary traumatic stress, and VT prior to deployment, in addition to stress management and self-care education and training (See Chapter 6 this book).

While all staff are expected to make every effort to report to work in the immediate aftermath of a large-scale disaster, a supportive social and physical work environment is a practical strategy that promotes resilience. Simple and successful accommodation management practices such as reduced hours, more flexible schedules, job rotations, location rotations, and work/rest/nourishment cycles reduce job stress (Spangler, 2013). Proactive outreach by a supervisor or an EAP for crisis support and linkage to disaster resources or work/life balance programs, instead of waiting for workers to access resources, can mitigate the negative outcomes of a massive disaster when everyone is presumed to have varying degrees of disaster exposure. Some organizations have disability management specialists who can facilitate earlier identification of those workers who experience work-related difficulties and implement "stay at work" strategies for absence and disability prevention as well as "return to work" strategies (Spangler, 2013).

There is substantial research evidence suggesting a direct relationship between a high caseload of trauma victims and an increased risk of symptoms of VT or secondary traumatic stress in mental health workers (Brady et al., 1999; Chrestman, 1999; Creamer & Liddle, 2005; Devilly, Wright, & Varker, 2009; Kassam-Adams, 1999; Lind, 2000). In the later stages of a catastrophic event, supervisors can mitigate disruption of the control domain in VT by managing the number of disaster survivor cases and ensuring a balanced caseload whenever possible.

Intimacy

> Self: *to feel connected to oneself*
> Other: *to feel connected to others*

Strategies

- Workplace social connectedness
- Peer care techniques
- Peer consultation
- Liaison with community disaster partners

Walter and Amy were paired as "buddies" during a departmental orientation for disaster preparedness. They participated in a peer consultation exercise using actual cases and both found the exercise to be helpful. When an explosion leveled a local factory, both clinicians found themselves experiencing extraordinary personal and professional challenges. They decided to meet twice weekly to discuss cases, check in regarding self-care and effective work balance. Both found that their meetings helped them feel less isolated in an extremely busy clinic, particularly as they dealt with listening to repeated stories of traumatic injury and loss from their patients. The clinic manager cleared two extra hours per week for their peer supervision meetings, resulting in fewer days out sick and more effective clinical practice. Three months following the disaster, they reduced their meetings to once per week and agreed to continue meeting both as means of managing vicarious trauma and as preparation for any future disaster.

Holding workplace social activities, such as team-building retreats, workplace celebrations, and resource groups, not only promotes an organizational culture of social connectedness and collegiality but also encourages workers to share the responsibilities for wellness and safety. In the wake of a massive disaster, the workplace can be effective in restoring a sense of community and connectedness, providing social support that has been identified as a powerful protective factor (Brewin, Andrews, & Valentine, 2000). Studies have indicated that post-disaster distress tends to prolong when there is a decline in social support and social participation (Norris & Kaniasty, 1996).

Peer care techniques is a disaster mental health competency proposed by the DEEP Center (Center for Disaster & Extreme Event Preparedness, 2003) and examples include establishing a "buddy system" in the pre-disaster stage and holding town hall meetings during the acute phase. The utility of a buddy system as a way to check-and-balance each other's stress level and as a source of social support has long been reiterated in stress management trainings for disaster workers (Hartsough & Myers, 1985).

Consultation with colleagues may help reduce feelings of isolation and increase feelings of efficacy (Figley, 1995; Pearlman & Saakvitne, 1995). In the event of a disaster, organizations can modify the work environment for mental health clinicians by providing opportunities for formal and regular peer supervision where challenging cases can be discussed without compromising privacy issues. Scheduling conference calls, establishing listservs, and exchanging contact information are ways to strengthen communication and collaboration between colleagues effectively decreasing the risk of disruption of the intimacy domain in VT.

Prior to disaster impact, forming a liaison and developing collaborative relationships with community disaster response partners, including the local police and fire department, allows groups to form a collective alliance and work together in disaster preparation, adding another layer of social support that can decrease feelings of isolation during a disaster.

References

Abrams, D.B. (1991). Conceptual models to integrate individual and public health interventions: The example of the workplace. In M. Henderson (Ed.), *Proceedings of the International Conference on Promoting Dietary Change in Communities* (pp. 173-194). Seattle, WA: The Fred Hutchinson Cancer Research Center.

Baker, E., Israel, B., & Schurman, S. (1996). The integrated model: Implications for worksite health promotion and occupational health and safety practice. *Health Education Quarterly, 23*, 175–188.

Blewett, V., & Shaw, A. (1995). Health promotion, handle with care: Issues for health promotion in the workplace. *Journal of Occupational Health Safety, 11*, 461–465.

Bober, T., & Regehr, C. (2006). Strategies for reducing secondary or vicarious trauma: Do they work? *Brief Treatment and Crisis Intervention, 6*(1), 1–9.

Brady, J.L., Guy, J.D., Poelstra, P.L., & Browkaw, B. (1999). Vicarious traumatization, spirituality, and the treatment of sexual abuse survivors: A national survey of women psychotherapists. *Professional Psychology Research and Practice, 30*(4), 386–393.

Brewin, C.R., Andrews, B., & Valentine, J.D. (2000). Meta-analysis of risk factors for post-traumatic stress disorder in trauma-exposed adults. *Journal of Consulting and Clinical Psychology, 68*, 748–766.

Brondolo, E., Wellington, R., Brady, N., Libby, D., & Brondolo, T.J. (2008). Mechanism and strategies for preventing post-traumatic stress disorder in forensic workers responding to mass fatality incidents. *Journal of Forensic and Legal Medicine 15(2)*, 78–88.

Business for Social Responsibility. (2004). Corporate social responsibility. *Issue Brief: Health and Wellness, Vol. 2004.*

Center for Disaster & Extreme Event Preparedness. (2003). Competencies. *DEEP PREP: All-Hazards disaster behavioral health training.* Retrieved from: www.umdeepcenter.org. Accessed March 1, 2013.

Chrestman, K.R. (1999). Secondary exposure to trauma and self-reported distress among therapists. In B.H. Stamm (Ed.), *Secondary traumatic stress: Self care issues for clinicians, researchers, and educators* (2nd ed.; pp. 29–36). Baltimore, MD: Sidran Press.

Chu, C., Driscoll, T., & Dwyer, S. (1997). The health-promoting workplace: An integrative perspective. *Australian and New Zealand Journal of Public Health, 21*, 377–385.

Cox, R.S. (n.d.) *Disaster Psychosocial Services Competency Matrices.* World Association for Disaster and Emergency Medicine. Retrieved from: http://www.wadem.org/. Accesssed April 7, 2013.

Creamer, T.L., & Liddle, B.J. (2005). Secondary traumatic stress among disaster mental health workers responding to the September 11 attacks. *Journal of Traumatic Stress, 18*(1), 89–96.

DeJoy, D., & Southern, D. (1993). An integrative perspective on worksite health promotion. *Journal of Medicine, 35*, 1221–1230.

Devilly G.J., Wright, R., & Varker, T. (2009). Vicarious trauma, secondary traumatic stress, or simply burnout? Effect of trauma therapy on mental health professionals. *Australian and New Zealand Journal of Psychiatry, 43*, 373–389.

Driskell, J., Salas, E., & Johnston, J. (1999). Does stress lead to loss of team perspective? *Group Dynamics, 3*, 1–12.

European Network for Workplace Health Promotion (1997). *The Luxembourg declaration on workplace health promotion in the European Union.* Presented at the European Network for Workplace Health Promotion Meeting, Luxembourg.

Figley, C.R. (1995). Compassion fatigue as secondary traumatic stress disorder: An overview In C. Figley (Ed.), *Compassion fatigue: Coping with secondary traumatic stress disorder in those who treat the traumatized* (pp. 1–20). New York, NY: Brunner/Mazel.

Follette, V.M., & Batten, S.V. (2000). The role of emotion in psychotherapy supervision: A contextual behavioral analysis. *Cognitive and Behavioral Practice, 7*, 306–312.

Green, K.L., & Johnson, J.V. (1990). The effect of psychological work organization on patterns of cigarette smoking among male chemical plant employees. *American Journal of Public Health, 80*, 1368–1371.

Hamilton, A. (1943). *Exploring the dangerous trades: The autobiography of Alice Hamilton, MD.* Boston, MA: Little Brown and Company.

Hartsough, D.M., & Myers, D.G. (1985). *Disaster work and mental health: Prevention and control of stress among workers* (DHHS Publication No. ADm 85–1422). Rockville, MD: National Institute of Mental Health.

Hernandez, P., Gangsei, D., & Engstrom, D. (2007). Vicarious resilience: A new concept in work with those who survive trauma. *Family Process, 46(2),* 229–241.

Hobfoll, S.E., Watson, P., Bell, C.C., Bryant, R.A., Brymer, M.J., & Friedman, M.J. (2007). Five essential elements of immediate and mid-term mass trauma intervention: Empirical evidence. *Psychiatry: Interpersonal & Biological Processes, 70,* 283–369. PMID:18181708; http://dx.doi. org/10.1521/psyc.2007.70.4.283.

Kantor, E.M. & Beckert, D.R. (2011) Preparation and systems issues: Integrating into a disaster response. In F.J. Stoddard, A. Pandya, & C.L. Katz (Eds.). *Disaster psychiatry: Readiness, evaluation, and treatment.* Arlington, VA: American Psychiatric Publishing.

Kassam-Adams, N. (1999). The risks of treating sexual trauma: Stress and secondary trauma in psychotherapists. In B.H. Stamm (Ed.), *Secondary traumatic stress: Self-care issues for clinicians, researchers, and educators* (2nd ed.; pp. 37–50). Baltimore, MD: Sidran Press.

Levy, B.S., & Wegman, D.H. (2000) *Occupational health: Recognizing and preventing work-related disease and injury*, Philadelphia, PA: Lippincott, Williams and Wilkins.

Lind, E.W. (2000). Secondary traumatic stress: Predictors in psychologists. *Dissertation Abstracts International, 61,* 3283.

Lusk, S.L., & Raymond, D.M. (2002) Impacting health through the worksite. *Nursing Clinics of North America, 37:,* 247–256.

Mental Health Commission of Canada (2013). *Psychological health and safety in the workplace—Prevention, promotion, and guidance to staged implementation.* Toronto, Canada: Canadian Standards Association. Retrieved from: http://www.mentalhealthcommission.ca/English/node/5346#sthash.GlhP18rd.EFAhN7PO.dpuf. Accessed January 10, 2014.

Motowildo, S.J., Packard, J.S., & Manning, M.R. (1986). Occupational stress: Its causes and consequences for job performance. *Journal of Applied Psychology, 71(4),* 618–629.

Munroe, J.F. (1999). Ethical issues associated with secondary trauma in therapists. In B.H. Stamm (Ed.), *Secondary traumatic stress: Self-care issues for clinicians, researchers, and educators* (2nd ed.; pp. 211–229). Baltimore, MD: Sidran Press.

Myers, D., & Wee, D.F. (2005). *Disaster mental health services.* New York, NY: Routledge.

National Institute of Mental Health (2002). Mental health and mass violence: Evidence-based early psychological intervention for victims/survivors of mass violence. In *A workshop to reach consensus on best practices,* NIH Publication No. 02–5138. Washington DC: US Government Printing Office. Retrieved from: http://www.nimh.nih.gov/health/publications/massviolence.pdf. Accessed December 22, 2013.

National Institute for Occupational Safety and Health (1999). *National occupational research agenda: Organization of work, Vol. 2004.* Centers for Disease Control and Prevention.

National Institute for Occupational Safety and Health (2008). *Essential elements of effective workplace programs and policies for improving worker health and well-being,* DHHS(NIOSH) Publication No. 2010–140. Retrieved from: www.cdc.gov/niosh. Accessed December 22, 2013.

National Institute for Occupational Safety and Health (2012). The Research Compendium: The NIOSH Total Worker Health Program, *Seminal research papers 2012.* Retrieved from: www.cdc.gov/niosh/docs/2012–146/. Accessed December 22, 2013.

Ng, A.T., & Kantor E.M. (2010). Psychological first aid. In F.J. Stoddard, C.L. Katz, J.P. Merlino (Eds.), *Hidden impact: What you need to know for the next disaster: A practical mental health guide for clinicians.* Sudbury, MA: Jones & Bartlett.

Norris, F. & Kaniasty, K. (1996). Perceived and received social support in times of stress: A test of the social support deterioration deterrence model. *Journal of Personality and Social Psychology, 71*, 499–511.

O'Donnell, M.P. (Ed.). (2002). *Health promotion in the workplace* (3rd ed.). Toronto, ON: Delmar Thomson Learning.

Palm, K.M., Polusny, M.A., & Follette, V.M. (2004). Vicarious traumatization: Potential hazards and interventions for disaster and trauma workers. *Prehospital and Disaster Medicine, 19*(1), 73–78.

Pearlman, L.A., & Saakvitne, K.W. (1995). *Trauma and the therapist: Countertransference and vicarious traumatization in psychotherapy with incest survivors.* New York: W.W. Norton & Co.

Quick, J., Nelson, D., & Hurrell, J., Jr. (1997). *Preventive stress management in organizations.* Washington, DC: American Psychological Association.

Roelofs, C., Barbeau, E., Moure-Eraso, R., & Ellenbecker, M.J. (2003). Prevention strategies in industrial hygiene: A critical literature review. *American Industrial Hygiene Association Journal, 64*, 62–67.

Saakvitne & Pearlman (1996). *Transforming the pain: A workbook on vicarious traumatization.* New York, NY: W.W. Norton & Company.

Seligman, M.E., Steen, T., Park, N., & Peterson, C. (2005). Positive psychology progress: Empirical validation of interventions. *American Psychologist, 60*(5), 410–421.

Sorensen, G., & Barbeau, E. (2004). Steps to a healthier US workforce: Integrating occupational health and safety and worksite health promotion: State of the science. Commissioned paper for the NIOH Steps to a Healthier US Workforce Symposium. Washington, D.C.

Sorensen, G., Barbeau, E., Hunt, M.K., & Emmons, K. (2004). Reducing social disparities in tobacco use: A social contextual model for reducing tobacco use among blue-collar workers. *American Journal of Public Health, 94*, 230–239.

Spangler, N.W. (2013). *Employer practices for addressing stress and building Resilience.* Arlington, VA: Partnership for Workplace Mental Health. Retrieved from: www.workplacementalhealth.org. Accessed December 10, 2013.

Spangler, N.W., Koesten, J., Fox, M.H., & Radel, J. (2012). Employer perceptions of stress and resilience intervention. *Journal of Occupational and Environmental Medicine, 54*(11), 1421–1429.

Van der Klink, J.J., Blonk, R.W., Schene, A.H., & Van Dijk, F.J. (2001). The benefits of interventions for work-related stress. *American Journal of Public Health, 91*(2), 270–276.

Walsh, D.W., Jennings, S.E., Mangione, T., & Merrigan, D.M. (1991). Health promotion versus health protection? Employees' perceptions and concerns. *Journal of Public Health Policy, 12*, 148–164.

World Health Organization. (1997). *Jakarta statement on healthy workplaces.* Jakarta, Indonesia: World Health Organization.

World Health Organization. (1999). *Regional guidelines for the development of healthy workplaces.* Shanghai, China: World Health Organization.

World Health Organization. (2000). *Anexo 6: Estrategia de promocion de la salud en los lugares de trabajo de America Latina y el Caribe.* Geneva, Switzerland: World Health Organization.

Young, B.H., Ruzek, J.I., Wong, M., Salzer, M.S., & Naturale, A.J. (2006). Disaster mental health training: Guidelines, considerations and recommendations. In E.C. Ritchie, P.J. Watson, & M.J. Friedman (Eds.), *Interventions following mass violence and disaster* (pp. 54–79). New York: Guildford Press.

PERSONAL REFLECTIONS

My 9/11

I was in the Mount Sinai Medical Center's Psychiatric Emergency Department on the morning of 9/11, exactly one week into my new job directing it and having just begun morning rounds. The phone rang and was handed to me—"Craig. . . ? It's Anand. . . . did you hear that a plane went into the World Trade Center. . .?" I have no recollection of what I said or did beyond hanging up and resuming rounds. I had no idea what else to do, but I was going to need to figure that out quickly.

That's not because our emergency department was overrun with people in need but rather because I had co-founded Disaster Psychiatry Outreach (DPO) exactly three years earlier, with Anand and two other psychiatric friends and colleagues. Right in New York City, DPO is and was a charitable organization devoted to using psychiatrists to help people affected by disaster, and we had all spent the last years, the very first of our years after residency, preparing for disaster. We had already responded to two aviation disasters, including one that had given us our start, and a Central American earthquake, and all made us feel like the cavalry riding to the rescue. I was the President and led the charge.

Rounds inevitably ended and for me everything changed. Grand rounds were cancelled so that I could address our department about the basics of mental health and disasters. Next I was planning out how to staff our emergency department for the psychological casualties that were expected. Somewhere amid all of that, I was meeting people from all over the hospital who suddenly wanted to know me and what I knew. I had not even begun to turn my attention to DPO when I walked home late that night amid the motionless and still streets of Manhattan. Where had everyone gone?

The next day DPO sprang into action thanks to the trailblazing of my good friend and fellow DPO Board member, Tony, who utilized his and our connections with local officials to establish DPO's presence at the Family Assistance Center (FAC) that had been opened at the Lexington Avenue Armory and soon moved to Pier 94 on the Hudson River. What followed were days and weeks of staffing the FAC, and even Ground Zero, with hundreds of psychiatrists from around New York City and elsewhere who had flocked to us as they never had before. My office at Mount Sinai became our operations center where DPO's very first paid staff person, an administrative assistant who was just hired in August, was based.

My life became all about 9/11. Thanks to the largess of Mount Sinai, I usually left the emergency department in the able hands of my chief resident as I ran back and forth to the FAC, Ground Zero, daily departmental briefings, and so many other places. My fledgling private practice took a backseat, and my wife, a high-octane child psychiatrist and pediatrician, even joined DPO for the first time in order to lead our child psychiatry efforts.

When the FAC eventually closed and Ground Zero became too filled with heavy machinery to be safe for us, I next turned my attention to working with my Mount Sinai colleagues in occupational medicine to raise funds for and set up a mental health program for 9/11 responders that opened its doors in July 2002. I had thought the program would operate for a year, but as I write in 2012 it remains open and bustling and funded for at least the next four years. I stepped down from directing it in 2006 but remain involved in small ways still as a supervisor and historian for the staff, most of whom have turned over since we began the program.

I am not sure what memory best defines my relationship with 9/11. There are so many memories but many more gaping holes. I wish I had kept a journal just like I did when I went to overseas disasters, but when a disaster affects where you live, you are not so level headed. I have spent most of my 9/11 story dealing with psychiatrists, medical students, residents, and representatives from other disaster response agencies than I have with our 9/11 affected patients. So, the memory that comes to my mind does not involve a patient. Instead, it is of coming home from the FAC about two weeks after 9/11 and breaking into tears after a senior psychiatrist who had been a pre-9/11 supervisor of mine before becoming a post-9/11 DPO volunteer criticized our efforts as a "disaster." Just two years out of residency, I had to cover my eyes from the bright spotlight of leadership.

I did not lose anyone on 9/11 and am ashamed to admit that most of my memories of it have nothing to do with the very patients I entered psychiatry to treat or started to DPO to help. And, therein lies my own inexplicable lesson from 9/11—I need to be with patients but repeatedly deprive myself of that chance. In 2006, I stepped down from directing the World Trade Center mental health program for responders and finally stepped down as President of DPO just a few months ago. Yet, I still feel the tug of organizing and advocacy and run a program at Mount Sinai that conducts psychiatric development work in low-income countries and communities. I edit books on disaster psychiatry, give lots of talks on the subject, and just travelled to post-tsunami Japan this past January all the while juggling my practice, my role at the school of medicine as a faculty advisor, and being a father to my post-9/11 children. I am still trying to figure out how to stop and dread what it would mean if another 9/11 was to strike again in New York City.

Craig L. Katz, MD
Director, Professional Development Program in Mental Health
Associate Clinical Professor of Psychiatry and Medical Education
Mount Sinai School of Medicine

Navigating Resources on Vicarious Trauma and Disasters

13

WHAT RESOURCES ARE AVAILABLE ON VICARIOUS TRAUMA?

Mudassar Iqbal, Tamar Lavy, and Mark R. Evces

While there has been substantial interest in the phenomena of vicarious trauma and compassion fatigue, the organization and availability of resources is still emerging. There are organizations and individuals who have done considerable work in this field and listed below are some of the resources available to those who are interested in or are experiencing vicarious trauma. We faced a number of challenges while compiling the list of resources. Most of the information was obtained from Internet websites and not all organizations could be contacted directly for their input. Some of the entities are well-known to practitioners in the field but for those new to these areas, the names might not be familiar. It was also a challenge to identify people and groups who have been making significant efforts in a diverse and changing world of resources. In this chapter, we attempt to provide an objective account of the nature of services offered by these organizations, but for more specific queries, these organizations should be contacted directly. The resources cited in this chapter are limited to those based in the United States and some parent organizations are described in the next chapter, Chapter 14, on the resources for disaster response. We note that some of these organizations or services are non-profit while others are for-profit. The organizations are divided into private and governmental/professional organizations, and we included a subcategory of private organizations providing caregiving support services as we believe that this is an important specialized area of indirect trauma. We have listed some current printed literature that can build a broader base of understanding of the phenomena of vicarious trauma and compassion fatigue. These books or chapters can be used as an adjunct to this text. Descriptions are adapted from online and printed resources listed immediately following each program summary.

Organizations

Private Organizations Addressing Vicarious Trauma

Proqol.org
http://www.proqol.org/

This nonprofit organization offers training in the research, clinical, and organizational use of the Professional Quality of Life (ProQOL) assessment instrument and the theory of compassion satisfaction and compassion fatigue. Trainings are customized to each audience. The organization's website has an extensive data bank of cases as well as scientific literature on compassion fatigue and vicarious trauma. Beth Hudnall Stamm, Ph.D., is the developer of the ProQOL and serves as the director of ProQOL.org. In addition to offering training courses, Dr. Stamm also gives motivational talks about her experiences as a traumatic brain injury survivor, and how addressing experiences of compassion satisfaction, compassion fatigue, and professional quality of life helped her return to her work and to full participation in her community.

The Figley Institute
http://www.figleyinstitute.com/
141 Robert E Lee Boulevard, #255
New Orleans, LA 70124

The Figley Institute offers training and continuing education programs to those who provide relief to emotionally traumatized individuals, families, businesses, governmental agencies, and communities. These programs were developed by Dr. Charles R. Figley and Dr. Kathlee Regan Figley. The Institute's mission is to alleviate human suffering that results from traumatic life experiences by providing laypersons and professionals with high-quality training in treating trauma.

Vicarious Trauma Institute
http://www.vicarioustra
uma.com/
Vicarious Trauma Institute
8010 East Morgan Trail, Suite One
Scottsdale, AZ 85258
Tel: (480) 991–4119

The Vicarious Trauma Institute offers individualized training and educational presentations on vicarious traumatization and compassion fatigue for helping professionals and others experiencing vicarious trauma. Half-day, multi-day, and weekend workshops are available.

Headington Institute
http://headington-institute.org/
Headington Institute
402 S. Marengo Avenue
Pasadena, CA 91101
Tel: (626) 229–9336
Fax: (626)229–0514

The Headington Institute assists humanitarian workers and other professional helpers learn skills, utilize social support and organizational resources, and foster public interest needed to maintain their well-being and thrive in their work. Their mission statement includes a focus on

Wendt Center for Loss and Healing

http://www.wendtcenter.org
Wendt Center Main Office
4201 Connecticut Ave NW, Suite 300
Washington, DC 20008
Tel: (202) 624–0010
Fax: (202) 624–0062
E-Mail: info@wendtcenter.org

Sidran Institute

http://www.sidran.org
http://www.riskingconnection.com/
Sidran Institute for Traumatic Stress Education & Advocacy
200 E. Joppa Road, Suite 207
Towson, MD 21286
Tel: (410) 825–8888, (410) 337–0747

The Green Cross

http://greencross.org/
Green Cross Academy of Traumatology
P.O. Box 352
Becker, MN 55308 USA
Tel: (320) 743–3639
Fax: (320) 743–4119

Trauma Research, Education and Training Institute (TREATI)

http://www.treati.org
22 Morgan Farms Dr., Suite 5
South Windsor, CT 06074
Tel: (860) 644–2541

Compassion Fatigue Awareness Project / Health Caregiving, L.L.C.

www.compassionfatigue.org
www.healthycaregiving.com

caring for others by providing support to humanitarian workers by working with local organizations and staff in need. Emphasis is placed on spiritual resources, collaboration, and advocacy.

The Wendt Center provides educational presentations, trainings, and research related to counseling for grief and trauma, including support for providers and volunteers.

The Sidran Institute is a non-profit organization that develops and delivers trauma-focused media and educational resources and programs, and designs and consults for professional and layperson consumers who are interested in learning about collaborative, individualized trauma services. The Institute's "Risking Connection" program teaches a relational approach to helping others recover from trauma as effectively, efficiently, and safely as possible for both providers and survivors.

The Green Cross Academy of Traumatology (GCAT) is non-profit international humanitarian organization including trauma and compassion fatigue treatment specialists. GCAT offers Compassion Fatigue Educator (CFE) Certification for those interested in specialized training in the study and prevention of compassion fatigue. A Compassion Fatigue Therapist (CFT) Certification is also offered for those seeking to further specialize in the assessment and treatment of secondary traumatic stress.

The Trauma Research, Education, and Training Institute, Inc. (TREATI) provides training for helping professionals interested in the study and treatment of the impact of trauma on both survivors and the professionals who treat them.

The Compassion Fatigue Awareness Project collects and distributes information on compassion fatigue. Founder Patricia Smith is available for Compassion Fatigue presentations. Healthy Caregiving, LLC is

(*Continued*)

Patricia Smith
Founder
Healthy Caregiving, LLC
E-mail: patricia@
  healthycaregiving.com
Gift From Within
http://www.giftfromwithin.org/
16 Cobb Hill Rd.
Camden, ME 04843 USA
Tel: (207)236–8858
Fax: (207) 236–2818
E-mail: JoyceB3955@aol.com

the parent organization of the Compassion Fatigue Awareness Project. Founded by Patricia Smith, this website offers a variety of media related to the prevention of compassion fatigue.

Gift From Within is a non-profit organization dedicated to those who suffer post-traumatic stress disorder (PTSD), those at risk for PTSD, and those who care for traumatized individuals. It develops and disseminates educational material on PTSD and compassion fatigue, including videotapes, DVDs, articles, books, and other resources through its website.

Caregiver Wellness
  Compassion Fatigue and
  Chronic Sorrow Workshops
http://www.caregiverwellness.ca
Jan Spilman, MEd. RCC
PO Box 44062
Burnaby, BC V5B 4Y2
Tel: (604) 297–0609
Email: caregiverwellness@shaw.ca

Caregiver Wellness Workshops offers compassion fatigue, resilience-building, and self-care presentations to professionals, volunteers, and family caregivers.

Compassion Unlimited
http://www.
  compassionunlimited.com
Compassion Unlimited
3205 South Gate Circle, Suite 2
Sarasota, FL 34239
Tel: (941) 720–0143
Fax: (941) 827–9459
E-mail: info@
  compassionunlimited.com

Compassion Unlimited, Inc., provides training in and consultation for the treatment of posttraumatic stress and compassion fatigue for professionals, survivors, and families affected by trauma.

Self-Care Academy / Nurse
  Fit
http://self-careacademy.com/sca/
www.nursefit.com
Self-Care Academy
Tel: (303) 904–9803
Email: kim@self-careacademy.com
  and kimrichards@nursefit.com

Self-Care Academy offers consultation, training, and online media for the prevention and treatment of compassion fatigue.

Compassion Fatigue Solutions
http://www.compassionfatigue.ca
Compassion Fatigue Solutions
Françoise Mathieu
837 Princess St. Suite 300
Kingston, On K7L 1G8 Canada
Tel: (613) 547–3247
Fax: (613) 547–0655
Email: whp@cogeco.ca

Compassion Fatigue Solutions provides training and for individuals and organizations including health care workers, police officers, paramedics, mental health professionals, and teachers, to address effects of working with trauma and in stressful work environments.

The Sanctuary Model
http://www.sanctuaryweb.
com/sanctuary-model.php
Tel: (888) 538–2134

The Sanctuary Model provides consultation and educational training for groups and organizations working with trauma survivors, focusing on the environmental and organizational effects of stress and trauma.

Private Organizations Providing Resources for Caregiving

National Family Caregiving Association (NFCA)
www.thefamilycaregiver.org
www.nfcacares.org
National Alliance for Caregiving
www.caregiving.org

10400 Connecticut Avenue Suite 500,
Kensington, MD 20985
Tel: (301) 942–6430
Fax: (301) 942–2302
4720 Montgomery Lane, 5th Floor
Bethesda, MD 20814
Tel: (301) 718–8444
E-mail: info@caregiving.org

Rosalyn Carter Institute for Caregiving
www.rosalynncarter.org
www.rci.gsw.edu

Georgia Southwestern State University
800 GSW Drive
Americus, GA 31709
Tel: (229) 928–1234, (229) 931–2663
E-mail: rci@rci.gsw. edu

Joyful Heart Association
http://www.joyfulheartfoundation.org

Joyful Heart is a national organization with locations in New York, Los Angeles, and Honolulu.
Tel: New York: (212) 475–2026
Los Angeles: (310) 405–0135
Honolulu: (808) 531–3520
E-mail: info@joyfulheartfoundation.org

Red Cross Family Caregiving Program
http://www.redcross.org

2025 E. St NW
Washington, DC 20006
Tel: (202) 303–4498

Professional Organizations and Government Programs

International Society for Traumatic Stress Studies
http://www.istss.org
111 Deer Lake Road, Suite 100
Deerfield, IL 60015
Tel: (847) 480–9028
Fax: (847) 480–9282
National Center for PTSD and PILOTS http://www.ptsd.va.gov/
http://www.ptsd.va.gov/professional/
pilots-database/pilots-db.asp
U.S. Department of Veterans Affairs
810 Vermont Avenue, NW
Washington, DC 20420

The International Society for Traumatic Stress Studies is a professional organization for trauma-focused researchers, clinicians, and policy makers.

The National Center for PTSD (NCPTSD) is part of the United States Veterans Affairs health care system. The Center supports and provides research, education and training on trauma and PTSD and includes the Published International

Literature on Traumatic Stress (PILOTS) database. The PILOTS Database is an online guide to international academic and lay literature on traumatic stress and PTSD.

SAMHSA-National Center for Trauma-Informed Care (NCTIC)
www.samhsa.gov/nctic/
National Center for Trauma-Informed Care
66 Canal Center Plaza, Suite 302
Alexandria, VA 22314
Telephone: (866) 254–4819
Fax: (703) 548–9517
E-mail: NCTIC@NASMHPD.org

The United States Substance Abuse and Mental Health Services Administration (SAMHSA) established the NCTIC to provide trauma-informed training and education for publicly funded programs and organizations.

Books

At the time of publication, we were unaware of any book entirely dedicated to vicarious traumatization in disasters. The references below indicate chapters devoted to the subject within a book on disaster psychiatry. It is noteworthy that the majority of materials in print that discuss the topic present secondary traumatization as a form of countertransference or burnout. Very few discuss it as a defined phenomenon.

Merlino, J. P. (2011). Rescuing ourselves: Self-care in the disaster response community. In F. J. Stoddard, Jr., A. Pandya, & C.L. Katz (Eds.), *Disaster psychiatry: Readiness, evaluation, and treatment* (pp. 35–48). Arlington, VA: American Psychiatric Publishing, Committee on Disasters and Terrorism, Disaster Psychiatry.

This chapter provides an overview of the core concepts of self-care among clinician responders providing disaster mental health care. The author discusses potential challenges and solutions with the goal of mitigating the negative psychological impact of disaster response work.

Charney, A. E., & Pearlman, L. A. (1998). The ecstasy and the agony: The impact of disaster and trauma work on the self of the clinician. In P. M. Kleespies (Ed), *Emergencies in mental health practice: Evaluation and management* (pp. 418–435). New York, NY: Guilford Press.

This chapter provides a theoretical framework for understanding the psychological process by which a clinician is affected by providing care to the traumatized. The focus is mostly on disasters as the cause of trauma but the authors suggest that the information can be applied to other causes as well.

Ehrenreich, J. H. (2006). Managing stress in humanitarian aid workers: The role of the humanitarian aid organization. In G. Reyes & G.A. Jacobs (Eds.), *Handbook of international disaster psychology: Interventions with special needs*

This is a chapter of a multi-volume work produced by the American Psychological Association that informs readers on the psychological effects of humanitarian aid work on aid workers specifically. This target population can include mental health clinicians. Aid

(Continued)

populations (Vol. 4; pp. 99–112). Westport, CT: Praeger Publishers/ Greenwood Publishing Group.

workers' professional lives are uniquely characterized by long hours, living and working in unpleasant or unsafe conditions, being physically demanding, having limited privacy and personal space, heavy workloads amidst limited resources, and separation from families for extended periods of time. At times, they are themselves exposed to the same ongoing threat during post-disaster conditions experienced by those they are trying to help. The chapter addresses not only vicarious traumatization but also PTSD, depression, grief, anxiety, and psychosomatic complaints.

Myers, D. & Wee, & D. F. (2005). *Disaster mental health services: A primer for practitioners.* Brunner-Routledge Psychosocial Stress Series. New York, NY: Brunner-Routledge.

This book aims to educate clinicians already in the practice of treating the traumatized on skills specifically targeted for helping survivors of disasters. Chapter 4 of Part II is entitled, "Stress Management and Prevention of Compassion Fatigue for Psychotraumatologists" and provides an overview of the variety of psychological demands and challenges faced by providers. A focused discussion of vicarious trauma was not the aim of the chapter.

Wee, D. F., & Myers, D. (2002). Stress responses of mental health workers following disaster: The Oklahoma City bombing. In C.R. Figley (Ed.), *Treating compassion fatigue.* Psychosocial Stress Series, no. 24 (pp. 57–83). New York, NY: Brunner-Routledge.

The book *Treating compassion fatigue* is one of 36 works in the Psychosocial Stress Series by Routledge. There are two chapters in this book that address compassion fatigue in disaster responders: Chapter 3, "Stress responses of mental health workers following disaster" and Chapter 10, "Strategies for managing disaster mental health worker stress." The former is a study presenting the results of a questionnaire applied to the disaster mental health workers of the Oklahoma City bombing. This is an informative case review style presentation but obviously not generalizable. The latter provides practical strategies to prevent or mitigate psychological trauma in disaster mental health workers that can be applied at three stages of intervention: before, during, or immediately after the disaster.

Dass-Brailsford, P. (2009). Secondary trauma among disaster responders. In P. Dass-Brailsford (Ed.), *Crisis and disaster counseling: Lessons learned from hurricane Katrina and other disasters.* (pp. 213–218). New York, NY: Sage.

This chapter provides an overview by defining common terms used to describe psychological reactions among disaster mental health responders, highlights warning signs of those adversely affected, discusses the challenges faced by workers, and suggests strategies to mitigate the effects.

Orloff, L. (2011). *Managing spontaneous community volunteers in disasters: A field manual.* Boca Raton, FL: CRC Press.

This is a general field manual produced by the American nonprofit organization, World Cares Center, that helps train and educate volunteers for disaster preparedness and response. This manual contains a chapter entitled "Building a Resilient Team" that provides an introduction to basic concepts on mental health issues in volunteer responders; however, it is not a manual made specifically for mental health workers. The author defines and describes various psychological phenomenon (trauma and stress disorders, secondary/vicarious trauma, PTSD), signs of stress, and strategies for self-care.

Wee, D., & Myers, D. (1998). Disaster mental health: Impact on the workers. In K. Johnson, (Ed). *Trauma in the lives of children: Crisis and stress management techniques for teachers, counselors, and student service professionals* (pp. 257–263). Auburn Hills: Hunter House.

This book focuses on providers who care for traumatized children. The appendix entitled, "Disaster Mental Health: Impact on the Workers," provides an introduction to the study of stress reactions in responders and goes on to present a study entitled "The Northridge Earthquake Crisis Counselor Study."

Online Resources

Resources for Professionals Working With Traumatized Children and Families
https://www.childwelfare.gov/Adoption/preplacement/caring_addressing.cfm
http://www.mollydragiewicz.com/VTguidebook.pdf
Fact Sheet about Vicarious Trauma by American Counseling Association
http://www.counseling.org/docs/trauma-disaster/fact-sheet-9—-vicarious-trauma.pdf?sfvrsn=2
Vicarious Traumatization and Spirituality in Law Enforcement
http://www.fbi.gov/stats-services/publications/law-enforcement-bulletin/july-2011/vicarious-traumatization
Vicarious Trauma and Organization Structure
http://vawnet.org/Assoc_Files_VAWnet/PrevVicariousTrauma.pdf
Self-Care for Trauma Psychotherapists and Caregivers: Individual, Social and Organizational Interventions
http://www.melissainstitute.org/documents/Meichenbaum_SelfCare_11thconf.pdf
Brief Tips about Self-Care and Self-Help Following Disasters. A National Center for PTSD Fact Sheet
http://www.ncptsd.va.gov/facts/disasters/fs_self_care_brief.html

14

HOW DO WE NAVIGATE RELEVANT INFORMATION ON DISASTERS?

Helen Ryu, Tamar Lavy, and Mark R. Evces

Introduction

Large-scale, organized psychological response to disasters in America was documented as early as the Chicago Fire in 1871 (Bulling & Harvey, 1999). The Congressional Charter of 1905 established the American Red Cross, which recognized the need for organized efforts to provide comfort and relief to survivors of disaster. Stress response phenomenon was established in the *Diagnostic and Statistical Manual (DSM) I* in 1952 (American Psychiatric Association, 1952) as Gross Stress Reaction, eventually evolving to be called Posttraumatic Stress Disorder (PTSD) from the *DSM-III* (American Psychiatric Association, 1980) until the present. It is argued that the first introduction as a diagnostic category by the American Psychiatric Association was based on the contributions of Freud and his conceptualization of traumatic neurosis (Wilson, 1995).

Beyond the labeling and analysis of the phenomenon, disaster mental health response has been evolving to include efforts from multiple tiers of government, private and nonprofit organizations, both locally and internationally. They provide a wide variety of services from preparedness, to Psychological First Aid, and even longer term follow-up. In addition, research, service coordination, and education have also been in development to better understand and enhance the mental health response to disaster. Unlike other fields within the health professions, this field is a rather new one and its identity is still unclear. In this chapter, we have compiled a list of major organizations involved in disaster mental health response to provide readers with a starting point towards navigation of the immense, and at times overwhelming, world of disaster resources. Descriptions are taken from online and printed resources listed immediately following each program summary.

Government Programs

There are three major federal agencies involved in disaster mental health response: the Department of Health and Human Services, the Department of Homeland Security, and the Department of Defense. The Department of Health and Human Services (DHHS) oversees the most number of agencies and offices that facilitate disaster related mental health care. Of them, the Assistant Secretary of Preparedness and Response (ASPR) is responsible for interagency coordination. With the combined efforts of the agencies and coordination with DHHS, they are active in a broad range of activities that can be organized into the following categories—services, research, planning/preparedness, coordination/integration/technical assistance, and training—as outlined in the Summary of Disaster Behavior Health Assets and Capabilities prepared by the DHHS (http://www.phe.gov/Preparedness/planning/abc/Documents/sum-hhs-disasterbehavioral health.pdf).

Department of Health and Human Services

Medical Reserve Corps
http://www.medicalreservecorps.gov/
   HomePage
Division of the Civilian Volunteer
   Medical Reserve Corps
The Tower Building
1101 Wootton Parkway, Room 181
Rockville, MD 20852
Tel: (240) 453–2839
Fax: (240) 276–8873
E-mail: MRCcontact@hhs.gov

Founded shortly after 9/11, it is a national network of citizen volunteers who have health service skills and are trained and prepared to respond to emergencies and include those in the mental health field such as psychiatrists, psychologists, and social workers. They also function to provide education and outreach in their own community throughout the year. They also provide assistance to existing emergency response systems such as American Red Cross, local public health, police, fire, ambulance services.

Emergency System for the Advance Registration of Volunteer Health Professionals (ESAR-VHP)
http://www.phe.gov/esarvhp/Pages/
   default.aspx
U.S. Department of Health and Human
   Services
Office of the Assistant Secretary for
   Preparedness and Response
200 Independence Avenue, S.W.
Room 638G
Washington, D.C. 20201

The ESAR-VHP is a state-based volunteer registration system that allows prompt identification and mobilization of health professional volunteers. Mental health provider volunteers include psychiatrists, psychologists, clinical social workers, and mental health counselors. It is a state-based system but volunteer information is shared between states to optimize resources if needed.

National Disaster Medical System (NDMS)
http://ndms.fhpr.osd.mil/

The NDMS is administered by the ASPR and made up of federal employees that are divided into teams dispersed geographically across the nation to form a single integrated national medical

Commissioned Corps
http://www.usphs.gov/

Center for Disease Control (CDC)
http://emergency.cdc.gov/mentalhealth/
Centers for Disease Control and
 Prevention
1600 Clifton Rd.
Atlanta, GA 30333
Tel: (800) CDC-INFO
TTY: (888) 232–6348

**National Institute of Mental Health
(NIMH)**
http://www.nimh.nih.gov/index.shtml
E-mail: nimhinfo@nih.gov

**Substance Abuse and Mental
 Health Services Administration
 (SAMHSA)**
*Center for Mental Health
 Services—Emergency Mental Health and
 Traumatic Stress Services Branch (CMHS)*

response that assists the military as well as
state and local authorities during major
peacetime disasters.
The Commissioned Corps is one of the
uniformed services that operates under
the DHHS. Each officer is assigned to
a specific team. There are four types of
teams including the Mental Health Team.
There are five mental health teams at this
time, each with a minimum of 28 officers
made up of social workers, psychologists,
psychiatrists in addition to leadership and
administrative staff. Each month, there is
a minimum number of officers on call
ready to be deployed. Their role is to treat
individuals affected by major disasters, help
local response teams, and provide behavioral
health care to the officers themselves.
The CDC funds relevant research including
developing community resilience, policy
formulation, and personnel management for
disaster response. They also provide expertise
in communications for disaster response
operations and information dissemination
systems to share best practices and educational
material. They have an abundance of data that
helps inform resource allocation decisions
in emergency situations. The CDC provides
senior level health officials within each state
health department to assist in making their
expertise accessible. They provide relevant
information to educate and advise directly
to communities in addition to disseminating
information to local authorities, health
service providers, and other Federal agencies.
The CDC has developed several training
courses for HHS employees and contractors,
the Commissioned Corp and the public.
The NIMH funds studies looking at the
consequences of stress and trauma across
multiple domains of basic science, clinical
practice, and health systems for both
civilians, military personnel and veterans
with the goal of better informing efforts
to improve risk assessment, diagnosis,
interventions, and recovery.
SAMHSA a major source of expertise in
all-hazards disaster planning and cultural
competence in disaster mental health
programs. In collaboration with FEMA,
SAMHSA funds crisis counseling grants.
Through their Disaster Technical Assistance

(*Continued*)

http://www.mentalhealth.samhsa.gov/
cmhs/emergencyservices
1 Choke Cherry Road, Sixth Floor
Rockville, MD 20850
Tel: (800) 789–2647
Fax: (240) 276–1844
*Substance Abuse and Mental Health
Services Administration Disaster Technical
Assistance Center (DTAC)*
http://www.samhsa.gov/dtac
4350 East West Highway, Suite 1100
Bethesda, MD 20814
Phone: 800–308–3515
Fax: 800–311–7691
E-mail: dtac@esi-dc.com

Center (DTAC), they provide telephone
consultation, logistical support, technical
assistance, and information dissemination.
They also developed the National Mental
Health Information Center, which is a
website that provides training materials
for responders and publications on
emergency mental health and traumatic
stress.

Office of Disability
http://www.hhs.gov/od/

The United States Office of Disability
advises the HHS on the needs of people
with disabilities, including those with
serious mental illness in the context of
emergency preparedness.
A compilation of DHHS resources including
disaster mental health can be found at
http://www.hhs.gov/emergency/index.
shtml#post

Department of Homeland Security

**Federal Emergency Management
Agency (FEMA)**
http://www.fema.gov/public-assistanc
e-local-state-tribal-and-non-profit/
recovery-directorate/crisis-counseling
Federal Emergency Management Agency
500 C Street S.W.
Washington, D.C. 20472
Tel: (800) 621-FEMA (3362)
TTY: (800) 462–7585

FEMA operates under the direction of
the Department of Homeland Security
and its role is to provide supplemental
assistance when local and state resources are
overwhelmed. For the purposes of disaster
mental health, FEMA provides funding
for and implements the Crisis Counseling
Assistance and Training Program (CCP)
together with SAMHSA's Emergency
Mental Health and Traumatic Stress
Services Branch of the Center for Mental
Health Services. The CCP is designed to
assist disaster survivors through counseling
and education as well as providing technical
assistance, consultation, and training to local
and state authorities and mental health
providers in the administration of the
program. The program provides funding
through two grants—the Immediate
Services Program (up to 60 days of service)
and the Regular Services Program (up
to nine months of service). The former
program is monitored by FEMA and the
latter is monitored by SAMHSA.

Department of Defense

Center for the Study of Traumatic Stress
http://www.cstsonline.org/
Center for the Study of Traumatic Stress
Uniformed Services University of the
  Health Sciences
Department of Psychiatry
4301 Jones Bridge Road
Bethesda, MD 20814–4799
Telephone: 301–295–2470
Fax: 301–319–6965
E-mail: cstsinfo@usuhs.mil

The Center was established in 1987 to advance the understanding of the psychological and health implications of exposure to trauma related to military work, terrorism, natural, and human-made disasters in response to concerns raised by the Department of Defense. It is a part of the Department of Psychiatry of the Uniformed Services University (USU) and affiliated with the Defense Centers of Excellence (DCoE) for Psychological Health and Traumatic Brain Injury. They are most productive in research but also provide consultation to governmental and non-governmental organization. It also offers a 2-year fellowship in Disaster and Preventive Psychiatry to military medical personnel.

Professional Organizations

American Psychiatric Association (APA)
http://www.psychiatry.org/practice/
  professional-interests/disaster-psychiatry
American Psychiatric Association
1000 Wilson Boulevard
Suite 1825
Arlington, VA 22209
Tel: 1–888–35-PSYCH or 1–888–35–77924
Tel from outside the U.S. and Canada: (703)
  907–7300
E-mail: apa@psych.org

The APA established a Task Force on Psychiatric Dimensions of Disaster in 1993. The Committee on Psychiatric Dimensions of Disasters works towards providing training and research from psychiatrists and effective, evidence-based care for disaster victims, and publishes a disaster psychiatry handbook.

American Psychological Association Disaster Response Network (DRN)
http://www.apa.org/practice/programs/
  drn/index.asx;
http://www.apa.org/news/press/response/
  disaster-training.aspx;
http://www.apa.org/research/action/
  trauma.aspx
American Psychological Association
750 First Street, NE
Washington, DC 20002–4242
Tel: (800) 374–2721 or (202) 336–5500

The APA Disaster Response Network (DRN) is a group of over 2,000 licensed psychologists with training in disaster response who volunteer to help people prepare for and cope with disasters. The DRN also provides education and training for publicly funded and private groups and organizations.
APA Road to Resilience Brochure:
  http://www.apa.org/helpcenter/
  road-resilience.aspx

Society for Disaster Medicine and Public Health (SDMPH)

SDMPH is a group of health professionals who collaborate in the creation of

(*Continued*)

http://sdmph.org/
Disaster Medicine and Public Health
Preparedness
Editor(s): James J. James, MD, DrPH, MHA

World Association for Disaster and Emergency Medicine (WADEM)
http://www.wadem.org/

policies and programs on disaster health globally. They publish *Disaster Medicine and Public Health Preparedness,* a peer-reviewed journal on disaster medicine and public health.

WADEM is a multidisciplinary international organization created in 1976, originally as the Club of Mainz, committed to the advancement of emergency and disaster research. They strive to disseminate scientific evidence and best practices in prehospital and emergency health care, public health, and disaster health and preparedness. They publish the peer-reviewed journal *Prehospital and Disaster Medicine* and sponsor biennial congresses worldwide.

Local Non-Profit Organizations

American Red Cross
www.redcross.org

The American Red Cross is a non-profit organization and the official American Affiliate of the International Federation of Red Cross. Red Cross Mental Health Services provides support to volunteers participating in disaster relief operations as well as services for victims of disasters. The Red Cross trains professional helpers who wish to volunteer to become Disaster Mental Health workers to provide acute mental health support and service coordination. Service availability varies by chapter but volunteers and their services can be deployed nationally if local resources are not available.

Disaster Psychiatry Outreach (DPO)
http://disasterpsych.org/
Disaster Psychiatry Outreach, Inc.
Tel: (646) 867–3514
E-mail: info@disasterpsych.org

The DPO is an organization of psychiatrists with an expertise in disaster mental health response. DPO personnel train and organize volunteer psychiatrists who provide immediate mental health services following a disaster by both interacting directly with victims and also by guiding and collaborating with government or private charitable agencies in providing appropriate care. They are also involved in research and policy development in the field of disaster mental health.

Mental Health America
http://www.mentalhealthamerica.net/
2000 N. Beauregard Street,
6th Floor Alexandria, VA 22311
Tel: (703) 684–7722
(800) 969–6642
Fax (703) 684–5968

**National Volunteer Organizations
Active in Disasters (NVOAD)**
http://www.nvoad.org/
1501 Lee Highway, Suite 170
Arlington, VA 22209–1109
Tel: (703) 778–5088
Fax: (703) 778–5091

MHA is an advocacy organization addressing mental health issues including access to and provision of quality services. MHA operates in 41 states to promote mental health and mental health services including survivors of disasters.

National Voluntary Organizations Active in Disaster (NVOAD) is a non-profit, membership-based organization that serves as the forum for organizations to share knowledge and resources throughout the disaster cycle—preparation, response, and recovery—to help disaster survivors and their communities.

International Non-Profit Organizations

Doctors Without Borders
http://www.doctorswithoutborders.org/
Doctors Without Borders—USA
Headquarters
333 7th Avenue, 2nd Floor
New York, NY 10001–5004
Tel: (212) 679–6800
Fax: (212) 679–7016

Doctors Without Borders/Médecins Sans Frontières (MSF) is an international medical humanitarian organization providing independent, impartial assistance to people threatened by violence, neglect, or catastrophe, primarily due to armed conflict, epidemics, malnutrition, exclusion from health care, or natural disasters. MSF provides advocacy and for people and communities in crisis and inadequate or abused aid systems and inadequate medical treatment.

**International Committee of the
Red Cross (ICRC)**
http://www.icrc.org/eng/
19 Avenue de la Paix CH 1202 Geneva
Tel: +41 22 734 60 01
Fax: +41 22 733 20 57

The ICRC is an international, nonprofit organization funded by governments and Red Cross and Red Crescent Societies. It provides humanitarian help for people affected by conflict and armed violence and promotes the laws that protect victims of war.

International Medical Corps
https://internationalmedicalcorps.org/
International Medical Corps
1919 Santa Monica Blvd.
Suite 400
Santa Monica, CA 90404
Tel: (310) 826–7800
24-Hour Donation Hotline: 800–481–4462
Fax: (310) 442–6622

Founded by volunteer doctors and nurses, the International Medical Corps is a non-profit, international humanitarian organization providing health care training and international health interventions and health care system development to communities in acute need.

E-mail: inquiry@
internationalmedicalcorps.org
DC Office
1313 L St. NW
Suite 220
Washington, DC 20005
PHONE: 202–828–5155
FAX: 202–828–5156
International Medical Corps UK
1st Floor
254–258 Goswell Road
London
EC1V 7EB
PHONE: +44 (0) 207 253 0001
FAX: +44 (0) 207 250 3269
Email: info@internationalmedicalcorps.
org uk

International Rescue Committee
www.rescue.org
International Rescue Committee, 122
42nd Street
New York, NY 10168 USA
Phone: (212) 551 3000

The nonprofit International Rescue Committee offers a variety of forms of assistance to refugees forcibly relocated from their homes by conflict or disaster in over 40 countries and across the United States.

Pan American Health Organization (PAHO)
http://www.paho.org/usa/
Regional Office of the World Health
Organization
525 Twenty-third Street, N.W.,
Washington, DC 20037
Tel.: (202) 974–3000
Fax:(202) 974–3663

The Pan American Health Organization (PAHO), a member of the United Nations system, is also a regional Office for the Americas of the World Health Organization. PAHO provides expert intervention and coordinates groups and organizations to address health and wellness issues in countries of the Americas.

United Nations Disaster Assessment and Coordination (UNDAC)
http://www.unocha.org/what-we-do/
coordination-tools/undac/overview

The United Nations Disaster Assessment and Coordination (UNDAC) is part of the international disaster response system to help the United Nations and governments of disaster-affected countries. UNDAC also assists in the coordination of acute international relief offered at no cost to a country in need.

United Nations Office for Disaster Risk Reduction (UNISDR)
http://www.unisdr.org/
UNISDR
Palais des Nations
CH1211
Geneva, Switzerland
Tel: +41 229178907–8
Fax: +41 229178964
E-mail: isdr@un.org

UNISDR assists countries in reducing the risk of disasters by working to proactively address risk factors for large-scale disasters.

Global Disaster Alert and Coordination System (GDACS)
www.gdacs.org

GDACS is a United Nations system for cooperating professionals to share and coordinate information as part of an acute disaster response.

United Nations Office for Coordination of Humanitarian Affairs (UNOCHA) http://www.unocha.org/	OCHA is a UN organization responsible for coordinating organizational responses to humanitarian crises, including prevention, preparation, and advocacy services for both acute and sustainable humanitarian response.

References

American Psychiatric Association. (1952). *Mental Disorders.* American Psychiatric Publishers. Washington, DC: Author.

American Psychiatric Association. (1980). *Diagnostic and statistical manual of mental disorders,* (3rd ed.). Washington, DC: Author.

Bulling, D., & Harvey, J. (1999). *Introduction to Disaster Mental Health Response for Emergency Managers.* Nebraska Emergency Management Agency.

Wilson, J.P. (1995). The historical evolution of PTSD diagnostic criteria. In Everyl, J. S. & Lating, J. M. (Eds.), *Psychotraumatology* (pp. 9–26). Boston, MA: Springer US. doi:10.1007/978–1–4899–1034–9_2

APPENDIX

Measures

TABLE A.1 Trauma Attachment Belief Scale—Scores and Sample Items

TABS Scores and Sample Items

TABS Scale	No. of Items	Sample Item
Total	84	
Self-Safety (S-S)	13	54. I feel threatened by others.
Other-Safety (O-S)	8	6. I never feel anyone is safe from danger.
Self-Trust (S-T)	7	19. I don't trust my instincts.
Other-Trust (O-T)	8	26. Trusting people is not smart.
Self-Esteem (S-E)	9	3. I don't feel like I deserve much.
Other-Esteem (O-E)	8	39. People are no good.
Self-Intimacy (S-I)	7	53. I hate to be alone.
Other-Intimacy (O-I)	8	35. I feel cut off from people.
Self-Control (S-C)	9	56. I have problems with self-control.
Other-Control (O-C)	7	78. I can't do good work unless I am the leader.

From: Pearlman, L.A. (2003). *Trauma Attachment Belief Scale Manual.* Torrance, CA: WPS.

Impact of Event Scale—Revised

INSTRUCTIONS: Below is a list of difficulties people sometimes have after stressful life events. Please read each item, and then indicate how distressing each difficulty has been for you **DURING THE PAST SEVEN DAYS** with respect to _____, which occurred on _____. How much were you distressed or bothered by these difficulties?

Not at all = 0   A little bit = 1   Moderately = 2   Quite a bit = 3   Extremely = 4

---

1. Any reminder brought back feelings about it.
2. I had trouble staying asleep.
3. Other things kept making me think about it.
4. I felt irritable and angry.
5. I avoided letting myself get upset when I thought about it or was reminded of it.
6. I thought about it when I didn't mean to.
7. I felt as if it hadn't happened or wasn't real.
8. I stayed away from reminders of it.
9. Pictures about it popped into my mind.
10. I was jumpy and easily startled.
11. I tried not to think about it.
12. I was aware that I still had a lot of feelings about it, but I didn't deal with them.
13. My feelings about it were kind of numb.
14. I found myself acting or feeling like I was back at that time.
15. I had trouble falling asleep.
16. I had waves of strong feelings about it.
17. I tried to remove it from my memory.
18. I had trouble concentrating.
19. Reminders of it caused me to have physical reactions, such as sweating, trouble breathing, nausea, or a pounding heart.
20. I had dreams about it.
21. I felt watchful and on-guard.
22. I tried not to talk about it.

The Intrusion subscale is the **MEAN** item response of items 1, 2, 3, 6, 9, 14, 16, 20. Thus, scores can range from 0 through 4.
The Avoidance subscale is the **MEAN** item response of items 5, 7, 8, 11, 12, 13, 17, 22. Thus, scores can range from 0 through 4.
The Hyperarousal subscale is the **MEAN** item response of items 4, 10, 15, 18, 19, 21. Thus, scores can range from 0 through 4.

Citations: Weiss, D.S. & Marmar, C.R. (1997). The Impact of Event Scale-Revised. In J.P. Wilson, & T.M. Keane (Eds.), *Assessing Psychological Trauma and PTSD: A Practitioner's Handbook.* (pp. 399–411). New York, NY: Guilford.
Weiss, D. S. (2004). The Impact of Event Scale-Revised. In J.P. Wilson, & T.M. Keane (Eds.), *Assessing psychological trauma and PTSD: A practitioner's handbook* (2nd ed., pp. 168–189). New York, NY: Guilford Press.

Professional Quality of Life Scale (ProQOL 5)

Compassion Satisfaction and Compassion Fatigue (ProQOL) Version 5 (2014)

When you *[help]* people you have contact with their lives. You may have found that your compassion for people you *[help]* can affect you in positive and negative ways. Below are some questions about your positive and negative experiences, as a *[helper]*. Consider the questions about you and your current work situation. Select the number that represents how you experienced these things in the *last 30 days*. There are no right or wrong answers. If you do not know an answer just give it your best guess.

1=Never	2=Rarely	3=Sometimes	4=Often	5=Very Often

1. I am happy.
2. I am preoccupied with more than one person I *[help]*.
3. I get satisfaction from being able to *[help]* people.
4. I feel connected to others.
5. I jump or am startled by unexpected sounds.
6. I feel invigorated after working with people I *[help]*.
7. I find it difficult to separate my personal life from my life as a *[helper]*.
8. I am not as productive at work because I am losing sleep over the traumatic experiences of a person I *[help]*.
9. I think that I might have been affected by the traumatic stress of people I *[help]*.
10. I feel trapped by my job as a *[helper]*.
11. Because of my *[helping]*, I have felt "on edge" about various things.
12. I like my work as a *[helper]*.
13. I feel depressed because of the traumatic experiences of the people I *[help]*.
14. I feel as though I am experiencing the trauma of a person I have *[helped]*.
15. I have beliefs that sustain me.
16. I am pleased with how I am able to keep up with *[helping]* techniques and protocols.
17. I am the person I always wanted to be.
18. My work makes me feel satisfied.
19. I feel worn out because of my work as a *[helper]*.
20. I have happy thoughts and feelings about those I *[help]* and how I could help them.
21. I feel overwhelmed because my case *[work]* load seems endless.
22. I believe I can make a difference through my work.
23. I avoid certain activities or situations because they remind me of frightening experiences of the people I *[help]*.

24. I am proud of what I can do to *[help]*.
25. As a result of my *[helping]*, I have intrusive, frightening thoughts.
26. I feel "bogged down" by the system.
27. I have thoughts that I am a "success" as a *[helper]*.
28. I can't recall important parts of my work with trauma victims.
29. I am a very caring person.
30. I am happy that I chose to do this work.

Your Scores on the ProQOL: Professional Quality of Life Screening

Based on your responses, place your personal scores below. If you have any concerns, you should discuss them with a physical or mental health care professional.

Compassion Satisfaction _____

Compassion satisfaction is about the pleasure you derive from being able to do your work well. For example, you may feel like it is a pleasure to help others through your work. You may feel positively about your colleagues or your ability to contribute to the work setting or even the greater good of society. Higher scores on this scale represent a greater satisfaction related to your ability to be an effective caregiver in your job.

The average score is 50 (SD 10; alpha scale reliability .88). About 25% of people score higher than 57 and about 25% of people score below 43. If you are in the higher range, you probably derive a good deal of professional satisfaction from your position. If your scores are below 40, you may either find problems with your job, or there may be some other reason—for example, you might derive your satisfaction from activities other than your job.

Burnout_____

Most people have an intuitive idea of what burnout is. From the research perspective, burnout is one of the elements of Compassion Fatigue (CF). It is associated with feelings of hopelessness and difficulties in dealing with work or in doing your job effectively. These negative feelings usually have a gradual onset. They can reflect the feeling that your efforts make no difference, or they can be associated with a very high workload or a non-supportive work environment. Higher scores on this scale mean that you are at higher risk for burnout.

The average score on the burnout scale is 50 (SD 10; alpha scale reliability .75). About 25% of people score above 57 and about 25% of people score below 43. If your score is below 43, this probably reflects positive feelings about your ability to be effective in your work. If you score above 57 you may wish to think about what at work makes you feel like you are not effective in your position. Your score may reflect your mood; perhaps you were having a "bad day" or are in need of some time off. If the high score persists or if it is reflective of other worries, it may be a cause for concern.

Secondary Traumatic Stress_____

The second component of Compassion Fatigue (CF) is secondary traumatic stress (STS). It is about your work-related, secondary exposure to extremely or traumatically stressful events. Developing problems due to exposure to other's trauma is somewhat rare but does happen to many people who care for those who have experienced extremely or traumatically stressful events. For example, you may repeatedly hear stories about the traumatic things that happen to other people, commonly called Vicarious Traumatization. If your work puts you directly in the path of danger, for example, field work in a war or area of civil violence, this is not secondary exposure; your exposure is primary. However, if you are exposed to others' traumatic events as a result of your work, for example, as a therapist or an emergency worker, this is secondary exposure. The symptoms of STS are usually rapid in onset and associated with a particular event. They may include being afraid, having difficulty sleeping, having images of the upsetting event pop into your mind, or avoiding things that remind you of the event.

The average score on this scale is 50 (SD 10; alpha scale reliability .81). About 25% of people score below 43 and about 25% of people score above 57. If your score is above 57, you may want to take some time to think about what at work may be frightening to you or if there is some other reason for the elevated score. While higher scores do not mean that you do have a problem, they are an indication that you may want to examine how you feel about your work and your work environment. You may wish to discuss this with your supervisor, a colleague, or a health care professional.

What Is My Score and What Does It Mean?

In this section, you will score your test so you understand the interpretation for you. To find your score on **each section,** total the questions listed on the left and then find your score in the table on the right of the section. The scoring system below is based on data from over 3,000 people around the world. It may or may not be representative of your individual situation so please consider your results as they apply to you and your work.

Compassion Satisfaction Scale

Copy your rating on each of these questions on to this table and add them up. When you have added then up you can find your score on the table to the right.	3. ____ 6. ____ 12. ____ 16. ____ 18. ____ 20. ____ 22. ____ 24. ____ 27. ____ 30. ____ **Total:** ____		

The Sum of My Compassion Satisfaction Questions Is	So My Score Equals	And My Compassion Satisfaction Level Is
22 or less	43 or less	Low
Between 23 and 41	Around 50	Average
42 or more	57 or more	High

Burnout Scale

On the burnout scale you will need to take an extra step. Starred items are "reverse scored." If you scored the item 1, write a 5 beside it. Our research has shown that reversing some items makes the ProQOL more accurate. For example, reversing the score on question 1. "I am happy" helps us learn about the effects of helping that can make a person unhappy. Learning about both the positive and negative effects the scale is more accurate.

★1. ____ = ____
★4. ____ = ____
8. ____
10. ____
★15. ____ = ____
★17. ____ = ____
19. ____
21. ____
26. ____
★29. ____ = ____
Total: ____

The Sum of My Burnout Questions Is	So My Score Equals	And My Burnout Level Is
22 or less	43 or less	Low
Between 23 and 41	Around 50	Average
42 or more	57 or more	High

You Wrote	Change to
1	5
2	4
3	3
4	2
5	1

Secondary Traumatic Stress Scale

Just like you did on Compassion Satisfaction, copy your rating on each of these questions on to this table and add them up. When you have added then up you can find your score on the table to the right.

2. ____
5. ____
7. ____
9. ____
11. ____
13. ____
14. ____
23. ____
25. ____
28. ____
Total: _____

The Sum of my Secondary Trauma Questions is	So My Score Equals	And My Secondary Traumatic Stress level is
22 or less	43 or less	Low
Between 23 and 41	Around 50	Average
42 or more	57 or more	High

INDEX

Note: page numbers in *italics* indicate figures and tables.